British Social Attitudes

the
1987
report

Edited by
Roger Jowell
Sharon Witherspoon
& Lindsay Brook

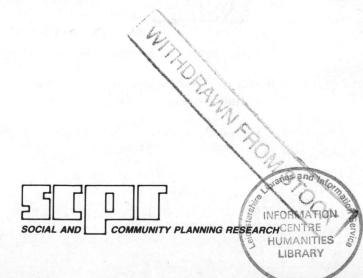

Gower

scpr

SOCIAL AND **COMMUNITY PLANNING RESEARCH**

Published by
Gower Publishing Company Limited,
Gower House,
Croft Road,
Aldershot,
Hants GU11 3HR
England

Gower Publishing Company,
Old Post Road,
Brookfield,
Vermont 05036,
U.S.A.

Cover photograph by Brian Astbury

Typeset by
Graphic Studios (Southern) Ltd, Godalming, Surrey.
Printed and bound in Great Britain by
Billing and Sons Limited, Worcester.

British Library Cataloguing in Publication Data

British social attitudes: the 1987 report.
  1. Public opinion — Great Britain   2. Great Britain — Social conditions
  — 1945-
  I. Jowell, Roger   II. Witherspoon, Sharon   III. Brook, Lindsay
  941.085'8   HD400.P8

ISSN 0-267-6869
ISBN 0-566-00740 1
ISBN 0-566-00753 3 (Pbk)

Contents

CHAPTER 3.   POLITICAL CULTURE
by Anthony Heath and Richard Topf **51**

CHAPTER 4.   NUCLEAR REACTIONS
by Ken Young **71**

CHAPTER 5.   FOOD VALUES: HEALTH AND DIET
by Aubrey Sheiham and Michael Marmot with Don Rawson
and Nicola Ruck **95**

CHAPTER 8. INTERIM REPORT: PARTY POLITICS
by John Curtice **171**

APPENDIX I. Technical details of the survey **187**

APPENDIX II. Notes on the tabulations **195**

APPENDIX III. The questionnaires **197**

SUBJECT INDEX **255**

Introduction

The aim of this series, now five years old, is to measure and, where possible, explain stability or change in British public attitudes, values and beliefs. Our general strategy is a simple one: by repeatedly asking the same carefully designed sets of questions of random samples of the population at intervals, we chart trends over the years (see Appendices I and III for technical details). We do not always succeed in that aim. For instance, some questions, despite piloting, turn out not to work very well and have to be adjusted or discarded; most, however, survive unscathed into future rounds.

A design of this sort, based on repeat measurements, is ideal for monitoring changes. Its intrinsic advantage is that, by keeping the measurement *methods* more or less constant over time, the products of those measurements are less likely to be artefacts and more likely to reflect real changes. Its intrinsic disadvantage, however, is that the regular repetition of questions is inescapably dull. Moreover, an all too familiar feature of repeat measurements is that nothing much changes between one reading and another – hardly the sort of revelation to command rapt attention. As a result, many survey time-series have a reputation for being estimable rather than exciting.

This series, though, has been fortunate in two respects. First, we had anticipated having each year to extol the virtues of measuring the absence of movement, pointing out that changes in attitudes tend to be gradual rather than sudden, and so on. In general, this remains true. Yet, sooner than expected, we have discerned several clear and sustained movements, sometimes sizeable ones, in public attitudes (see for instance Chapters 1, 4 and 8). Justifiably or not, such changes do tend to excite more interest than does the repeated discovery that things *are* what they used to be.

Second, each annual round of the survey has, in fact, been very different from its predecessors: this has been reflected in the coverage of each of the four books to date. Although each module of questions on a particular topic remains constant as far as possible between one measure and the next, we do not include each module annually. Thus some new modules are introduced each year, and others are repeated. This sort of mixture of new topics with hardy perennials helps to refresh a time-series, principally because it encourages diversity, as can be seen from the following list of topics from each of our annual Reports to date.

	The 1984 Report	The 1985 Report	The 1986 Report	The 1987 Report
Politics and political culture	x	x	x	x
Economic issues & expectations	x	x		
Social policy, welfare & public spending	x		x	x
Education	x		x	
Housing	x		x	
Health services	x			x
Food & health				x
Work and the work ethic			x	
Defence and international issues		x	x	x
Local government		x		
Environment & the countryside		x	x	x
Business & industry				x
Sex roles and gender issues		x		
Race and class	x		x	
Moral and family issues	x		x	x
Right & wrong in social & financial transactions		x		
US-British differences			x	
Attitude measurement, changes & consistency	x	x	x	

Our ability to cover such a variety of topics owes much to the help we have received from specialist advisers and contributors. Thirty chapters by over twenty authors in four years is testimony to the extent to which we have relied on contributions from colleagues both inside and outside SCPR. We depend upon them not only for writing chapters but also for their advice on questionnaire coverage and about the series in general. We are extremely grateful for their help.

The future of the series is now assured until 1990, and we hope its momentum will carry it forward well beyond then. In common with any *series* it is an appreciating asset, as the growing use of the dataset in the ESRC Archive at Essex seems to suggest. The 1987 survey fieldwork took place as usual this spring and will duly be reported on in *The 1988 Report*. But, with the permission of our core-funders, the Sainsbury Family Trusts, and with further support from the ESRC and Pergamon Press, we decided to bring forward the 1988 survey budget and devote it to conducting a post-election study as part of the *British General Election* series. The link between these two series, which started with some joint ESRC-supported methodological work (see Chapters 3 and 8), is thus more firmly established than ever.

With the replacement of the 1988 fieldwork round, *The 1989 Report* in the series is now planned to be a five-year review of stability and change in attitudes, instead of the customary annual report. In the same year, a book on the 1987 general election (a sequel to *How Britain Votes*) will then describe and interpret the attitudes and values which lay behind the election results; it will also report on some of the regular *British Social Attitudes* measurements on political beliefs and values.

The other important link we have established is with eight other countries (Australia, Austria, Eire, Hungary, Italy, the Netherlands, the USA and West Germany) in what we have called the *International Social Survey Programme* (ISSP). At the time of writing, most of these countries have conducted three annual surveys employing identical (or at least equivalent) questions on different topics: the role of government, family support networks, and social inequality. Several further annual rounds (including some repeat measurements) are in preparation. As we were able to glimpse from James Davis' chapter in *The 1986 Report*, a comparison of attitudes across nations and continents can be even more illuminating than national data in revealing our peculiarly British views and preoccupations. We want to pay a special tribute to our colleagues in each of these countries for the economical (and cordial) method we have jointly developed to tackle the notoriously difficult task of setting up and maintaining a cross-national, cross-cultural time-series. The ISSP promises to provide a wealth of valuable data.

The sample size for many of the topic areas covered in this Report is 3100, much larger than that in previous rounds. This increase was welcome, since for a number of topics small sizes of subgroups had hampered useful analyses. For other topics, however, we considered that the larger sample size would be somewhat extravagant. So we split the sample into two, asking some questions of *both* random subsamples, others of only one (1500 or so). This has added substantially to the effective questionnaire 'space' at our disposal, on this and future surveys, enabling us to continue introducing new topics alongside our repeat questions. Appendix III has full details of the structure and yield of the design.

By now the reader will have gleaned how fortunate the series is to have such sympathetic funders. The Sainsbury Family Trusts deserve most of the credit. Their trustees and directorate have been, and continue to be, not only steadfast supporters of the series but also assiduous and helpful critics. They have safeguarded the series from loss of independence and have responded swiftly to its changing needs. We are immensely indebted to them.

But these funds, generous as they are, are only core funds. To survive on this scale and with this degree of diversity, the series needs substantial additional support which it has been fortunate enough to receive from a variety of sources. The Department of Employment has committed itself to six years of annual funding to date, to enable us to continue including (and reporting on) our labour market questions. The Countryside Commission has so far provided funding for three years in succession for us to devise questions and monitor 'green' issues (see Chapter 7). The Department of Trade and Industry has committed three years of funding, starting with the 1986 survey (see Chapter 2), to devise and repeat questions on public attitudes to business and industry.

The Department of the Environment has similarly provided three years of support for a series of questions on housing. Marks and Spencer plc and Shell UK Ltd have both provided support to three annual rounds of the series as a general contribution towards its future.

In addition to these various *regular* sources of funds, the survey in some years benefits from occasional contributions, such as from the ESRC and the Nuffield Foundation. Three organisations – the Department of Transport, the Health Education Council (see Chapter 5) and the Centre for the Study of Individual and Social Values (see Chapter 6) – contributed funds towards the 1986 survey reported here. In each case, the aim is to repeat these measures in a future, but as yet unspecified, round of the series. These contributions are important not only on financial grounds, but also because they help to ensure that the dataset continues to be of practical value.

We are grateful to all these funders both for their support and for the spirit in which it is provided. A series of this kind needs to protect its independence; its coverage, the questions asked and the interpretations placed on its findings must all be the final responsibility of the investigators rather than of the funders. Otherwise the survey will always risk the accusation of deliberately having omitted topics or results it should properly have included, and vice versa. Core funding at a high level from a 'disinterested' source is, of course, the best means of promoting such impartiality, but it also depends on the willingness of other funders to accept these 'ground rules'. We are aware that such concessions have on occasion caused difficulties, particularly for some government departments, and we greatly appreciate the efforts that were made to overcome them.

Our colleagues in SCPR who have made the survey happen each year, and who have criticised and improved it, have our warmest appreciation. Fieldwork controllers, interviewers, computer programmers, coders, secretaries, other researchers, administrative staff all become involved in the study in one way or another and we depend heavily upon their skills. The study's research assistant over the past year, Kate Melvin, has made an invaluable contribution and we have all come to rely – rather too much, perhaps – on her impressive work.

Most important of all, we once again pay special tribute and reiterate our thanks to 3100 anonymous respondents.

RMJ
SFW
LLB

1 Citizenship and Welfare

*Peter Taylor-Gooby**

The Beveridge plan for social provision embodied a notion of welfare citizenship that was both comprehensive and limited. All members of society would have access to a range of social services at adequate minimum standards for an agreed range of needs, and these services would be financed through mass taxation. The better off would, however, still have the opportunity to pay for private welfare if they believed that its purchase would provide higher standards.

As the welfare state developed, private provision has generated inequalities, mainly in housing and pensions, and to some extent in access to health care and education. The extension of means-testing has further widened the gap, implicit in Beveridge, between provision for special groups – often seen as 'undeserving' – and for the common needs of the majority (most notably served through national insurance). The continuing expansion of the private sector, subsidised by the state through tax relief and other policies, has exacerbated these inegalitarian tendencies, as has an increasing divergence in living standards between the comfortable majority and certain poor minorities within it. In any case, universalism may not itself guarantee equality; it has been argued by academics from Titmuss (1955) to Le Grand (1982) that the least well off are often the least able to take full advantage of comprehensive social provision.

Welfare citizenship has always put the provision of health and other social services before redistribution *per se*, and the freedom to exercise privilege before equality. This compromise, between class division and the claims of need, was endorsed by a political consensus until the mid-1970s. There are now signs that the structure of attitudes that supported this settlement is breaking down. A party committed to public spending restraint, privatisation and the targeting of resources was returned to power with large majorities in 1979, 1983

* Reader in Social Policy, University of Kent.

and 1987. Allied to this are two important trends which call into question the traditional pattern of social provision: the marked expansion of non-state welfare and the continuing high level of unemployment. All of these developments might reasonably raise doubts about the stability of popular endorsement of welfare state citizenship.

Since 1983, the *British Social Attitudes* series has collected data in such areas as the level of support for state welfare spending, attitudes to private services, the needs of unemployed people, satisfaction with welfare provision, opinions about poverty and the legitimacy of income redistribution. So the 1986 survey and its predecessors provide the foundations for an assessment of current attitudes towards the role of the state in welfare provision, and valuable evidence of such changes as have occurred over the last three years.

Priorities for social spending

Current support for the welfare state

In 1986, as in earlier years, responses reveal a consistent pattern of strong public support for spending on the core welfare state services – the National Health Service, education and pensions. Together these services exhibit the main characteristics of the Beveridge citizenship settlement: the assurance of national minimum standards (alongside a recognition of the inevitability of substantial inequalities *within* state provision), a flourishing private sector (encouraged by the present government), and until recently a strong tradition of commitment by all major political parties. These three services also account for more than two thirds of all welfare state spending. Four-fifths of respondents described "providing a decent standard of living for the old" as "definitely" a legitimate area of state responsibility. Eighty-four per cent said the same about the provision of health care. Only one per cent was prepared to say that these activities should not fall within the scope of government. In contrast, rather less than half the sample saw the "reduction of income differences between the rich and poor" as legitimate, and just under two fifths thought it was "the government's responsibility to provide a decent standard of living for the unemployed". (See **Table 1.1** for further details.)

Willingness to pay taxes to finance welfare spending is evidence of the widespread acceptance of welfare citizenship: less than one-twentieth want tax cuts at the cost of welfare cuts – a remarkable degree of consensus. The real debate is between retaining the status quo and increasing welfare spending through raising tax levels. On this choice, the sample is split almost equally (see **Table 1.2** for details). However, the public is highly discriminating between different areas of provision. When presented with ten government activities and asked to select their first priority for extra spending, nearly half our respondents plump for the NHS. Education comes second, endorsed by over a quarter of respondents. No other area of spending is mentioned by more than eight per cent; these include non-welfare programmes such as roads, public transport and overseas aid, and more politically salient issues such as defence, police and prisons and help for industry. Other welfare programmes – social security and public housing, where the beneficiaries are fewer – receive far lower levels of support than does the heartland of the welfare state (see **Table 1.3**). When people are asked for their next highest priority, education tops the list (with 30% supporting extra spending), followed by the NHS (at 28%). Housing trails behind at 14% (see **Table 1.4**).

What seems to emerge is a consensus on priorities in the major areas of welfare spending, coupled with a less than wholehearted support for the needs of the traditionally 'undeserving'. This is strengthened by the pattern of responses to a question on priorities for spending on social security benefits. Pensions top the list with 40% support, followed by benefits for disabled people at 25%. The traditionally 'undeserving' unemployed receive 16%, and single parents only seven per cent. On second choices, disabled people receive the support of 33% of our sample but the priority given to the unemployed stays almost the same and that given to single parents climbs to only 11% (see **Table 1.5**).

Changes over time

The overall pattern of support for state welfare coupled with concern – albeit highly selective – about provision for less advantaged groups reflects the findings of many other surveys over the post-war period (for example, Klein, 1974; Taylor-Gooby, 1985). Over the period covered by the *British Social Attitudes* series, readiness to pay increased taxes to provide valued welfare services has grown substantially, particularly between 1983 and 1985, from around a third of the population to nearly half.

	1983 %	1984 %	1985 %	1986 %
Reduce taxes and spend *less* on health, education and social benefits	9	6	6	5
Keep taxes and spending on these services *at the same level* as now	54	50	43	44
Increase taxes and spend *more* on health, education and social benefits	32	39	45	46

So too has support grown for spending on the National Health Service and state education, largely at the expense of help for industry:

Highest priority for extra government spending*

	1983 %	1984 %	1985 %	1986 %
Health	37	51	47	47
Education	24	20	23	27
Help for industry	16	10	9	8
Housing	7	6	8	7
Social security benefits	6	7	5	5

* Defence, public transport, roads, police and prisons and overseas aid received no more than four per cent support in any year and so are omitted.

However the pattern of differential support for 'favoured' and 'unfavoured' social security benefits has hardly altered.

Highest priority for extra social benefit spending

	1983 %	1984 %	1985 %	1986 %
Retirement pensions	41	43	41	40
Benefits for disabled people	24	21	26	25
Benefits for the unemployed	18	18	16	16
Child benefits	8	9	10	11
Benefits for single parents	8	7	6	7

These public attitudes run counter to the policies of the 1979 and 1983 Conservative governments which have tended to advocate tax cuts at the expense of welfare spending, private provision in place of state welfare and targeted services rather than universal standards of social provision and care. Presumably the electoral success of the Conservatives cannot be explained by public support for their policies on welfare spending.

The politics of social spending

Evidence from this series over its first four years suggests that the policies of Margaret Thatcher's governments have failed to alter the widespread public acceptance of the advantages of limited welfare citizenship. The pattern of consensus on the major areas of state spending is reaffirmed when the data are broken down by support for the major political parties. Endorsement of higher spending has risen among all three groups and the division between Conservative supporters on the one hand and Labour and Alliance supporters on the other, is essentially between support for the *status quo* (perhaps not surprising among adherents of the party of government) and support for increased expenditure.

Tax versus social spending

	Conservative		Alliance		Labour	
	1983 %	1986 %	1983 %	1986 %	1983 %	1986 %
Less tax and social spending	10	5	6	3	8	5
Status quo	63	54	54	37	46	36
More tax and social spending	24	36	36	55	42	55

The structure of priorities for extra spending shows some interesting divisions. Labour party supporters are noticeably keener than those of the Conservative party and the Alliance on extra spending on health and, moreover, their enthusiasm has risen substantially since 1983. They are also more likely to endorse higher spending on housing and social security benefits than are supporters of the other two main political groupings. The priority given to education by the Alliance has sharply increased, and the enthusiasm among Conservatives for more health and education spending has also grown. Increased support for spending on education may reflect its reappearance close to the top of the political agenda, a development partly stimulated by the continuing school teachers' dispute.

Highest priority for extra spending

	Conservative		Alliance		Labour	
	1983	1986	1983	1986	1983	1986
	%	%	%	%	%	%
Health	34	43	43	46	39	53
Education	24	31	24	33	24	22
Housing	5	5	6	6	10	9
Social security benefits	3	2	4	4	9	7

When we come to look at specific areas of social security spending, we see that Labour Party supporters are rather more likely than Alliance supporters and considerably more likely than Conservatives to give priority to unemployment and child benefits. Both Labour and Alliance endorsement of the needs of the retired has declined slightly since 1983 and support for child benefits has increased by a similar margin. So there is considerable room for party differences within the overall pattern of support for maintaining or extending tax-financed welfare state expenditure.

Highest priority for social benefits

	Conservative		Alliance		Labour	
	1983	1986	1983	1986	1983	1986
	%	%	%	%	%	%
Retirement pensions	40	46	40	37	41	37
Benefits for disabled people	30	29	24	27	19	20
Benefits for the unemployed	11	11	20	17	25	22
Child benefits	7	8	7	10	8	13
Benefits for single parents	11	6	6	8	6	7

Interestingly, supporters of the two main opposition groupings show substantially more sympathy for the needs of the less favoured (currently met to a large extent by means-tested provision). The largest groups in all parties, however, support the traditional heartland of the welfare state – the National Health Service, education and pensions.

Dissatisfaction with the NHS

One finding of the 1986 survey which appears to contradict the evidence of growing public support for state health care is the increasing public dissatisfaction with some aspects of the NHS. In 1983 we asked whether a range of British institutions was well run or not, and repeated the question in 1986. Concern about the quality of organisation and management of the NHS rose from 42 to 63% over this period. Answering a separate question about 'the way the NHS is run nowadays', about a quarter of the sample described themselves as "quite" or "very dissatisfied" in 1983. By 1986 the proportion had risen to two fifths (see **Table 1.6**).

More detailed questions reveal it is in-patient and out-patient hospital treatment within the NHS, rather than GP or domiciliary services, which is the focus of increasing public concern (see **Table 1.7**). However, the rise in dissatisfaction with existing health provision in the state sector does not necessarily conflict with evidence elsewhere in the 1986 survey of support for state spending on the NHS. Dissatisfaction may lead to a decline in support for the service if alternatives are readily available; or alternatively, to redoubled demands for better provision, if a basic sympathy for its aims prevails (see Hirschman, 1970). In the *British Social Attitudes* survey, as in other work (for example Taylor-Gooby, 1987), dissatisfaction is associated with support for more state spending in general and on health care in particular. The link is, if anything, stronger among those with ready access to private treatment through health insurance.

Satisfaction with the NHS and support for state spending on health care

	Satisfied %	Neither %	Dissatisfied %
Support for social spending generally			
Less tax and social spending	6	5	4
Status quo	50	51	34
More tax and social spending			
– all	40	40	56
– those covered by health insurance	38	33	60
– those not covered	40	41	55
Highest priority for extra spending			
NHS highest priority (all)	45	45	51
– those covered by health insurance	34	31	43
– those not covered	47	48	52

It therefore seems reasonable to conclude that there is no evidence of a decline in support for the *principle* of socialised medicine as a component in citizenship; rather a valued public service is seen to have been damaged by spending cuts. Apparently it would take more than increased opportunities to use the private sector to turn dissatisfaction into disaffection or disloyalty towards the National Health Service.

Less favoured needs

Many surveys have shown that certain needs (particularly council housing, and benefits for the unemployed, for single parents and for children) receive much less public support than do the NHS, state education and state pensions (see for example Golding and Middleton, 1982; Mack and Lansley, 1985). This relative lack of sympathy for minority needs contrasts sharply with 'citizenship consensus' in favour of welfare spending on universal services. We have already noted the low priority given to council housing and social security – in particular benefits for the unemployed, children and single parents – among supporters of all parties, and ambivalence as to whether unemployment benefits should be the government's responsibility. Suspicion permeates attitudes to the needs of the unemployed and the poor.

Welfare for the unemployed

Well over three million people were registered as unemployed at the time of the survey – the highest figure in the history of the welfare state. Nonetheless there are marked divisions in sympathy for this group, and little evidence of a shift of opinion in their favour since 1983. A large majority of the electorate recognises unemployment as a serious social problem and increasingly as a more important priority for government policy than inflation.

	1983	1984	1985	1986
	%	%	%	%
Highest priority should be given to:				
keeping down inflation	27	26	22	20
keeping down unemployment	69	69	73	75

Those who give measures to reduce unemployment priority over the control of inflation outnumber by nearly four to one those who see inflation as the greater threat. This is particularly striking since just over half our sample sees inflation as the greater concern for themselves and their families.

Concern at probable increases in unemployment has fluctuated somewhat over the past four years but remains high. Moreover, the proportion of the sample predicting a fall in the jobless total has declined steadily.

In a year from now, do you expect unemployment to have gone up, to have stayed the same, or to have gone down?

	1983 %	1984 %	1985 %	1986 %
To have gone up	68	56	67	65
To have stayed the same	17	31	23	25
To have gone down	13	12	9	8

Any altruistic sentiments towards the plight of unemployed people do not seem however to extend to views on the level of benefit they should enjoy. We asked respondents to choose between two contrasting statements: whether benefits for the unemployed are *too low* and cause hardship *or* whether these benefits are *too high* and discourage people from finding jobs. Just under half the sample (44%) agreed with the first statement and 33% were in agreement with the second.* A similar division is evident in a pair of questions asking about 'scrounging' and low take-up. Concern about both issues, already at a high level in the early 1980s, has if anything increased.

	1983 %	1984 %	1985 %	1986 %
Large numbers of people *falsely* **claim benefits**				
Agree strongly	40	37	43	45
Agree slightly	25	27	24	25
Large numbers of people who are eligible for benefits *fail* **to claim them**				
Agree strongly	49	46	50	49
Agree slightly	32	33	34	34

While these changes and other changes noted earlier are fairly small, the high level of concern about these issues does indicate a failure of opposition parties to force the needs of the unemployed to the forefront of the political debate – especially at a time when unemployment has only just fallen from the highest recorded level.

Poverty

The hesitancy shown by our respondents about including the needs of unemployed people in welfare citizenship is also reflected in their attitudes to poverty, which we asked them to define:

---

* It should be noted that about one in five respondents in 1986 were unable to choose between the two statements, and answered "neither" or "both" or "don't know".

Would you say someone in Britain was or was not in poverty if . . .

		Yes	No
. . . they had enough to buy the things they really needed, but not enough to buy the things most people take for granted?	%	25	72
. . . they had enough to eat and live, but not enough to buy other things they needed?	%	55	43
. . . they had not got enough to eat and live without getting into debt?	%	95	3

While almost everyone agreed that they would describe someone as in poverty who had "not enough to eat and live without getting into debt", there was a large measure of dissensus on the other two descriptions of poverty, on the extent of poverty and on its relation to social benefits. The definition given above refers to the extreme of brutal need. The harshness of a level of living where income is below minimum subsistence is tempered by assumptions about opportunities to borrow. For academics, the debate over recent years has been between minimum subsistence and relative notions of poverty (Townsend, 1979). These latter define need in terms of inability to reach the living standards considered normal by the great majority of the population, rather than as lack of access to the bare essentials of life. Less than a quarter of the sample saw poverty in these terms and only about half assented to an intermediate position, "[having] enough to eat and live, but not enough to buy other things [they needed]". Similarly, there was little agreement on the extent of poverty, or on whether it has increased in the last few years or will increase in the future. Only about half those asked agreed that poverty was widespread, or that it was on the increase. However, less than a sixth of the sample saw it as on the wane.

Supporters of different political parties are more sharply divided on attitudes to poverty than they are in their attitudes to welfare spending and to priority areas. Conservatives are roughly twice as likely as Labour supporters to say there is very little poverty and to think that the numbers in poverty are not growing, although nearly one third *do* take this view.

	Conservative %	Alliance %	Labour %
Very little real poverty in Britain	59	37	27
Quite a lot	37	61	71
Poverty has been increasing over the last 10 years	34	51	66
Poverty will increase over the next 10 years	27	44	58

Party divergences on the *relative* conception of poverty are much more striking than those on the 'minimum subsistence' definition.

	Conservative %	Alliance %	Labour %
Conceptions of poverty			
– relative ("not enough to buy the things most people take for granted")	19	22	33
– minimum subsistence ("enough to eat and live, but not enough to buy other things")	50	54	62
– below minimum subsistence ("not enough to eat and live without getting into debt")	96	96	95

A question designed to discover how our respondents explained poverty showed that over a third adopted a fatalistic approach, while around about a quarter attributed poverty to social injustice, and smaller proportions thought that it resulted from fecklessness or ill luck. These statistics may be set against the results of the Breadline Britain survey carried out in 1983 and the EEC's poverty Eurobarometer of 1976.

Why do you think there are people who live in need?

	Eurobarometer 1976 %	Breadline Britain 1983 %	British Social Attitudes 1986 %
Because they have been unlucky	10	13	11
Because of laziness or lack of willpower	43	22	19
Because of injustice in our society	16	32	25
It's an inevitable part of modern life*	17	25	37

* 'progress' in Eurobarometer. The comparisons can be only tentative due to differences in sampling method and small differences in question wording.

The pattern of answers indicates a substantial decline since the mid-1970s in moralistic explanations of poverty. These have been supplanted mainly by fatalistic accounts, although concern about injustice has somewhat increased. This interpretation is supported by Golding and Middleton (1982) in their account of the growth of 'scrounger-phobia' in the mid-1970s, and Rose *et al* in their analysis of reasons given for Britain's economic decline (Rose, Vogler, Marshall and Newby, 1984). If moralistic contempt predominantly excluded the poor from welfare citizenship in the 1970s, the experience of recession appears to have engendered a fatalistic indifference rather than an active moral commitment to alleviate their plight.

As in the responses to earlier questions about the extent of poverty in Britain, and how it should be defined, our respondents divided sharply along party political lines. Labour supporters are far more likely to attribute poverty to injustice rather than to laziness, while Alliance supporters stress inevitability and Conservatives emphasise both the claim that it is simply a brute fact of life and, to a lesser extent, the moralistic interpretation. **Tables 1.8** and **1.9** give full details.

We then asked four questions designed to relate perceptions of poverty to impressions of the living standards of two groups of social benefit recipients – pensioners and the unemployed. In the first two questions, respondents were asked whether "a married couple without children living only on unemployment benefit" and "a married couple living only on the state pension" were "really poor", "hard up", "[had] enough to live on" or "[had] more than enough". In the following two questions, we substituted the rough cash value of unemployment benefit and the basic rate pension for the category of recipient.* Responses are shown below.

	Unemployed couple %	Couple on £50 a week %	Pensioner couple %	Couple on £62 a week %
Really poor	12	39	19	23
Hard up	47	51	51	49
Have enough to live on	28	8	23	25
Have more than enough	1	1	–	1

Relatively few people see a couple on unemployment benefit or on the basic state pension as having enough to live on. And respondents are rather more likely to see pensioners as in poverty, compared with the unemployed. But when we introduced the rough cash benefits received, the number seeing the unemployed as "really poor" increases by more than three times. In the case of pensioners, however, the number increases only slightly.

Unemployment benefits have been set at a lower rate than basic state pensions for some two decades. It appears that the popular perception of pensioners as more deserving than the workless extends to the impression that

---

* Many people on both kinds of benefit also of course receive housing benefit. But since the amount of housing benefit varies widely from person to person, we (reluctantly) decided not to add in even a notional sum to cover it.

their poverty is more severe. At the same time, the real living standards of unemployed people – when these are brought home in cash terms – are seen as extremely low by nearly 90% of the population. As **Table 1.10** shows, Labour supporters are particularly likely to see both groups of beneficiaries as poor. In the case of the unemployed, the party gap narrows when benefits are given cash values.

The contrast between the widespread support for state spending on universal services benefiting groups at all levels in society and the more divided and niggardly attitudes to the poor is further clarified when we look at attitudes to redistribution.

Redistribution and equality

Citizenship in the welfare state has traditionally been concerned with redistribution in the direction of *needs* arising from age, sickness, unemployment and so on. Redistribution from better to worse off in the direction of greater *equality* has received much less attention. A number of questions scattered through the questionnaire, but brought together in the table below, addresses these issues. As we can see, support for egalitarian measures declines as one moves at one extreme from a simple endorsement of the principle of progressive taxation to the other extreme of redistribution from the better off to the less well off. The sequence of questions brings the issue of who pays to benefit whom uncomfortably nearer home to the majority of the population.

Proportion that those with higher incomes should pay in taxes compared with those with lower incomes

	%
Much larger/larger	77
Same	19
Small/much smaller	1

Should it be the government's responsibility to reduce income differences between rich and poor?

	%
Definitely/probably should	72
Can't choose	4
Probably/definitely should not	23

It is the responsibility of government to reduce the differences in income between people with high incomes and those with low incomes

	%
Agree strongly/agree	59
Neither	20
Disagree/disagree strongly	21

Government should redistribute income from the better off to those who are less well off

	%
Agree strongly/agree	43
Neither	25
Disagree/disagree strongly	30

While progressive taxation, the Robin Hood attack on the rich and the view that income gaps are too large* are enthusiastically received, the prospect of a few more pence on one's own income tax to benefit a less fortunate neighbour receives only lukewarm response. Similarly, while progressive taxation is supported in principle, a question about tax rates shows that just over two-thirds of all households think their own tax rate is too high and less than one per cent think it too low. Whatever you think about tax rates and income inequalities, redistribution has more charm when it enables you to put your hand in someone else's pocket.

As might be expected, questions on redistributive policies expose wide party divisions. Labour and Alliance supporters are keener on egalitarian policy than Conservatives but even Labour supporters are ambivalent: while over 90% see the narrowing of income differences as definitely a government responsibility, only one in five agree strongly that government should redistribute from the better off to the less well off **(Table 1.11)**. In the formulation of policy for the 1987 general election campaign, the party leaderships may have been wise to stress that any tax increases they propose would fall on a comfortably distant minority of higher rate taxpayers. The prospects for a radically egalitarian party gaining popular support seem remote. The weakness of egalitarian sentiments is highlighted in three questions about the legitimacy of privileged access to welfare services. We asked:

- *Do you think that health care should be the same for everyone, or should people who can afford it be able to pay for better health care?*
- *Should the quality of education be the same for all children, or should parents who can afford it be able to pay for better education?*
- *And do you think that pensions should be the same for everyone, or should people who can afford it be able to pay for better pensions?*

As the table below shows, rather more respondents thought that the better off should be allowed to pay for better health care and education than favoured equal standards for all. The ratio between tolerance of privilege and equality rises to nearly two to one for pensions. Cross-tabulation by party allegiance shows a downward gradient in support for privileged access from Conservative through Alliance to Labour. However, over a third of Labour supporters are content to see the rich get better education, over two fifths tolerate privilege in health care and nearly half in pensions. Similarly, over half those in the lowest

---

* Note that the question does not assume that anything should be done about these gaps.

Access to welfare services

	Health care %	Education %	Pensions %
Should be			
– same for everyone	46	47	36
– able to pay			
for better services	53	52	61

income category (under £5,000 a year) would not debar anyone from getting better services if they were prepared to pay for them (see **Table 1.12**).

The tolerance of privileged access for the better off is reflected in attitudes to one of the major mechanisms whereby such privilege is exercised – private welfare.

Private medicine and private schooling

In 1986, as in earlier years, we asked people's opinions about the balance of private and state health care and education. And in 1986, as in earlier surveys in the series, only small minorities support the abolition or restriction of the private sector in schooling and hospitals and some three fifths of the sample think NHS GPs and dentists should be free to take on private patients. Nearly half our respondents want private treatment restricted to private hospitals, but two out of five respondents think private treatment should be allowed in NHS hospitals. (For further details see **Table 1.13**.) Questions which contrast freedom with restriction tend to load choice in favour of freedom, because many people think that freedom is good in itself; even so these findings indicate strong support for the continuance of private welfare services and a measure of support for their coexistence with, and integration into, state provision. And despite official party policy, less than a fifth of Labour supporters want private health care or education restricted, and only about half endorse the limiting of NHS GPs' and dentists' private practice. On the issue of private welfare the battle lines are drawn up between supporters of the *status quo* and private sector expansionists. Abolitionists form only a minority rearguard of opinion.

As we have seen, there is strong support for tolerance of privileged access to better health care, but only 27% of the sample took the view that state provision should be available only to the poor. Even Conservatives, with their keen support for an expanded private sector, were unenthusiastic about this proposal.

> *It has been suggested that the National Health Service should be available* only to those with lower incomes. *This would mean that contributions and taxes could be lower and most people would then take out medical insurance or pay for health care. Do you support or oppose this idea?*

	Conservative %	Alliance %	Labour %
Support	33	26	23
Oppose	62	70	73

Tolerance of privilege and of the private sector, coupled with the earlier evidence of support for state spending and of widespread enthusiasm for universal provision (at least for 'favoured' needs) show continued endorsement of the Beveridge ideal. This may be interpreted in two ways. Universal services have often benefited higher social groups – the same people who are most likely to have access to the private sector: thus the pattern of attitudes may simply reflect acquiescence in the existing structure of privilege. An alternative explanation would emphasise the role of universal provision in binding society together, allowing everyone to have access to basic standards in essential services, irrespective of social class or income. This latter interpretation is lent some support by the fact that those with access to private health care are only slightly less likely than others to oppose the restriction of the NHS to low income groups. Similarly, those with private health insurance are as likely to endorse welfare state spending in general as is the population at large.

Some evidence, however, points to a more discriminating public mind than either of the above interpretations suggests. For example, those who have access to private medicine – especially through personal contract rather than as a perquisite of employment – are much less likely to make the NHS their highest priority for state spending.

	No private health insurance %	Health insurance through employer %	Health insurance not through employer %
NHS highest priority for extra spending	49	34	38

So self-interest may undermine support for particular aspects of the welfare state without necessarily extending to all of them. This may lead to a gradual attrition of support, even for highly favoured services, as the corresponding private sector provision expands. But further work is needed to clarify the position.

Conclusions

Our latest survey shows that public opinion continues to support in broad outline the structure of citizenship embodied in the welfare settlement of the past four decades. While there is growing opposition to those government policies which bring about cuts in universal services, to the targeting of provision on specific low-income minorities and to the substitution of private for state services, the idea of egalitarian welfarism meets with little approval. There is a strong contrast between a high level of support for the NHS, state education, state pensions and benefits for disabled people and much greater ambivalence about spending on the unemployed, council tenants and single parents. Few voters of any party want radical redistribution – or are ready to pay for it. There is little consensus on the nature, extent and cause of poverty. Few people regard major groups of beneficiaries as really poor even when benefit levels are spelt out in cash terms, although they may see pensioners and the unemployed as hard up. In any case, there is widespread ignorance of the levels of benefit payment. There is no agreement either on the priority that should be given to the unemployed nor on the level of hardship they suffer – nor indeed how 'deserving' they are of sympathy: the unemployed are lower in the pecking order of legitimate government responsibilities than are pensioners or the NHS. Inequality in access to welfare, even in the areas of the most valued state services, and the continuance of the private sector, are widely supported. People want a welfare state, but they also want it carefully limited – a limitation which will inevitably perpetuate existing inequalities in society.

A number of social changes over the past 40 years suggest that limited welfare state citizenship ideals will produce an even more unequal society in the future. Two are likely to be particularly important. First, unemployment has recently reached the highest recorded level. Although it is likely to fall somewhat (in part due to the decreasing rate at which young people are entering the labour market), it is unlikely to return to the levels of the 1950s, 1960s and early 1970s in the foreseeable future. A considerable volume of work indicates that the unemployed figure prominently among those in poverty (for example, Moylan, Miller and Davies, 1984). If the scale of their need is inadequately recognised in public opinion, it is possible that their poverty – and associated health and social problems – may even increase.

Second, private provision in housing, education, pensions and some aspects of health care is expanding. Increasing access to the private sector may well undermine support for those state services for which private welfare can offer a substitute. The high level of tolerance towards private provision (often at higher standards than state welfare is currently able to afford) is unlikely to produce an equilibrium – rather a tendency for the support of some groups to slip gradually from state to private sector.

In the past year, however, attitudes to welfare in Britain have hardened against further constraints in spending and against the philosophy of targeting state services exclusively on defined groups in need. Nonetheless if Margaret Thatcher has misjudged the public mood on welfare spending and cuts in services, she may well have struck a chord of sympathy in popular attitudes to privatisation, redistribution to the poor and welfare for unemployed people. There is thus little in the pattern of public attitudes to hearten those who believe in social equality or in a high standard of provision for those in need. A continuing high level of long-term unemployment and the growth of private welfare are likely to move public opinion even more out of sympathy with these goals, although it is probably over-pessimistic to predict that eventually this is likely to undermine welfare state citizenship altogether.

References

GOLDING, P. and MIDDLETON, S., *Images of Welfare*, Martin Robertson, Oxford (1982).

HIRSCHMAN, A., *Exit, Voice and Loyalty*, Harvard University Press, Harvard, United States (1970).

KLEIN, R., 'The Case for Elitism', *Political Quarterly*, vol. 45, no. 3 (1974), pp. 401-27.

LE GRAND, J., *The Strategy of Equality*, Allen and Unwin, London (1982).

MACK, J. and LANSLEY, S., *Poor Britain*, Allen and Unwin, London (1985).

MOYLAN, S., MILLER, J. and DAVIES, R., *For Richer, For Poorer? DHSS Cohort Study of Unemployed Men*, DHSS Research Report No. 11, HMSO, London (1984).

ROSE, D., VOGLER, C., MARSHALL, G. and NEWBY, H., 'Economic Restructuring: the British Experience', *Annals of the American Academy of Political and Social Science*, no. 475 (1984), pp. 137-57.

TAYLOR-GOOBY, P., 'Welfare Attitudes: Cleavage, Consensus and Citizenship', *Quarterly Journal of Social Affairs*, vol. 3, no. 3 (1987).

TAYLOR-GOOBY, P., *Public Opinion, Ideology and Social Welfare*, Routledge and Kegan Paul, London (1985).

TITMUSS, R., 'The Social Division of Welfare', *Essays on the Welfare State*, Allen and Unwin, London (1955).

TOWNSEND, P., *Poverty in the United Kingdom*, Penguin, Harmondsworth (1979).

1.1 AREAS OF GOVERNMENT RESPONSIBILITY (B226)
by age, compressed Goldthorpe class schema and party identification

DEFINITELY/PROBABLY SHOULD BE THE GOVERNMENT'S RESPONSIBILITY TO	TOTAL	AGE+							COMPRESSED GOLDTHORPE CLASS SCHEMA+						PARTY IDENTIFICATION+			
		18-24	25-34	35-44	45-54	55-59	60-64	65+	Never had a job	Sal-ariat	Routine non-manual	Petty Bourg-eoisie	Manual foremen	Working class	Cons.	Alliance	Labour	Non-aligned
	%	%	%	%	%	%	%	%	%	%	%	%	%	%	%	%	%	%
A ... provide a job for everyone who wants one	62	70	65	61	56	60	61	60	74	46	59	66	62	71	42	62	81	59
B ... keep prices under control	89	90	90	86	91	89	87	91	89	80	88	91	92	96	85	88	94	89
C ... provide health care for the sick	98	95	99	97	100	99	96	99	96	97	97	99	99	99	97	98	99	97
D ... provide a decent standard of living for the old	98	94	98	99	99	99	95	100	98	98	96	98	97	99	97	99	98	96
E ... provide industry with the help it needs to grow	87	85	88	88	86	92	91	86	92	84	88	86	87	88	84	88	92	77
F ... provide a decent standard of living for the unemployed	83	80	82	85	81	84	82	87	90	80	81	86	86	85	74	85	91	76
G ... reduce income differences between the rich and poor	72	76	76	68	74	70	75	70	80	58	69	72	81	82	53	74	88	77
BASE: B RESPONDENTS Weighted	1315	211	250	273	204	92	77	205	106	298	293	85	77	439	451	225	468	91
Unweighted	1321	197	245	226	216	98	79	207	94	301	298	86	81	443	452	227	471	88

1.2 SOCIAL SPENDING AND THE LEVEL OF BENEFITS (Q57)
by age, compressed Goldthorpe class schema and party identification

	TOTAL	AGE+							COMPRESSED GOLDTHORPE CLASS SCHEMA+						PARTY IDENTIFICATION+			
		18-24	25-34	35-44	45-54	55-59	60-64	65+	Never had a job	Sal-ariat	Routine non-manual	Petty Bourg-eoisie	Manual foremen	Working class	Cons.	Alliance	Labour	Non-aligned
	%	%	%	%	%	%	%	%	%	%	%	%	%	%	%	%	%	%
GOVERNMENT SHOULD																		
- reduce taxes, lower social spending	5	6	3	4	5	4	6	6	7	4	3	9	4	6	5	3	5	8
- keep same as now	44	49	44	38	42	48	41	45	33	44	44	48	42	44	54	37	36	47
- increase taxes, increase social spending	46	38	47	52	48	42	47	43	52	48	47	42	50	44	36	55	55	34
none/don't know	6	7	5	5	5	6	6	6	8	4	6	2	4	6	5	5	4	11
not answered	*	-	*	*	-	-	1	*	-	*	*	-	-	*	*	-	*	-
BASE: ALL RESPONDENTS Weighted	3066	454	570	611	484	232	204	509	238	680	668	193	183	1051	1035	535	1072	231
Unweighted	3100	436	557	615	506	241	211	521	228	694	684	194	185	1062	1054	542	1080	226

1.3 FIRST PRIORITY FOR EXTRA GOVERNMENT SPENDING (Q53) by age, compressed Goldthorpe class schema and party identification

FIRST PRIORITY	TOTAL	AGE+							COMPRESSED GOLDTHORPE CLASS SCHEMA+						PARTY IDENTIFICATION+			
		18-24	25-34	35-44	45-54	55-59	60-64	65+	Never had a job	Sal-ariat	Routine non-manual	Petty Bourg-eoisie	Manual foremen	Working class	Cons.	Alliance	Labour	Non-aligned
	%	%	%	%	%	%	%	%	%	%	%	%	%	%	%	%	%	%
Health	47	44	47	44	48	54	51	49	46	41	53	39	50	49	43	46	53	50
Education	27	22	31	35	29	20	22	20	23	36	24	34	26	24	31	33	22	20
Help for industry	8	10	8	8	9	8	5	7	6	9	8	10	7	8	9	8	6	9
Housing	7	12	7	5	6	4	7	9	8	5	7	6	8	8	5	6	9	10
Social security benefits	5	6	2	3	4	6	8	7	11	2	4	4	2	6	2	4	7	4
Police and prisons	3	2	2	2	2	2	4	4	2	3	2	3	4	2	4	1	1	2
Defence	1	1	1	1	1	2	1	1	2	1	1	2	-	1	3	*	*	1
Roads	1	2	1	1	2	2	1	1	1	2	1	3	1	1	2	1	1	3
Public transport	*	1	*	-	1	1	1	*	-	1	*	-	1	*	1	-	*	-
Overseas aid	*	1	1	1	1	-	-	*	2	1	1	-	1	-	-	1	1	-
BASE: ALL RESPONDENTS Weighted	3066	454	570	611	484	232	204	509	238	680	668	193	183	1051	1035	535	1072	231
Unweighted	3100	436	567	615	506	241	211	521	228	694	684	194	185	1062	1054	542	1080	226

1.4 SECOND PRIORITY FOR EXTRA GOVERNMENT SPENDING (Q53)
by age, compressed Goldthorpe class schema and party identification

SECOND PRIORITY	TOTAL	AGE+							COMPRESSED GOLDTHORPE CLASS SCHEMA+						PARTY IDENTIFICATION+			
		18-24	25-34	35-44	45-54	55-59	60-64	65+	Never had a job	Sal-ariat	Routine non-manual	Petty Bourg-eoisie	Manual foremen	Working class	Cons.	Alliance	Labour	Non-aligned
	%	%	%	%	%	%	%	%	%	%	%	%	%	%	%	%	%	%
Education	30	31	33	35	31	29	25	21	31	36	31	24	26	27	27	34	31	32
Health	28	24	31	32	29	26	23	22	26	25	31	32	27	27	29	31	25	20
Housing	14	17	14	11	13	11	12	17	17	14	11	9	17	16	10	11	17	20
Help for industry	8	9	7	8	10	10	13	7	7	7	9	14	6	9	12	6	8	5
Social security benefits	7	8	7	3	7	7	9	9	8	5	4	6	11	9	4	6	11	7
Police and prisons	5	4	3	4	4	8	8	7	5	6	6	6	3	4	8	4	3	4
Defence	3	2	2	2	2	3	2	5	1	3	3	5	5	1	4	2	2	2
Public transport	2	2	1	1	1	2	3	4	2	2	1	1	3	2	2	1	2	2
Roads	2	2	1	2	3	2	2	4	1	2	3	2	2	2	3	2	2	1
Overseas aid	1	2	1	*	1	-	2	1	2	2	1	1	-	*	*	2	1	2
BASE: ALL RESPONDENTS Weighted	3066	454	570	611	484	232	204	509	238	680	668	193	183	1051	1035	535	1072	231
Unweighted	3100	436	567	615	506	241	211	521	228	694	684	194	185	1062	1054	542	1080	226

1.5 FIRST AND SECOND PRIORITY FOR SPENDING ON SOCIAL BENEFITS (Q54) by age, compressed Goldthorpe class schema and party identification

	TOTAL	AGE+							COMPRESSED GOLDTHORPE CLASS SCHEMA+						PARTY IDENTIFICATION+			
		18-24	25-34	35-44	45-54	55-59	60-64	65+	Never had a job	Salariat	Routine non-manual	Petty Bourgeoisie	Manual foremen	Working class	Cons.	Alliance	Labour	Non-aligned
	%	%	%	%	%	%	%	%	%	%	%	%	%	%	%	%	%	%
FIRST PRIORITY																		
Old age pensions	40	17	32	43	43	45	53	59	31	41	37	44	60	40	46	37	37	34
Disabled benefits	25	18	19	24	30	33	28	29	29	26	26	26	19	23	29	27	20	28
Unemployment benefits	16	32	19	13	15	13	12	7	23	15	15	8	11	18	11	17	22	13
Child benefits	11	19	21	11	5	5	3	2	10	9	11	12	7	12	8	10	13	15
Single parent benefits	7	14	9	8	6	3	3	2	6	7	10	8	3	6	6	8	7	8
SECOND PRIORITY																		
Disabled benefits	33	25	31	36	36	32	36	48	28	34	33	32	38	33	35	31	31	33
Old age pensions	24	17	26	26	25	30	25	22	28	25	25	26	17	24	25	27	24	25
Unemployment benefits	17	15	18	17	19	21	18	13	18	16	16	16	21	17	15	16	19	15
Child benefits	13	20	17	12	10	7	9	9	11	11	12	13	11	14	10	13	14	15
Single parent benefits	11	22	12	11	9	8	10	5	12	12	12	8	11	10	11	11	11	9
BASE: ALL RESPONDENTS																		
Weighted	3066	454	570	611	484	232	204	509	238	680	668	193	183	1051	1035	535	1072	231
Unweighted	3100	436	567	615	506	241	211	521	228	694	684	194	185	1062	1054	542	1080	226

1.6 SATISFACTION WITH THE NATIONAL HEALTH SERVICE (Q58)
(Comparison over time)

	SURVEY YEAR		
	1983	1984	1986
	%	%	%
SATISFACTION WITH THE WAY THE NATIONAL HEALTH SERVICE RUNS NOWADAYS			
Very satisfied	11	11	6
Quite satisfied	44	40	34
Neither satisfied nor dissatisfied	20	19	19
Quite dissatisfied	18	19	23
Very dissatisfied	7	11	16
Not answered	*	*	*
BASE: ALL RESPONDENTS			
Weighted	1719	1645	3066
Unweighted	1761	1675	3100

1.7 SATISFACTION WITH DIFFERRENT PARTS OF THE NHS (Q59)
(Comparison over time)

	PARTS OF THE NATIONAL HEALTH SERVICE											
	LOCAL DOCTORS/GPS		NHS DENTISTS		HEALTH VISITORS		DISTRICT NURSES		IN HOSPITAL AS INPATIENT		ATTENDING HOSPITAL AS OUTPATIENT	
	1983	1986	1983	1986	1983	1986	1983	1986	1983	1986	1983	1986
	%	%	%	%	%	%	%	%	%	%	%	%
SATISFACTION WITH THE WAY EACH OF THESE PARTS OF THE NATIONAL HEALTH SERVICE RUNS NOWADAYS												
Very satisfied	33	27	24	19	14	12	22	19	34	25	21	14
Quite satisfied	47	51	49	55	34	37	38	41	40	42	40	41
Neither satisfied nor dissatisfied	7	8	15	14	39	29	31	25	17	15	16	14
Quite dissatisfied	9	10	7	7	4	6	1	3	5	10	15	19
Very dissatisfied	3	4	3	3	2	2	1	1	1	3	6	10
Don't know	*	*	2	3	6	14	6	12	2	4	2	3
BASE: ALL RESPONDENTS												
Weighted	1719	3066	1719	3066	1719	3066	1719	3066	1719	3066	1719	3066
Unweighted	1761	3100	1761	3100	1761	3100	1761	3100	1761	3100	1761	3100

1.8 EXPLANATIONS OF POVERTY (B77)
by age, compressed Goldthorpe class schema and region

WHY ARE THERE PEOPLE WHO LIVE IN NEED?	TOTAL	AGE+							COMPRESSED GOLDTHORPE CLASS SCHEMA+						REGION					
		18-24	25-34	35-44	45-54	55-59	60-64	65+	Never had a job	Sal-ariat	Routine non-manual	Petty Bourg-eoisie	Manual foremen	Working class	Scot-land	North	Mid-lands	Wales	South	Greater London
	%	%	%	%	%	%	%	%	%	%	%	%	%	%	%	%	%	%	%	%
Because they have been unlucky	11	11	10	10	11	8	10	15	8	11	13	8	10	11	8	12	9	12	13	10
Because of laziness/lack of willpower	19	18	12	16	19	33	22	24	15	16	16	33	15	22	10	20	23	17	19	20
Because of injustice in society	25	34	32	26	21	20	24	13	35	24	25	18	21	26	33	29	23	31	20	23
Inevitable part of modern life	37	31	36	39	41	32	38	39	32	39	38	38	48	34	42	33	41	38	37	35
Because of ignorance	1	*	1	-	2	1	3	1	1	2	1	-	1	1	-	*	1	-	1	3
BASE: B RESPONDENTS Weighted	1548	255	284	306	246	103	93	257	132	336	329	106	87	531	163	406	252	82	485	160
Unweighted	1548	239	274	308	259	110	96	259	119	335	335	105	91	533	147	409	261	84	481	166

1.9 EXPLANATIONS OF POVERTY (B77)
by annual household income and party identification

WHY ARE THERE PEOPLE WHO LIVE IN NEED?	TOTAL	ANNUAL HOUSEHOLD INCOME+					PARTY IDENTIFICATION+			
		Under £5,000	£5,000-£7,999	£8,000-£11,999	£12,000-£17,999	£18,000	Conservative	Alliance	Labour	Non-aligned
	%	%	%	%	%	%	%	%	%	%
Because they have been unlucky	11	12	13	10	9	10	11	11	9	14
Because of laziness/lack of willpower	19	21	20	17	18	21	27	14	13	22
Because of injustice in society	25	27	28	27	24	23	10	23	41	21
Inevitable part of modern life	37	35	33	41	39	38	42	44	32	29
Because of ignorance	1	1	2	*	1	1	1	2	*	2
BASE: B RESPONDENTS Weighted	1548	353	260	295	250	184	505	264	553	125
Unweighted	1548	259	260	296	250	188	508	265	552	120

1.10 ATTITUDES TOWARDS STATE BENEFITS AND POVERTY (B79a, B79b) by age, compressed Goldthorpe class schema and party identification

WOULD YOU SAY THAT A MARRIED COUPLE ON UNEMPLOYMENT BENEFIT/STATE PENSION ARE:

	TOTAL	AGE+							COMPRESSED GOLDTHORPE CLASS SCHEMA+						PARTY IDENTIFICATION+			
		18-24	25-34	35-44	45-54	55-59	60-64	65+	Never had a job	Sal-ariat	Routine non-manual	Petty Bourg-eoisie	Manual foremen	Working class	Cons.	Alliance	Labour	Non-aligned
	%	%	%	%	%	%	%	%	%	%	%	%	%	%	%	%	%	%
UNEMPLOYMENT BENEFIT																		
Really poor	12	12	12	9	13	17	22	11	14	12	10	11	15	13	7	12	18	9
Hard up	47	51	47	51	48	50	45	38	53	51	49	38	48	45	46	46	50	37
Have enough to live on	28	32	29	27	24	21	19	36	21	26	30	36	24	29	35	26	22	38
Have more than enough	1	1	1	1	1	-	-	1	-	1	1	-	-	1	1	1	*	1
STATE PENSION																		
Really poor	19	16	20	19	18	15	28	23	25	21	16	13	25	19	14	18	26	13
Hard up	51	50	53	57	49	57	49	44	45	55	53	55	55	47	51	54	50	47
Have enough to live on	23	26	18	21	26	25	18	28	19	20	26	25	18	25	30	21	17	26
Have more than enough	*	1	*	1	-	1	1	-	1	*	-	-	-	1	*	*	1	-
BASE: B RESPONDENTS																		
Weighted	1548	255	284	306	246	103	93	257	132	336	329	105	87	531	505	264	553	125
Unweighted	1548	239	274	308	259	110	96	259	119	335	335	105	91	533	508	265	552	120

1.11 ATTITUDES TO REDISTRIBUTIVE POLICIES (B205, B231I)
by compressed Goldthorpe class schema, annual household income and party identification

	TOTAL	COMPRESSED GOLDTHORPE CLASS SCHEMA+						ANNUAL HOUSEHOLD INCOME+					PARTY IDENTIFICATION+			
		Never had a job	Sal-ariat	Routine non-manual	Petty Bourg-eoisie	Manual foremen	Working class	Under £5,000	£5,000-£7,999	£8,000-£11,999	£12,000-£17,999	£18,000+	Cons.	Alli-ance	Labour	Non-aligned
	%	%	%	%	%	%	%	%	%	%	%	%	%	%	%	%
IT IS THE RESPONSIBILITY OF THE GOVERNMENT TO REDUCE THE DIFFERENCES IN INCOME BETWEEN PEOPLE WITH HIGH INCOMES AND THOSE WITH LOW INCOMES																
Agree strongly	24	38	13	19	21	28	32	36	32	26	12	8	12	20	37	30
Agree	35	29	32	36	35	37	38	33	37	40	34	32	29	42	35	39
Neither agree nor disagree	17	16	20	23	25	13	18	19	17	16	23	21	23	17	18	18
Disagree	17	15	26	18	15	18	10	10	12	15	25	29	27	19	8	12
Disagree strongly	4	2	8	4	4	4	1	1	2	3	7	11	8	2	1	1
GOVERNMENT SHOULD REDISTRIBUTE INCOME FROM THE BETTER OFF TO THOSE WHO ARE LESS WELL OFF																
Agree strongly	11	18	6	8	6	17	17	16	16	13	5	2	4	9	21	9
Agree	32	33	29	28	33	35	36	38	37	33	28	27	18	32	43	40
Neither agree nor disagree	25	26	23	26	26	29	26	25	27	26	25	21	26	29	22	30
Disagree	25	18	33	28	28	19	19	16	16	21	33	42	39	26	11	14
Disagree strongly	5	2	9	8	5	1	1	2	3	5	9	8	11	3	1	6
BASE: B RESPONDENTS *Weighted*	1315	106	298	293	85	77	439	288	233	270	218	161	451	225	468	91
Unweighted	1321	94	301	298	86	81	443	293	233	270	220	167	452	227	471	88

1.12 ATTITUDES TOWARDS THE WELFARE STATE (B81a, B81b, B81c)
by compressed Goldthorpe class schema, annual household income and party identification

	TOTAL	COMPRESSED GOLDTHORPE CLASS SCHEMA+						ANNUAL HOUSEHOLD INCOME+					PARTY IDENTIFICATION+			
		Never had a job	Sal-ariat	Routine non-manual	Petty Bourg-eoisie	Manual foremen	Working class	Under £5,000	£5,000-£7,999	£8,000-£11,999	£12,000-£17,999	£18,000+	Cons.	Alli-ance	Labour	Non-aligned
DO YOU THINK THAT HEALTH CARE/ EDUCATION/PENSIONS SHOULD BE THE SAME FOR EVERYONE OR SHOULD PEOPLE WHO CAN AFFORD IT PAY FOR BETTER SERVICES?	%	%	%	%	%	%	%	%	%	%	%	%	%	%	%	%
HEALTH CARE																
Same for everyone	46		54	42	39	38	49	42	45	50	48	39	32	46	57	44
Able to pay for better	53		45	58	58	62	49	56	54	51	51	61	66	53	42	53
EDUCATION																
Same for everyone	47		44	45	37	47	49	45	45	49	46	43	29	47	62	63
Able to pay for better	52		54	53	61	52	50	54	54	50	53	56	69	51	37	37
PENSIONS																
Same for everyone	36		29	35	28	31	42	39	39	35	32	26	23	33	49	39
Able to pay for better	61		69	61	68	67	55	56	59	63	66	72	74	65	47	57
BASE: B RESPONDENTS *Weighted*	1548	132	336	329	106	87	531	353	260	295	250	184	505	264	553	125
Unweighted	1548	119	335	335	105	91	533	359	260	296	250	188	508	265	552	120

1.13 ATTITUDES TOWARDS PRIVATE MEDICINE AND PRIVATE SCHOOLING (Qs62, 63, 65a) by compressed Goldthorpe class schema, annual household income and party identification

	TOTAL	COMPRESSED GOLDTHORPE CLASS SCHEMA+						ANNUAL HOUSEHOLD INCOME+					PARTY IDENTIFICATION+			
		Never had a job	Sal-ariat	Routine non-manual	Petty Bourg-eoisie	Manual foremen	Working class	Under £5,000	£5,000-£7,999	£8,000-£11,999	£12,000-£17,999	£18,000+	Cons.	Alli-ance	Labour	Non-aligned
	%	%	%	%	%	%	%	%	%	%	%	%	%	%	%	%
PRIVATE MEDICINE																
Private medical treatment in all hospitals should be abolished	11	17	10	7	7	12	13	15	9	11	8	9	3	9	19	12
Private medical treatment should be allowed in private hospitals but not in NHS hospitals	46	44	39	49	50	47	50	44	51	51	51	38	38	48	53	43
Private medical treatment should be allowed in both private and NHS hospitals	41	37	50	44	42	37	35	38	38	38	40	52	58	40	26	39
GPs should be allowed to take on private patients	57	48	63	61	64	56	53	54	57	58	54	65	68	62	44	60
GPs should not be allowed to take on private patients	38	45	34	36	35	41	42	40	39	40	43	34	29	36	51	34
NHS dentists should be free to give private treatment	62	51	68	65	68	61	57	58	62	62	61	71	73	66	49	64
NHS dentists should not be free to give private treatment	33	41	29	30	31	36	36	34	32	35	36	28	24	30	45	31
PRIVATE EDUCATION																
Should there be more private schools?	13	12	16	14	23	13	10	12	12	11	14	17	23	11	6	11
Should there be about the same number as now?	64	54	62	69	64	62	64	62	66	66	68	62	68	67	58	65
Should there be fewer private schools?	9	13	9	9	8	8	11	9	11	11	8	8	3	10	15	6
Should there be no private schools at all?	10	17	9	7	9	13	12	13	9	10	8	11	3	9	18	10
BASE: ALL RESPONDENTS Weighted	3066	238	680	668	193	183	1051	700	498	577	508	408	1035	535	1072	231
Unweighted	3100	228	694	684	194	185	1062	727	507	578	514	412	1054	542	1080	226

2 Business and industry

*Martin Collins**

The background to this examination of public attitudes towards industry is the designation of 1986 as 'Industry Year'. During the year various attempts were made to improve public attitudes towards industry. These results – for the spring of 1986 – provide a benchmark, with questions scheduled for inclusion in the 1987 and 1989 surveys to monitor any shifts in attitude that may have occurred.

In the programme for 'Industry Year', steps were taken to strengthen links between industry and society and to build public awareness of the indirect or direct role industry plays – through wages, taxes and profits – in supporting, for example, social services and other benefits. Schools were a particular target, the programme seeking to promote the attractions of a career in industry.

The impetus for such a programme is reflected by the report of the Select Committee on Overseas Trade (House of Lords, 1985), which states:

> A principal theme . . . is that of the national attitude towards trade and manufacturing . . . [which] needs to change – and change radically – if we are to avoid a major social and economic crisis. (Para. 7)

Later in the report, the theme is picked up, with references to:

> a general lack of awareness of the importance of manufacturing . . . reflected in the inadequate social esteem accorded to industry and trade in modern British culture. (Para. 126)

> This calls for a radical change of attitude from all sections of society. (Para. 130)

Our results do *not* confirm this reading of the problem. Industry and trade may or may not receive poor treatment in the mass media; they may or may not

* Director of SCPR's Survey Methods Centre and Visiting Professor in The City University Business School.

enjoy the consistent support of government and Civil Service or the esteem of many influential members of society. But, insofar as the Select Committee and 'Industry Year' were addressing the general public, they were preaching to the converted. Not only is the value of industry recognised, but the general public also echoes many of the other criticisms made by the Select Committee: of inadequate investment and training; of poor management and labour relations; of insufficient government support.

A general view of British industry

Our questions were wide-ranging, designed to cover different aspects of industry's role and image. One theme was the particular role of the private manufacturing sector as opposed to the service and public sectors. Another was the relative attractiveness of a job in manufacturing as opposed to the other sectors, on a series of different criteria. A third theme, which we will discuss first here, was an overall assessment of industry (along the lines of the Select Committee's broad assumptions), including the public's view of Britain's general industrial performance. We had tackled this latter question in previous rounds of the survey, so a comparison was already available.

The view that Britain needs industry, and its manufacturing industry in particular, is almost unanimous. People see the desirability of a strong manufacturing base, only 7% believing that we can manage without. Even those people who themselves work in service sectors of the economy are no less convinced of the role that manufacturing plays in the economy. (This is only the first of many indications of a consensus among those who work in different sectors: manufacturing and service; public and private.) Moreover there is widespread recognition that British industry deserves our support: by more than two to one (59% to 23%), the sample felt that we should make particular efforts to buy British goods, even when we have to pay a bit more for them.

As we will see, however, the majority view is that industry is not currently performing as it could. Expectations for the future are mixed: as many people anticipate a further decline in industrial performance as expect an improvement. Depressingly, given the unpleasant medicine industry has received to cure its ills, expectations in 1986 are actually worse than those observed in 1983.

Looking ahead over the next year, do you think Britain's general industrial performance will . . .

		Improve a lot	Improve a little	Stay the same	Decline a little	Decline a lot
1983	%	5	39	34	13	4
1986	%	3	22	47	16	7

Pessimism is more common in the parts of the country that have suffered most: 30% of those living in Scotland and 25% of those in Northern England expect further decline. It is also more common among the young: among the under 25s, only 16% (as opposed to 25% of the total sample) expect to see any improvement. But, even among the most optimistic groups – those living in the more protected South and the over 55s – substantial minorities expect further decline.

		Expect: Improvement	Decline
Total	%	25	23
Region: South	%	28	21
Greater London	%	26	22
Midlands/Wales	%	26	21
North	%	23	25
Scotland	%	18	30
Age: 55+	%	30	18
35–54	%	26	25
25–34	%	23	24
18–24	%	16	28

An important assumption behind allowing – or acquiescing in – the decline of Britain's manufacturing base is that industry will emerge leaner and fitter, more able to survive in a competitive world, and more efficient. Views as to whether this has been achieved already are mixed: 32% think that British industry is more efficient than it was five years ago, and 24% that it is less efficient. Moreover, only around a third (36%) expect the position to improve over the next five years. The majority expects no improvement.

Where do the problems lie?

No analysis of Britain's economy comes up with a single overriding factor to explain our ills. Nor does the general public see the problem in simplistic terms. Of ten possible causes of Britain's economic difficulties, the average respondent thought four to be "very important" and another four to be "quite important". Blame is widely distributed. The government is blamed by the largest number, nearly 60% thinking its failure to create jobs to be a very important contributory factor. But employers and managers are also criticised: about 50% blame lack of investment and poor management. And the workforce does not escape criticism: about 40% are critical of workers' resistance to change, and 33% think that "people are not working hard enough".

When this question was asked previously, in 1983, people were equally likely to blame a wide range of factors. But there have been some quite marked changes in the three intervening years.* More people now blame lack of

---

* This question was asked rather differently in 1983, so changes in responses should be treated with some caution.

government support (up by 14%), lack of investment (up by 14%) and bad management (up by 9%). Fewer blame environmental factors such as high energy costs (down by 8%) or the decline in world trade (down by 6%). The largest shift of all is in the perceived importance of manufacturing industry's failure to attract good recruits. The percentage identifying this as a *very* important factor is still relatively low (36%) but it has increased greatly over the 19% recorded in 1983.

	Very important factors	
	1983	1986
	%	%
Government not creating jobs	45	59
Employers not investing	34	48
Industry badly managed	39	48
Decline in world trade	50	44
Energy costs too high	48	40
Workers reluctant to change	37	39
Best leavers don't go into industry	19	36
People not working hard enough	36	33
Government spending too high	23	30
Wages too high	14	13

The signs of industrial decline are apparently easy for all to see: in factory closures, unemployment figures and in imported goods in the shops. Britain's relative failure in *international* trade is also clearly recognised by the general public, almost half of whom feel that Britain is "worse than most" of her international competitors at selling goods abroad. (Only one in ten thinks that Britain is "better than most" in this respect.)

In fact, Britain's exports of manufactured goods have risen over the last decade, but perhaps not nearly fast enough. Whilst exports, in volume terms, have risen by 15–20% over a ten-year period, imports have doubled. In 1983, for the first time, the balance of trade in manufactured goods was in deficit. There is a general trend in world trade against the older industrial countries, but this does little to explain the particularly poor British performance. Britain's share of manufacturing exports, among the 11 main industrial countries, as high as one-third at the turn of the century and still one fifth only 30 years ago, is now less than one tenth and continuing to decline.

The failure is not blamed on lack of imagination or an inability to make good products. In terms of invention and design, British industry is highly regarded. Here, about half the sample say Britain is better than most of her competitors and only around one in ten that she is worse. British marketing skills – tailoring the product to match consumer needs – are rather less well regarded. Views are evenly divided, with about one in four feeling that Britain is better than most and the same number thinking her worse than most at making the goods people want to buy.

But British industry's real problems are seen to lie in underinvestment and the poor quality of its staff. Industry is widely criticised for its failure to invest in new skills and new machinery, for its failure to attract good workers – in management and 'on the factory floor' – and for its poor industrial relations.

		In comparison with our industrial competitors, Britain is:	
		Better than most	**Worse than most**
Inventing new products	%	52	14
Designing products	%	47	10
Making goods people want	%	23	23
Training for new skills	%	17	35
Investing in new machinery	%	12	49
Attracting good managers	%	12	39
Attracting good workers	%	11	33
Industrial relations	%	11	43
Selling goods abroad	%	10	46

In most respects those who work in the public sector tend to be fractionally more critical than those who work in the private sector. But the differences are trivial. People from all sectors – public and private, manufacturing and services – see the same problems. British industry is believed to have the potential to succeed in the international arena, in terms of inventiveness and design skills, but it is ill-equipped to realise that potential in almost every other respect.

The role of government

We have already seen that Britain's economic problems are attributed more to government's failure to stimulate employment than to any other single factor. It is not surprising then to find the vast majority of the sample – 91% – favouring government-led construction projects to create more jobs. But a majority of the sample also approved of other ways of supporting British industry: 67% would favour import controls, 61% subsidies for private industry.

The significance of such support for industry wanes somewhat when placed in the context of other spending priorities. While the vast majority feel that the government should spend money to create jobs, around 90% would be opposed to cuts in spending on health and education. These social spending priorities are seen as more important than aid to industry. Thus, 75% see health and 57% education as first or second priority for extra spending, while only 16% see aid to industry as having similar importance. There has, in fact, been a reduction in support for such spending since 1983, when twice as many people included aid to industry as one of their first two priorities. The needs of the social services are apparently seen to be either greater, or more the responsibility of government, than are the needs of industry.

Government moves to help industry would be supported, but support for such intervention is not unselective. Some forms of aid to industry – to build new factories or start new businesses, to retrain staff or sell goods abroad – are popular. Other, more direct support – to finance research and development or to install new machinery – is less in demand. And the most direct form of aid – subsidising wages in declining industries – is opposed by the majority. Support tends to be for measures designed to facilitate industrial growth generally, not for measures that will help particular businesses, especially not those in decline.

	Should the government help to pay?		
	Definitely	Probably	No
For new factories	% 43	41	14
To start businesses	% 37	47	14
For training	% 36	43	19
To sell goods abroad	% 38	37	24
For research	% 23	38	37
For new machinery	% 19	36	44
To pay wages in declining industries	% 11	27	59

The call for government help – rather than government interference – can be seen elsewhere in the survey. Only 16% would favour more state ownership of industry, and 45% feel that "private enterprise is the best way to solve Britain's economic problems". Again, however, all things are relative: although nationalised industry is not well regarded – 66% thinking it is not well run, manufacturing industry fares little better – 55% thinking it is not well run.

The case for profits

After the failure to stimulate employment, the next most widely acknowledged problem in British industry is a lack of investment. A recurrent theme in industry's communications with the public is that such investment depends upon profits. Public opinion has been thought not to recognise this link. To quote again from the Lords' Select Committee report:

> Investment depends on profitability. The public must recognise the need for profit on investment. (Para. 232)

As in other respects, such comments may underestimate the sophistication of public attitudes. For instance, a link between private wealth creation and *public* spending is widely perceived to exist: 65% believe that the less profitable industry is, the less money is available to spend on things like education and health; 57% believe we would all be better off if industry made bigger profits; and only 18% believe that profits are already too high.

Where public opinion needs convincing is not that investment depends on profit, but that profit is likely to be devoted to investment. There is a striking discord between how people think profit *should* be used and how they think it *would* be used.

	Where should the profit go? %	Where would the profit go? %
Investment:		
New machinery	31 ⎫	20 ⎫
Training the workforce	12 ⎬ 53%	2 ⎬ 32%
Researching new products	10 ⎭	10 ⎭
Workforce benefits:		
Pay rise	21 ⎫ 28%	3 ⎫ 5%
Conditions	7 ⎭	2 ⎭
Customer benefit:		
Lower prices	13	2
Shareholders/managers:		
Increased dividends	4 ⎫ 4%	36 ⎫ 55%
Bonus to top management	* ⎭	19 ⎭

So British industry is thought to suffer from lack of investment, and the ability to invest is thought to depend on making profit; but that is not the same as saying that one problem will be solved by the other. Most people believe that a 'windfall' profit in a company ought to be channelled into investment: in machinery, employee training, or research and development. Others favour distribution to the workforce, through pay or improved conditions, or to the customer through reduced prices. Only a very small minority are in favour of the profits going primarily to shareholders or senior management. Yet according to more than half of the sample this is where such profits are *expected* to go. One third would expect them to go into investment, mostly in new machinery or new products; hardly anyone expects profits to be applied to the workforce through improved conditions or pay.

Shareowners in our sample (just over 15% of the total) did have somewhat different priorities for the use of profits, being more likely to favour investment, especially in new machinery (41%, compared with 29% of non shareowners), but still only 7% of them favoured distribution to shareholders through dividends. They were even more inclined, however, to believe that this is what would be done, as many as 47% thinking that a windfall profit would be used to increase dividends. Even among shareowners – most of whose different views can probably be attributed to social background – there is almost no support for the short-term profit-taking which is seen to be the most likely outcome (see **Table 2.1**).

This is the context in which acceptance of the profit motive should be seen. Answers to other questions only reinforce the position: 71% think that owners and shareholders are the groups who benefit most from the profits earned by industry, 20% that directors and managers benefit most, only 5% and 2% respectively see the general public or employees as the main beneficiaries. As many as 53% also agree (and only 12% disagree) that too much of the profit from British industry goes abroad.

'Profit' is not a dirty word to the British public. On the contrary, the message that profits are necessary appears not to be in dispute. But the uses to which profits *ought* to be put are seen to be radically different from the uses to which they *are* currently believed to be put. There are clearly more difficult messages for industry still to convey.

Management and labour relations

The theme of worker participation in profits crops up elsewhere in the survey, where 80% agree that industry should share more of its profits with its employees. This view is found among workers in all sectors of the economy, as much among workers in the public sector as among those in the private sector. The support for worker participation in profits is higher, for instance, than support for general views such as that "ordinary working people do not get their fair share of the nation's wealth" (66%), or that "there is one law for the rich and one for the poor" (59%). It is closer to the level of support given to *related* issues such as that employees who have shares in their companies tend to work harder (76%), and that the government should act to give workers more say in running the places where they work (80%).

The demand for worker participation is not simply the same as support for strong trade unions. Indeed, only 44% of the sample felt that employees needed strong trade unions to protect their interests. And very similar proportions thought that trade unions had too much power or favoured stronger legislation to control them. The demand seems to be related more to the generally critical view of management. Bad management is seen to be "very important" by 48%, and "quite important" by a further 41%, as an explanation of British economic decline. And less than one third of the sample felt that managers generally know what is best for a firm and employees ought to go along with it. Here at last we find close accord between public opinion and the views of the Lords' Select Committee:

> Many of the decisions which have to be taken by management will be taken with better results if the workforce are involved in the decision-making process . . . It is in the interest of everyone in industry – managers and workforce alike – and of the nation as a whole, that closer mutual understanding is achieved. (Para. 170)

The 1987 budget measures to encourage employee profit-sharing schemes will apparently therefore find support among the British public. (This is, perhaps, hardly surprising since *The 1986 Report* showed that about one half of all employees have some form of profit-linked incentive.) But, as before, public attitudes to these issues are tempered by a certain reserve. For instance, by more than two to one (57% to 23%), people feel that "full co-operation in firms is impossible because workers and management are really on opposite sides", and by nearly the same margin (52% to 27%) that "management will always try to get the better of employees if it gets the chance". An apparently strong belief exists that employers will not act in the interests of their workforces unless they are compelled to do so.

A career in industry

The importance of the quality of the workforce is a recurring theme in the Select Committee report and in government reaction. It occurs too in the 'Industry Year' campaign. The education system is questioned for its ability to provide the skills industry needs, skill training in employment is re-examined, and industry's need to attract the best school leavers and graduates is stressed. In all three respects, public attitudes appear to be solidly behind those who feel action is needed.

Thus, the Select Committee says that "the education system must be more responsive to the needs of industry" (Para. 232), and 72% of our sample say that Britain's schools fail to teach the kinds of skills that British industry needs. The Committee calls for more training in employment: "in many industrial firms a larger training effort is required" (Para. 168). And, as we have already reported, 79% of our sample think that the government should help to pay for skill training in industry. Also, by a majority of two to one, Britain is thought to be worse than most of her international competitors in providing such training.

Above all, perhaps, the Committee points to industry's failure to attract staff of the appropriate calibre. The public agrees: 73% think that this is an important cause of Britain's economic difficulties. Disagreement arises, however, over why this should be. The Committee believes that "industry needs to make itself more attractive to young people in terms of the career prospects it offers – in terms of pay, advancement, responsibility, job satisfaction, and status" and that the education system should "inculcate into schoolchildren a sense of the role of industry and commerce" (Para. 165). For these reasons it lends enthusiastic support to the initiatives planned for 'Industry Year'. The detailed results that follow show, however, that factors such as job satisfaction, pay and promotion are not among the main public concerns about industry. Jobs in industry may well be satisfying, interesting and reasonably well paid: the problem is seen to be that they may not last.

Choosing a job

Overwhelmingly, the advice that respondents would give to a school leaver choosing a first job is to look primarily for job security (57%) or work interest (26%). Future prospects of promotion, starting pay and working conditions receive far less emphasis. Even taking into account people's second priorities, although promotion is more widely mentioned (by 38% as first or second), security (75%) and work interest (54%) still dominate.

The continuing impact of unemployment on the nation's psyche can be seen in changes in responses to this question since 1983.* Then, job security was

* The question has undergone some modification since 1983 (see *The 1984 Report* (Q.202a) for details). The levels of changes we report here are, however, extremely unlikely to be artefactual.

already the most widely mentioned priority for a school leaver but, only three years on, half as many again choose it as the first priority. Longer-term criteria such as career development or opportunities for promotion have been pushed firmly into the background.

	First priority for school leavers	
	1983	1986
	%	%
Job security	38	57
Interest/satisfying work	22	26
Opportunities for promotion/development	28	9
Working conditions, starting pay, etc.	3	4

Men and women, and people of different ages, disagree hardly at all in their emphasis on job security. Nor is there any evidence that a person's employment sector has much influence on his or her views. There is, however, a small regional trend, with three recognisable groupings:

		Most important	
		Security	Interest
Northern England, Wales	%	64	20
Scotland, Midlands	%	58	27
London, South	%	51	31

Even in the relatively cushioned South, job security is the highest priority. But the added emphasis on security rather than interest in areas of high or rising unemployment is clear to see. More direct measures bring out the link more clearly. At the extreme, 70% of those who are themselves currently unemployed regard job security as the first priority for the young.

Confidence – or lack of it – plays a major part. Those who expect unemployment to rise and industrial performance to decline are especially likely to stress the importance of job security.

		Most important	
		Security	Interest
Unemployment will:			
go up a lot	%	63	22
go up a little	%	58	25
stay the same	%	47	34
go down	%	51	30
Industrial performance will:			
decline a lot	%	70	19
decline a little	%	56	28
stay the same	%	57	25
improve	%	54	31

The strongest pattern of all is the effect of the possession of educational qualifications. The less qualified the person, the more likely he or she is to stress job security. This may be due partly to lower expectations in general, but it is undoubtedly also a reflection of how the labour market is currently operating.

| | | Most important | |
		Security	Interest
No qualification	%	63	17
'O' level or CSE	%	60	26
'A' level or professional	%	49	37
Degree	%	27	53

More detailed figures are given in **Tables 2.2** and **2.3**.

The impact of unemployment is clear. Those under most threat from rising unemployment – such as those without formal qualifications – recommend the young to concentrate on finding a lasting job rather than one which has inherent interest or even rosy prospects. But what sort of job would that be? We asked about a range of different sectors.

Recommending a job

Surprisingly, perhaps – but less so in terms of the sorts of priorities we have just seen – the 'sunrise' industry of computer manufacturing comes second to the safe old Civil Service as a recommended first job for a young person. Asked to choose between six kinds of organisation, one in three people said they would advise a youngster to seek a job in the Civil Service; another one in five selected it as their second choice; and very few indeed would not recommend it. 'Older' industry, represented here by a large engineering factory, was not popular: only 18% would advise it as either first or second choice, while 20% would advise positively *against* it.

		Civil Service	Computer manu-facturer	Large accounting firm	Building society	Large engineering factory	Depart-ment store
First choice	%	32	24	18	11	7	1
Second choice	%	20	16	21	20	11	4
Not advised	%	6	7	3	5	20	50

The pattern of first and second choices reveals a clear division between manufacturing and service industries (or perhaps between manual and non-manual work). Thus those whose first choice was the Civil Service, accountancy or the building society were especially likely to make their second choice from the same three service jobs. Conversely, those whose first choice was either computer manufacturing or engineering were especially likely to name the other as their second choice.

In terms of this basic split between manufacturing and service sectors, no major differences emerge between men and women or between different age groups. Within the service jobs, however, differences are more marked. Men favour accountancy while women favour the building society; the under 25s are themselves markedly less enthusiastic about the Civil Service than their elders, young men favouring accountancy and young women the building society. Surprisingly, perhaps, no such age differences appear in the choice between computers and engineering (see **Table 2.4**).

Confidence in the future – in terms of employment prospects and industrial performance – has been seen to influence the *criteria* people think important in career choice. But it is not associated with any variation in terms of choice between our six jobs. Even the respondent's level of qualification, the strongest discriminator in terms of the choice between job security and work interest, shows only one small effect in terms of the choice between jobs: those with degrees or professional qualifications are especially likely to recommend accountancy.

Evaluating the jobs

As well as being asked to recommend jobs from the list of six, our respondents were asked to say which of them they thought was best in terms of each of the five criteria (security, interest, pay, promotion, conditions) examined earlier. There is, of course, a general tendency for the 'popular' jobs to be rated more highly than the 'unpopular' ones on all criteria. But a few sub-patterns do emerge:

- The Civil Service is especially well rated for job security: 49% think it the best in this respect, compared with the 32% selecting it as their first recommendation to a young person seeking a job. It suffers, however, in terms of perceptions of job interest, where only 16% rate it the best. So it is characterised as a safe but dull career, gaining 'first place' overall, mainly – it appears – as a result of a climate of uncertainty conditioned by unemployment.
- Accountancy, although well recommended overall, surprisingly has no clear specific attractions except, marginally, opportunities for promotion.
- The building society is especially linked with good working conditions. In this respect it is differentiated from the otherwise similar accountancy practice. It too fares relatively badly in terms of perceived job interest.
- Both engineering and computer manufacturing are rated comparatively highly for work interest and starting pay. These findings – especially the first one in respect of job interest – seem to challenge both the view of the Select Committee and one of the premises of 'Industry Year'. According to these results, the latter merely reiterates what the public already knows: that 'industrial' jobs are interesting. No fewer than 46% rated *either* the computer manufacturer or the engineering factory as offering the most interesting work, compared with only 32% for the *three-fold* combination of 'office jobs'. It is only in the admittedly crucial area of job security that these jobs – in the Civil Service, accountancy or a building society –

outscore manufacturing industry. Safeness nowadays, not surprisingly, is regarded as rather more important than excitement.

For further details see **Tables 2.5** and **2.6**. So the battle to stimulate *interest* in industrial employment is hardly a difficult one. In this respect the 'Industry Year' campaign seeks to achieve what even the most doubting analyst of the power of promotion and advertising would accept is achievable: to reinforce an existing view. If work interest were to displace job security as the primary quality to be sought in a job, we could expect to find a quite different pattern of career advice to a young person. The computer manufacturer would top the list, the engineering factory would move up to level second with the Civil Service; even the poorly rated department store would move up to a position comparable with the accountancy firm and the building society.

	Overall recommendation %
Civil Service	32
Computer manufacturer	24
Accountancy firm	18
Building society	11
Engineering factory	7
Department store	1
Office jobs	61
Manufacturing industry	31

	Job security %
Civil Service	49
Computer manufacturer	14
Building society	13
Accountancy firm	13
Engineering factory	5
Department store	1
Office jobs	75
Manufacturing industry	19

	Work interest %
Computer manufacturer	30
Engineering factory	16
Civil Service	16
Accountancy firm	10
Department store	9
Building society	6
Manufacturing industry	46
Office jobs	32

From industry's point of view what is needed therefore is a change of priorities between the criteria by which different jobs are judged. Unlike the 'image reinforcement' task, this objective is one which would deter even the most confident supporter of promotion and advertising. Changing an image which stems directly from experience of reality is an unenviable and possibly fruitless task.

We are able, of course, only to look in these results for the opinions of adults, not of the schoolchildren whom industry needs to attract. Yet no more encouragement is gained by separate examination of the youngest respondents, those aged from 18 to 24. For them too job security is still the paramount consideration, named as first priority by 58% (more or less the same proportion as of the total sample). Similarly, the three office jobs dominate their recommendations to a young person seeking their first job: 62% of them would recommend the Civil Service, accountancy or a building society, compared with only 30% recommending either the computer manufacturer or the engineering factory (again an almost identical split to that among all respondents).

Perhaps the most depressing feature of these results is the suggestion of a vicious circle. Legislators and the general public appear to agree that improved industrial performance depends to an important extent on industry's ability to attract a high-calibre workforce. Yet such people (that is those who have the choice) are likely to be deterred from working in industry by the insecurity arising from its recent past. So it seems that the recruits needed to assist industrial recovery may be attracted to industry only when they believe that recovery has been achieved, or at least begun. Further tabulations supporting these conclusions are given at the end of this chapter.

Big business, small business

The final aspect of public attitudes to industry that we examined was a comparison of big and small businesses. The pattern of findings is simple and plausible. Big business is seen to be more effective in respect of those activities which depend on resources: investing in new machinery and technology, attracting the best employees, providing them with skill training, paying good wages, and inventing new products.

At the same time, though, big business is seen to be relatively remote from and out of touch with its employees and its customers. (Yet again, the general public is in remarkably close accord with the Lords' Select Committee, which was equally critical of these aspects of British industry.) Small businesses are therefore regarded as being better at those activities which demand contact: labour relations, caring about customers, making goods that people want to buy, charging a fair price for them, and making well designed products.

		Big businesses better	Small businesses better	No difference
Investing in technology	%	77	8	13
Attracting best workers	%	59	18	21
Training employees	%	49	26	22
Inventing new products	%	42	26	29
Paying a fair wage	%	37	27	35
Making well designed products	%	26	39	32
Charging fair prices	%	22	39	37
Making goods people want	%	19	41	37
Caring about customers	%	5	71	22
Good employee relations	%	5	77	15

Conclusions

'Industry Year', initiated by the RSA (the Royal Society for the Encourage-ment of Arts, Manufactures and Commerce) defined industry to include the production and sale of tradeable services – a wider definition than that which concerned the Lords' Select Committee. But in each case, the focus of concern was that the British "hold industrial activity in low esteem". Britain's relative industrial failure was indeed blamed on this poor image, which was said to be "deeply embedded in our cultural attitudes".

Our results do not give much support to this view of British 'cultural attitudes'. On the contrary, they show considerable public sympathy with industry. We must wait for *The 1988 Report* to see if any shifts have occurred over the year, but our findings to date suggest that the campaign is likely to land on fertile ground.

The caricature of public opinion inherent, for instance, in the House of Lords Select Committee's remarks, may have arisen because general support for industry and its objectives is so clearly tempered by widespread public doubts about its ability to 'deliver'. Almost everybody believes that Britain still needs a strong manufacturing base and most think that – as individuals and as a society – we owe industry our support (for instance by buying British goods). But expectations are low, actually lower than they were three years ago. British industry is highly regarded in terms of inventiveness and design, but in other respects it is compared unfavourably with its overseas competitors.

Lack of investment – in jobs, plant and skills – is blamed for the problems. People generally acknowledge that such investment depends on industry's ability to make profits. They also acknowledge that public services like health and education depend on these profits. But they do not believe that profits are actually used very beneficially. Again, although industry would, it is believed, benefit from greater worker participation in management and profits, people do not see managements as likely collaborators in this process.

Crucially, given one of the thrusts of the 'Industry Year' campaign, the public believes firmly that industry needs to attract good workers, and that manufacturing jobs have high interest and starting pay. But, nowadays, these attributes count for little when compared with job security. And manufacturing industry, for all its interest, does not offer such security, not when compared with safe employers such as the Civil Service.

Public opinion offers industry sympathy and understanding. But it lacks confidence and belief. A few years of convincing industrial performance might change all that.

Reference

HOUSE OF LORDS, *Report from the Select Committee on Overseas Trade*, HMSO, London (1985).

Acknowledgements

We are grateful to the Department of Trade and Industry for its financial support which enabled a module on attitudes to business and industry to be devised and carried. Although we relied heavily on the Department for advice and help in deciding appropriate areas of questioning, the final responsibility for the questions and the interpretation must rest with SCPR and the author.

2.1 USE OF A LARGE PROFIT MADE BY A BIG BRITISH FIRM (B98a, B98c) by share ownership

WHICH ONE OF THESE THINGS DO YOU THINK IT WOULD BE MOST LIKELY TO DO?

	TOTAL	OWNS SHARES+	
		YES	NO
	%	%	%
Increase dividends to the shareholders	36	47	34
Give the employees a pay rise	3	3	3
Cut the prices of its products	2	2	2
Invest in new machinery/new technology	20	20	19
Improve employees' working conditions	2	*	2
Research into new products	10	8	11
Invest in training for the employees	2	*	3
Give a bonus to top management	19	14	20
BASE: B RESPONDENTS Weighted	1548	246	1287
Unweighted	1548	252	1281

WHICH ONE DO YOU THINK SHOULD BE ITS FIRST PRIORITY?

	TOTAL	OWNS SHARES+	
		YES	NO
	%	%	%
Increase dividends to the shareholders	4	7	4
Give the employees a pay rise	21	9	23
Cut the prices of its products	13	12	13
Invest in new machinery/new technology	31	41	29
Improve employees' working conditions	7	5	7
Research into new products	10	16	9
Invest in training for the employees	12	10	12
Give a bonus to top management	*	-	*
BASE: B RESPONDENTS Weighted	1548	246	1287
Unweighted	1548	252	1281

2.2 MOST IMPORTANT FACTOR AFFECTING JOB CHOICE (B94) by age within sex, region and highest educational qualification obtained

	TOTAL	AGE+ WITHIN SEX								REGION						HIGHEST QUALIFICATION OBTAINED			
		MALE				FEMALE				Scot- land	North	Mid- lands	Wales	South	Greater London	Degree	Professional/ 'A' level	'O' level/ CSE	None
		18-24	25-34	35-54	55+	18-24	25-34	35-54	55+										
	%	%	%	%	%	%	%	%	%	%	%	%	%	%	%	%	%	%	%
Good starting pay	3	4	4	4	5	3	3	1	3	4	3	5	2	3	2	3	1	2	5
Secure job for the future	57	60	57	54	53	57	60	57	57	58	64	57	63	51	51	27	49	60	63
Promotion opportunities	9	12	12	6	12	11	8	8	9	6	8	8	10	11	12	13	10	9	8
Interesting work	26	21	25	33	23	25	26	31	22	25	19	28	21	32	30	53	37	26	17
Good working conditions	4	3	2	4	6	4	3	2	7	6	6	3	1	2	4	4	2	2	6
BASE: B RESPONDENTS:																			
Weighted	1548	122	127	252	212	134	157	300	242	163	406	252	82	485	160	117	307	422	685
Unweighted	1548	112	122	258	217	127	152	309	248	147	409	261	84	481	166	113	309	419	689

2.3 MOST IMPORTANT FACTOR AFFECTING JOB CHOICE (B94)
by economic sector, and expectations for unemployment and industrial performance in next year

	TOTAL	ECONOMIC SECTOR+				EXPECTATIONS FOR UNEMPLOYMENT					EXPECTATIONS FOR INDUSTRIAL PERFORMANCE				
		Private manuf.	Private non-manuf.	Public service	Public manuf. and trans.	Go up a lot	Go up a little	Stay the same	Go down a little	Go down a lot	Improve a lot	Improve a little	Stay the same	Decline a little	Decline a lot
	%	%	%	%	%	%	%	%	%	%	%	%	%	%	%
Good starting pay	3	5	3	3	5	3	3	3	2	(7)	(-)	1	4	3	3
Secure job for the future	57	59	56	53	59	63	58	47	52	(41)	(62)	53	57	56	70
Promotion opportunities	9	11	9	8	11	7	10	11	10	(15)	(8)	9	10	9	7
Interesting work	26	22	29	31	18	22	25	34	30	(30)	(27)	32	25	28	19
Good working conditions	4	3	3	5	6	4	3	4	6	(7)	(4)	5	3	4	2
BASE: B RESPONDENTS:															
Weighted	1548	345	577	345	100	468	555	383	95	(14)	(47)	315	725	257	107
Unweighted	1548	351	578	346	101	468	554	384	97	(12)	(48)	321	715	258	110

2.4 RECOMMENDING A JOB (B96a)
by age within sex, economic sector and most important factor affecting job choice

JOB RESPONDENT WOULD BE MOST LIKELY TO RECOMMEND TO A YOUNG PERSON	TOTAL	AGE+ WITHIN SEX								ECONOMIC SECTOR+				MOST IMPORTANT FACTOR AFFECTING JOB CHOICE				
		MALE				FEMALE				Private manuf.	Private non-manuf.	Public service	Public manuf. and trans.	Good starting pay	Secure job for the future	Promotion opportunities	Interesting work	Good working conditions
		18-24	25-34	35-54	55+	18-24	25-34	35-54	55+									
	%	%	%	%	%	%	%	%	%	%	%	%	%	%	%	%	%	%
Building Society	11	9	8	8	5	29	16	13	7	9	12	12	12	(10)	12	12	9	17
Large firm of accountants	18	26	23	21	17	16	12	18	14	20	18	16	18	(14)	18	20	20	8
Large engineering firm	7	9	5	7	9	6	3	5	11	9	6	6	9	(10)	7	8	6	10
Department store	1	2	-	*	1	5	1	2	1	1	1	1	1	(6)	1	1	2	2
Civil Service	32	21	31	36	34	23	29	34	33	30	30	35	36	(33)	34	26	31	25
Large firm making computers	24	27	27	20	28	18	26	24	24	25	25	22	21	(20)	25	26	22	34
BASE: B RESPONDENTS Weighted	1548	122	127	252	212	134	157	300	242	345	577	345	100	(48)	875	144	408	60
Unweighted	1548	112	122	258	217	127	152	309	248	351	578	346	101	(47)	870	145	415	58

2.5 EVALUATION OF JOBS (B95)
by job recommended for security, interest and promotion opportunities

	TOTAL	RECOMMENDED JOB					
		Building Society	Large firm of accountants	Large engineering factory	Department store	Civil Service	Large firm making computers
SECURE JOB FOR THE FUTURE	%	%	%	%	%	%	%
Building society	13	53	10	9	(13)	7	10
Large firm of accountants	13	7	44	7	(9)	5	8
Large engineering factory	5	1	2	34	(9)	2	4
Department store	1	2	1	1	(13)	1	2
Civil Service	49	35	36	41	(36)	80	30
Large firm making computers	14	1	5	8	(19)	5	44
INTERESTING WORK							
Building society	6	31	4	2	(9)	5	1
Large firm of accountants	10	8	32	4	(-)	7	3
Large engineering factory	16	9	15	57	(9)	16	13
Department store	9	11	8	6	(40)	9	8
Civil Service	16	9	7	4	(2)	34	7
Large firm making computers	30	21	23	21	(31)	21	60
PROMOTION OPPORTUNITIES							
Building society	9	34	8	4	(6)	4	6
Large firm of accountants	17	15	39	15	(22)	12	11
Large engineering factory	9	7	7	32	(15)	5	9
Department store	5	5	8	6	(27)	4	5
Civil Service	34	26	24	27	(8)	60	19
Large firm making computers	18	7	8	10	(9)	10	46
BASE: B RESPONDENTS Weighted	*1548*	*171*	*277*	*108*	*(22)*	*488*	*373*
Unweighted	*1548*	*170*	*276*	*108*	*(21)*	*490*	*375*

2.6 EVALUATION OF JOBS (B95)
by job recommended for good starting pay and good working conditions

	TOTAL	RECOMMENDED JOB					
		Building Society	Large firm of accountants	Large engineering factory	Department store	Civil Service	Large firm making computers
	%	%	%	%	%	%	%
GOOD STARTING PAY							
Building Society	9	45	6	4	(13)	5	4
Large firm of accountants	13	6	41	6	(15)	9	6
Large engineering factory	13	11	12	55	(33)	8	9
Department store	2	3	1	3	(18)	1	2
Civil Service	24	14	12	10	(8)	54	9
Large firm making computers	30	16	23	20	(13)	17	66
GOOD WORKING CONDITIONS							
Building Society	24	66	29	24	(13)	17	15
Large firm of accountants	12	5	30	9	(21)	7	10
Large engineering factory	4	2	2	21	(-)	2	4
Department store	6	8	6	7	(25)	5	6
Civil Service	32	11	20	23	(13)	62	18
Large firm making computers	14	2	7	11	(9)	4	39
BASE: B RESPONDENTS							
Weighted	1548	171	277	108	(22)	488	373
Unweighted	1548	170	276	108	(21)	470	375

3 Political culture

*Anthony Heath and Richard Topf**

The rhetoric of politicians is not renowned for standing up to close scrutiny. Thus when Roy Jenkins invoked no less a revolutionary than Cromwell to assert that the new Alliance was 'Casting the Kingdoms old, Into another mould', further evidence for the claim was clearly needed.

There is no doubt, however, that things have been changing. The 'new mould' of British politics has manifested itself in numerous ways. Voters appear to be far more volatile. Compared with the stability of the 1950s and early 1960s, support for the political parties seems to fluctuate widely from month to month, and even from week to week. There have been large swings in by-elections, and the proportion of the electorate claiming an attachment to *any* of the political parties has fallen remarkably from 44% in 1964 to around 20% in the mid-1980s.

These changes all preceded the founding of the SDP and its Alliance with the Liberals, and so explanations other than the formation of a third major political force must be sought. Some writers have attributed the decline in attachment to the Conservative and Labour Parties to the inability of either, when in power, to resolve Britain's social and economic problems. On that thesis, the rise of the Alliance vote is seen as a protest against the ineffectiveness of the traditional parties of government. Other explanations emphasise changes in British society: the decline of traditional communities based on social class; increased upward social mobility into a growing middle class; and the emergence of a new generation of educated voters brought up in an affluent post-war society, and with political concerns different from those of their parents. These social changes, it is argued, have loosened voters' attachments to traditional social

* Anthony Heath is Official Fellow, Nuffield College, Oxford. Richard Topf is Senior Lecturer in Politics at City of London Polytechnic, and Member of Nuffield College.

relationships and modes of behaviour and have introduced a new element of instability into British politics.

It follows from both types of explanation that these changes in political behaviour should imply changes in British political culture as well. In his recent book on British politics, Kavanagh (1985) writes:

> Every political system is embedded in a political culture. At one time, historians, anthropologists and political scientists spoke of a 'national character'. Now we are more likely to refer to the political culture – the values, beliefs and emotions that give meaning to political behaviour. These are the values which create dispositions for people to behave in a particular way or which provide justifications for behaviour (p.46).

If changes in our values, beliefs and emotions have led to changes in political behaviour, have they also led to changes in our relationship with the political system itself? Is our weakening attachment to one particular political party or another reflected in a weakening attachment to the whole system of government?

Our central concern in this chapter is with political culture rather than with party politics. We are concerned with citizens' orientations towards the political system in general, and the part which they should play in it, rather than with their attitudes towards specific parties or the issues of party politics. Our central question is whether the political culture has undergone a transformation similar to that which we have seen in political behaviour.

The decline of the civic culture

The 1950s are seen by most commentators as the heyday of stable, two-party politics, and as the period when Britain had a balanced political culture underpinning its stable democracy. The main empirical basis for this interpretation was provided by the American writers Almond and Verba (1963) who conducted national attitude surveys in five western democracies, including Britain, early in 1959. They concluded that Britain (and the United States) exhibited an exemplary political culture. In Britain, they said, there was an essential balance between people's confidence in their ability to influence politics and their respect for political authority:

> The democratic citizen is called upon to pursue contradictory goals: he must be active, yet passive; involved, yet not too involved; influential, yet deferential (p.479).

The ideal democratic citizen, they believed, would have "a judicious mixture of respect for authority and sturdy independence" (Barry, 1970, p.48); an excess of either of these characteristics would spell dangers for democracy. Too much independence would lead to radical populism and 'ungovernability'; too much respect for authority would lead to the reverse dangers of an authoritarian government unconstrained by fear of public disapproval. It should not be forgotten that, at the time they were writing, Almond and Verba shared the widespread concerns about the events of the first half of the twentieth century when in many countries popular unrest led to communism on the one hand, and unduly powerful leaders encouraged fascism on the other.

Almond and Verba held that, in Britain and the USA *par excellence* (but not in the three other countries – Italy, West Germany and Mexico – which they studied) there was the necessary balance of self-confidence and deference that made a viable, stable democracy possible. This balance of self-confidence and deference they termed the civic culture.

By the mid 1970s, however, the increased volatility of the electorate and the decline of two-party politics led many writers to perceive a breakdown of the civic culture in Britain. Samuel Beer (1982) wrote:

> In the light of the survey evidence it is no exaggeration to speak of the decline of the civic culture as a 'collapse'. The change in attitudes towards politics and government since the 1950s has been deep and wide (p.119).

The evidence which Beer reviewed had two strands corresponding to the two elements of the civic culture identified by Almond and Verba. The first was survey evidence of widespread distrust of and dissatisfaction with governments of any party, for example from a survey conducted by Alan Marsh in early 1974 (Marsh, 1977). Britain, it was argued, no longer had a deferential political culture. Respect for the political authorities had declined to alarmingly low levels, with important implications for stable democracy.

The second strand of evidence was the increasing demand for participation in the political process. In summarising his findings, Marsh said:

> The British want to be secure, certainly, but they want to be consulted even more than they want to be rich and powerful. This finding seems to accord well with the general theme of this study: that deference is no longer a force in British political culture but has given way to a concern for influence in the decisions of the political community (pp.176-7).

Marsh himself saw this "concern for influence" as associated with an increased potential for political protest and for unconventional forms of political behaviour. And commentators such as Beer (1982) talked of a rise of populism and a "crisis of ungovernability". Other writers took a less pessimistic view of the changes, seeing them as new potentials for a genuinely participatory democracy. Tony Benn (1970), for example argued that "the new citizen wants and must receive a great deal more power than all existing authority has so far thought it right, necessary or wise to yield him" (p.23). There were, therefore, both optimistic and pessimistic interpretations of the changes that were occurring, but general agreement that the political culture *was* indeed changing.

Trust and deference

In 1986 we asked our *British Social Attitudes* respondents four questions to gauge attitudes towards the political system and the way the country is run. All had been asked in earlier studies.[1] Taken together the answers tend to present a picture of widespread public cynicism. We asked:

How much do you trust a British government of any party to place the needs of this country above the interests of their own political party?

	%
Just about always	5
Most of the time	34
Only some of the time	46
Almost never	11
Don't know/can't say	4

Two related questions yielded even more cynical answers. We asked respondents whether they agreed or disagreed with the statements that:

generally speaking, those we elect as MPs lose touch with people pretty quickly

and that

parties are only interested in people's votes, not in their opinions.

To both of these statements around two thirds of respondents gave what might be interpreted as cynical or disillusioned responses. These findings certainly dispel any notion that British voters are generally deferential towards and trusting of political leaders.

The other three questions on trust towards government and politicians replicate those asked by Marsh in 1974. The distributions of answers in the two surveys are very similar and lead us to conclude that levels of trust and cynicism have changed little over the last decade.[2]

% Agreeing that . . .	1974	1986
	%	%
Generally speaking those we elect as MPs lose touch with people pretty quickly	67	70
Parties are only interested in people's votes, not in their opinions	67	66
A British government of *any* party [cannot usually be trusted] to place the needs of this country above the interests of their own political party	60	57

To be sure, the commentators had argued that, by the time of Marsh's survey, the civic culture had already collapsed, and after reviewing the answers to these and similar questions, Marsh himself concluded "that results are unequivocal. Political trust in Britain is at a very low ebb" (p.119).

Yet there is little evidence that trust in politics and in politicians had ever been much higher. Even in their 1959 survey of Britain, Almond and Verba found that 58% of respondents agreed that "people like me don't have any say about what the government does" and 83% agreed that "all candidates sound good in their speeches but you can never tell what they will do after they are elected". Kavanagh (1971) has also collected evidence to show that similar expressions of distrust of politicians can be found in even earlier surveys. And he adds that, as far back as 1867, Walter Bagehot contrasted the social deference of the British towards their social superiors with their lack of political deference to the authorities. This suggested to Bagehot that the natural impulse of the "English people is to resist authority" (quoted in Kavanagh, 1971, p.335).

We have to conclude, therefore, that Almond and Verba were wrong in their original description of the British civic culture as one characterised by high levels of deference and respect for the political authorities. The cynicism which so startled commentators in the 1970s had also been present, but unstressed, in the 1959 survey. The questions to which Almond and Verba had given most attention, and on which their conclusions were based, concerned *public officials* rather than politicians. British citizens expressed considerable confidence in the evenhandedness of officials; but while the perceived fairness of public officials may well be an important feature of British political culture, it is not to be confused with deference to politicians.[3] As Kavanagh (1971) points out, "it is not immediately clear why the confidence of British voters that they would receive serious consideration from the police and the civil service is an indicator of deference" (p.339).

We must also distinguish between attitudes to politicians and attitudes towards the *political system* itself: it is unlikely that questions about MPs and political parties can properly be interpreted as telling us about citizens' respect for democratic political institutions. It is quite possible for a person to believe that MPs lose touch with people pretty quickly *and* to support the institutions of parliamentary democracy. Politicians may not be trusted but it does not follow that people reject representative government and prefer to take matters into their own hands by resorting to direct action. Indeed, lack of trust in politicians might lead to a willingness to strengthen constitutional checks on their power, rather than to disillusionment with constitutional procedures. None of these findings, then, implies that democracy in Britain is unstable.

In place of the 'collapse' or 'crisis' of British political culture which some commentators have seen, the truth would appear to be much more prosaic. Cynicism about politics and politicians is not a novel phenomenon brought about by the failures of recent governments to solve Britain's economic and social problems. Rather it is a long-standing feature of British political culture, which goes back at least as far as the 1950s when Britain was regarded as an exemplary stable democracy – and perhaps much further back than that.

Participation

We turn now to the second element of the political culture – to political participation and the citizen's confidence that he or she can influence political decision making. We asked respondents: *Suppose a law was being considered by Parliament which you thought was really unjust and harmful. Which, if any, of the things on this card do you think you would do?* We then asked whether or not they had actually done any of the things mentioned, and also how effective they thought the different courses of action would be.

	Would do	Had ever done	Believed 'very' or 'quite' effective
	%	%	%
Sign petition	65	34	45
Contact your MP	52	11	50
Contact radio, TV or newspaper	15	3	58
Speak to influential person	15	3	38
Contact government department	12	3	26
Go on protest or demonstration	11	6	21
Raise issue in organisation you already belong to	10	5	32
Form group of like-minded people	8	2	26

As can be seen, there is little relation between what people would do, what they say they have done and what they believe to be effective. For example, contacting the media is most frequently endorsed as effective, but is a course of action rarely followed. And, few people think that going on a demonstration is effective but it is, relatively speaking, one of the more popular courses of action. These discrepancies between perceived effectiveness and reported action suggest that political action cannot be explained in purely rational, instrumental terms: it almost certainly possesses a moral or expressive component as well.*

It is of some interest therefore that the two most popular courses of action are signing a petition and contacting their MP. Just over a third of respondents reported that they actually had signed a petition, and two thirds said that they would do so. About one half of the respondents said that they would contact their MP – and that it would be effective – and one in ten reported having done so.

These results, which have not changed in the past few years (see *The 1984 Report*, pp.20-22), contrast strikingly with our findings of cynicism towards government. Deference towards political authorities may be lacking, but the other element of the civic culture – confidence in one's own ability to affect the political process – is much more evident. To be sure, many more people thought that they *would* participate than actually *had* participated, but this is something that Almond and Verba too had found in 1959 and seen as indicative of a *potential* for action.

Whereas absence of deference seems to be a long-standing feature of British political culture, in contrast attitudes to participation, whether actual or potential, do appear to have changed over the past three decades. In their 1959 study, Almond and Verba asked four questions on which we have based our own. After an introductory question much like ours: *Suppose a law was being considered by Parliament which you consider very unjust or harmful, what do you think you would do?*, they asked a further three questions:

---

* The clearest example of this is of course voting. Few people can believe that their individual vote will make a difference to the election outcome. The fact that so many people *do* vote must be explained by their sense of civic obligation to vote, or by their desire to express their commitment (or opposition) to a particular party.

		Likely	Depends/ Don't know	Unlikely
If you made an effort to change this law, how likely is it that you would succeed?	%	12	25	62
If such a case arose, how likely is it you would actually try to do something about it?	%	35	19	47
		Yes	Don't know	No
Have you ever done anything to try to influence an Act of Parliament?	%	6	1	93

Source: The Civic Culture Study, ICPR edition (1974)

While these questions are clearly not identical to ours, they are similar enough to indicate that there have been marked changes over the last 30 years or so. Perceived chances of success, likelihood of participation, and actual participation all appear to be much higher in 1986. For example, only six per cent of respondents reported in 1959 that they actually had done something to try to influence Parliament, while by 1986, remarkably, 44% said that they had done something. Admittedly, the great majority of such actions were simply signing petitions; but if we exclude petitions we still find that 20% of our sample had done something in an attempt to influence Parliament. This growing citizen participation seems to mark an important change in the civic culture – although it is not quite the change that commentators had in mind when they talked of collapse and crisis. On Almond and Verba's line of argument it might indicate an ominous shift of balance away from passivity and towards action. And it might also indicate an increased potential for protest, for radical populism and the concomitant risk of ungovernability about which some commentators had warned.

However, our data do not support such dramatic interpretations. Our respondents were asked what they would do if a law was being considered by Parliament which they thought was *really unjust and harmful*. Even under such provocation, signing a petition (presumably aimed at Parliament) and contacting an MP are far and away the most popular courses for action. The protests that our respondents had in mind seem therefore to be of a rather orderly kind, directed *at* rather than *against* Parliament, and working *within* rather than *outside* the existing political system.

Support for democratic procedures can also be inferred from a separate group of questions about the various ways in which "people or organisations can protest against a government action they strongly oppose". Options ranged from "organising public meetings" to "seriously damaging government buildings".

% Saying that different forms of protest should 'definitely' or 'probably' be allowed

	%
Organising public meetings to protest against the government	83
Publishing pamphlets to protest against the government	78
Organising protest marches and demonstrations	58
Organising a nationwide strike of all workers against the government	28
Occupying a government office and stopping work there for several days	10
Seriously damaging government buildings	2

As can be seen, there are very high levels of support for orderly and conventional forms of protest, but support falls off sharply as we move down the list to forms of direct or violent action. Indeed, these data show strong support for another element of British political culture – freedom of speech and assembly – but little indication of support for direct action or violent forms of protest. Protecting freedom of speech and assembly can be seen as part of that "sturdy independence" (Barry, 1970) which makes up the 'active' component of the civic culture. Such evidence as we have suggests that this sturdy independence is increasing.

Interestingly, there is also evidence of the increased demand for participation that Tony Benn spoke of. In the *British General Election* studies of 1974, 1979 and 1983 and in the *British Social Attitudes* survey of 1986, we asked: *Do you think the government should give workers more say in running the places where they work?* The difference between responses in the 1970s and those given in the 1980s is striking:[4]

% Agreeing that workers should be given more say in running the places where they work

	%
1974*	56
1979*	54
1983*	68
1986	80

Source: British General Election studies.

What we have found, then, is evidence of widespread but long-standing distrust of politicians, coupled with a widespread and growing self-confidence on the part of the electorate to try to bring influence to bear on Parliament. There is no evidence, however, that either phenomenon implies any loss of respect for democratic procedures. We would agree with Kavanagh (1971) in his reassessment of Almond and Verba's work, that:

> Support for British political institutions does not coexist with widespread political passivity or deference but with comparatively high levels of political participation and widespread sense of political competence (p.353).

The question remains as to what relationship, if any, exists between these changes in political culture and the changes in party politics over the last quarter century. If distrust of politicians has been long-standing, clearly then we cannot relate it to the recent increases in electoral volatility, or to the decline of the two-party system and the emergence of the Alliance. The perceived inability of successive Conservative and Labour governments to solve Britain's long-standing problems may have undermined confidence in those two parties, but their ineffectiveness cannot be blamed for reducing confidence in the democratic system *per se*. A more promising theory, perhaps, is that social changes – such as the expansion of higher education and the growth of the middle classes – are producing increased numbers of citizens with the self-confidence to participate in politics, with new political concerns and with a greater wish to be consulted in the political process.

Political culture and political values

Writers such as Almond and Verba tend to take a rather narrow view of political culture, focusing on trust in government and on confidence to participate in the political process. A wider definition of political culture would also include attitudes towards the economic and social order. These attitudes and values, as we shall see, are closely associated with the particular phenomena of trust and participation and may perhaps help to explain them. In any event they must be included if we define political culture as encompassing ". . . the values which create dispositions for people to behave in a particular way or which provide justifications for behaviour" (Kavanagh, 1985, p.46).

On this broader definition of political culture, we need to consider two contrasting sets of values and perceptions. The first set relates to the economic order of society, in particular to economic equality and perceived conflicts – for example, between management and workers, rich and poor. The second set of values relates to social order and covers such matters as civil liberty and respect for the law. These two sets of values might be said to represent the two most fundamental ideological principles in contemporary society.[5]

Egalitarianism

There has been considerable debate in the sociological literature about the extent of class consciousness in society: whether the working class has a 'conflict model' of society and espouses radical values, or whether in contrast it accepts a 'dominant ideology' which endorses the existing economic order. (For a review, see Marshall, 1983.) The outcome of this debate has been unclear, but the results are much less ambiguous when we turn from these general images of society to more specific questions, such as the ones listed below, concerning rich and poor, management and workers.

		Agree	Neither agree nor disagree	Disagree
Ordinary working people do not get their fair share of the nation's wealth	%	65	19	14
There is one law for the rich and one for the poor	%	59	17	22
Full cooperation in firms is impossible because workers and management are really on opposite sides	%	57	19	23
Big business benefits owners at the expense of workers	%	54	26	19
Management will always try to get the better of employees if it gets the chance	%	52	20	27

As we can see, the balance of public opinion tends towards the radical or egalitarian. On none of the questions is there a consensus; but people who take a radical perspective are consistently and comfortably in the majority. Thus by a margin of almost five to one respondents agree that "ordinary working people do not get their fair share of the nation's wealth" and by approaching three to one they accept a conflict model of worker–manager relations.

Not surprisingly, the radical majority is even larger within the working class itself. Distinguishing three groups – the salariat (professional, managerial and administrative occupations), the intermediate classes (routine non-manual workers, foremen, technicians and the petty bourgeoisie) and the working class proper* – we find large differences in the percentages endorsing the radical alternative:

	% Agreeing with the radical alternative		
	Salariat	Intermediate classes	Working class
	%	%	%
Nation's wealth shared unfairly	53	61	76
One law for rich, one for poor	45	56	71
Management and workers on opposite sides	44	56	65

Within the working class there are large majorities with radical or egalitarian views, although even within the salariat surprisingly large numbers take a radical stance.

---

* For further details of this class schema, see Heath, Jowell and Curtice (1985).

Even bigger differences, however, can be found when we distinguish between people according to their political sympathies:

	% Agreeing with the radical alternative		
	Conservative identifiers %	Alliance identifiers %	Labour identifiers %
Nation's wealth shared unfairly	43	65	85
One law for rich, one for poor	36	62	78
Management and workers on opposite sides	49	55	67

As might be expected, attitudes towards economic equality are among those which discriminate most powerfully between Conservative, Labour and Alliance identifiers. It is, after all, values and beliefs such as these that are reflected in party political behaviour.

Since these questions have not yet been asked in a regular time-series (though the *British Social Attitudes* series intends to rectify that omission), it is impossible to know whether these divisions between the classes and parties are long-standing. Rather contradictory arguments, based on very little evidence, have been put forward at various times. In the late 1950s, when Almond and Verba were conducting their study, there was much discussion of the 'end of ideology'. It was alleged that there was broad consensus on the *objectives* of government policy and that the central political debates concerned *means* rather than ends. If this interpretation is valid, then current evidence would suggest that there has been a revival of ideology.

But against this a number of more recent writers have argued that ideological differences between the classes and the parties have actually been declining, and that this accounts for the rise of the Alliance. Rose and McAllister (1986), for example, argue for the proposition that 'We are all Alliance nowadays' and that voters for the different parties no long possess distinctive political principles. Such heroic assertions tend to flourish when there is a lack of evidence one way or the other. Earlier researchers such as Almond and Verba did not collect data on political principles and it is therefore unwise to be dogmatic about *trends*. Our evidence indicates that in British political culture these ideological differences may be long-standing, especially in the light of their relationship to the narrower aspects of political culture – such as trust and participation – distinguished by Almond and Verba. Radicalism is clearly associated with cynicism towards government; it is not however associated at all strongly with activism.

To demonstrate this point we constructed compressed measures of cynicism and egalitarianism.[6] From the individual questions on attitudes towards MPs and trust in government we constructed a composite index, distinguishing between respondents who scored high (the very cynical), medium (fairly cynical) and low (not cynical). We followed the same procedure with the individual questions on income redistribution, worker–management conflict and so on, and again distinguished between those who scored high, medium and low on this index. We shall use the terms 'left', 'centre' and 'right' respectively to describe these three groups.

As we can see, there is a strong association between cynicism and egalitarianism: people who are on the left on our egalitarianism index are markedly more cynical about politicians than are those on the right.*

Egalitarianism and cynicism

		Very cynical	Fairly cynical	Not cynical
Left	%	37	55	8
Centre	%	21	56	23
Right	%	7	42	50

With participation, however, the picture is very different. We divided our sample into three groups: those who said they had never done anything about a government action which they thought was unjust or harmful, those who had engaged in only one type of action and those who had engaged in more than one. This time the differences between those on the left of our egalitarian index and those on the right are small and not statistically significant.

Egalitarianism and participation

		Engaged in no 'protest' action	Engaged in one 'protest' action	Engaged in two or more 'protest' actions
Left	%	57	30	13
Centre	%	56	31	14
Right	%	52	34	14

Here, then, we have an important paradox. People who are furthest to the left – that is, people who tend to have conflict models of management–worker relations and who disapprove of the existing distribution of income and wealth – are the most cynical about politicians and the least trusting of government. They are also much more likely to feel that both government and business have too much power and that workers should be allowed more say in running the places where they work; and they are rather more likely to feel that the various forms of protest should be allowed. For example, 76% of those on the left agree that government has too much power whereas only 19% of those on the right agree. (For more details see **Tables 3.1** and **3.2**).

---

* Statistically, these differences are highly significant (chi-square = 179, 4 degrees of freedom, $p < .0001$).

So radical attitudes towards the economic order tend to go with radical attitudes towards the political order – but *not* with actual protest or participation. Economic radicals are more likely to be cynical about politicians, to feel that government has too much power and to support political liberties – for example, the freedom to organise protest meetings and protest marches. But they do *not* appear more likely to engage in these forms of protest themselves.

Moral traditionalism

A possible explanation of this paradox emerges when we turn to the other main ideological dimension – that concerned with civil (as opposed to political) liberty and with law and order. Again, we asked a number of questions to tap this dimension.

		Agree	Neither agree nor disagree	Disagree
Schools should teach children to obey authority	%	83	10	7
People who break the law should be given stiffer sentences	%	72	20	7
Censorship of films and magazines is necessary to uphold moral standards	%	66	15	18
Young people today don't have enough respect for traditional British values	%	66	20	13
The law should always be obeyed even if a particular law is wrong	%	45	22	31

Here we have a rather different story. While we have seen that a consistent – though narrow – majority of the population tends to be highly critical of the existing economic order, we also find that a majority supports the prevailing moral order and the rule of law. Simultaneously, then, we have economic radicalism *and* moral 'traditionalism'.

Many researchers have found that moral attitudes such as these are unrelated to egalitarian ones (see for example Himmelweit, Humphreys and Jaeger, 1985). The two ideological principles cross-cut each other. It is not, therefore, surprising to find that their relationships with two aspects of political culture (trust and participation) are reversed. We show below that attitudes towards the existing moral order prove to be unrelated to trust but more closely linked to participation.

As before, we constructed a composite index of the moral dimension, based on the questions listed above. We divided respondents into 'authoritarians' (who scored highest on the index), 'conformists' (the average scorers) and 'libertarians' (the low scorers).[7]

First, consider the relationship with political cynicism:

Moral traditionalism and cynicism

		Very cynical	Fairly cynical	Not cynical
Authoritarians	%	26	50	24
Conformists	%	21	54	25
Libertarians	%	19	52	29

The relationship between moral traditionalism and political cynicism is rather weak, and not statistically significant. This finding – that political cynicism and lack of trust in government bear little relation to people's attitudes towards law and order – is important. It suggests that authoritarian attitudes in the moral or socio-legal sphere are only loosely related to authoritarian attitudes in the political sphere. Take, for example, attitudes towards government power. As we mentioned earlier, economic radicals are much more likely than economic conservatives to think that government has too much power – the difference between the two groups reaching a remarkable 56 percentage points. But the difference between libertarians and authoritarians is much smaller – a mere 15 points. (For more details see **Tables 3.1** and **3.2**).

This finding emphasises that we are dealing not with general psychological traits (a theory that was particularly popular in discussions about the rise of fascism) but with cultural phenomena. The fact that attitudes to the economic order are powerfully related to political cynicism brings out how important are attitudes towards the economic order, not only in shaping party politics but also in shaping trust in politicians and government. In other words, our political culture connects *economic* and political values much more than it connects *moral* and political values.

When we turn to participation rather than values, however, the picture changes.

Moral traditionalism and participation

		Engaged in no 'protest' action	Engaged in one 'protest' action	Engaged in two or more 'protest' actions
Authoritarians	%	60	31	9
Conformists	%	57	32	12
Libertarians	%	47	31	22

Libertarians show a significantly greater tendency to participate in various forms of political action in protest against unjust government actions.*

---

* Chi-square = 25.3, 4 degrees of freedom, p<.0001.

Interestingly, moreover, they also show a higher tendency to turn out and vote. Nineteen per cent of authoritarians reported that they did not generally vote, compared with only nine per cent of libertarians. Libertarians then are not only more inclined to protest but also apparently more inclined to participate generally in the political process.

In a sense, then, the libertarian–authoritarian ideological dimension would also seem to be an active–passive dimension. In part this is because authoritarians tend to be older than libertarians, and in general the elderly are less likely to engage in political participation. But this is not the whole story. Even after taking age into account, we find that libertarians are likely to have received more formal education than authoritarians, and so education may be the key to our paradox.

Education and participation

Almond and Verba themselves had suggested that education socialised citizens into the democratic political culture, although their evidence indicated that this was less true in Britain than it was in the USA (possibly because they used a measure for education that was less appropriate to Britain). Our own evidence shows that those with educational qualifications, and graduates in particular, are more liberal in their moral values, more confident in their ability to understand politics and generally more inclined to participate in politics than are the unqualified.

It is not at all surprising that the highly educated have more confidence in their ability to understand politics and to handle paper and pencil activities like writing to MPs. But the effects of education seem to run further than this. Those with qualifications – particularly graduates – are more likely to have engaged in demonstrations (possibly at college or university?) as well as in signing petitions and writing to their MPs.

	Graduates	Those with intermediate qualifications	Those with no qualifications
	%	%	%
Have contacted MP	29	11	8
Have signed a petition	52	37	29
Have gone on demonstration	17	7	2

Our interpretation is that education assists the development of the self-confidence upon which a participant political culture may be built. And it is perhaps the growth in the numbers of the highly educated that has led to the growth of participation in recent years. Education may also give the self-confidence to question tradition as well as to participate – hence the connection between moral liberalism and political participation. Certainly, graduates are much less likely to agree with the proposition that *Young people today don't have enough respect for traditional British values,* and in general are markedly more libertarian than the educationally unqualified on other moral issues:

% Agreeing with the authoritarian alternative

	Graduates	Those with intermediate qualifications	Those with no qualifications
	%	%	%
Young people lack respect for traditional values	49	61	74
Even wrong laws should be obeyed	32	42	52
Schools should teach children to obey authority	67	80	88

Here we see that the differences between the graduates and the unqualified in their attitudes towards authority are as great as the ones we saw earlier between the classes in their attitudes towards equality and conflict.

Education then would seem to provide the sociological basis both for liberal moral attitudes and for increased political participation. It contrasts with class, which provides the basis for attitudes towards the economic order and in turn for political cynicism or lack of trust.

In other words, a subordinate position in the class structure tends to be associated with egalitarian values in the economic sphere and with cynicism and distrust in the political sphere. But it is education which produces the commitment and self-confidence to participate in politics. Thus working class people who have typically received less education than those in the middle classes are less likely to have the confidence needed to set about changing the society of which they disapprove.

Notes

1. These four questions are a selection from among those asked by Marsh (1977). He interprets some as measures of 'efficacy' and others as measures of 'trust', but notes that "we have a classic example of conceptual interpenetration between two scales" (p.262). For further details see Marsh (1977), Appendix 3.
2. We should note that there has been some change in coding between the two surveys. For the questions on MPs and parties, Marsh offered his respondents the options "agree strongly", "agree", "disagree", "disagree strongly" and "don't know". We offered the additional option of "neither agree nor disagree". The options for the trust question are, however, identical.
3. Q.220 in the 1985 *British Social Attitudes* survey asked about attitudes towards public officials. This showed marked differences between attitudes to officials and attitudes to politicians. See *The 1985 Report,* p.236, for full details of question wording and the distribution of responses.
4. There was a change of coding in 1986. Respondents were not offered the option "doesn't matter", available in earlier surveys.
5. For further discussion see Heath, Jowell and Curtice (1985), Chapter 8.
6. The egalitarianism scale was constructed from Qs.230B, 230D, 231D, 231E and 231F of version B of the self-completion questionnaire. Responses were scored

from 1 to 5 and summed. Not answered and "don't know" responses were assigned to the midpoint (i.e. score 3). The resulting scores were then divided (approximately) into the top and bottom quartiles and the middle 50%. The same procedure was followed with the cynicism scale, the questions used being 92A, 92C, 92D and 93 from version B of the interview questionnaire. The reliability of the egalitarianism scale is very high (Cronbach's alpha = 0.82); that of the cynicism scale was rather lower (Cronbach's alpha = 0.63).

7. The moral traditionalism scale was constructed in the same way as the egalitarianism scale, the questions used being selected from Q.232 on version B of the self-completion questionnaire. (Cronbach's alpha for the moral traditionalism scale was 0.71).

References

ALMOND, G.A. and VERBA, S., *The Civic Culture: Political Attitudes and Democracy in Five Nations*, Princeton University Press, Princeton (1963).
BARRY, B., *Economists, Sociologists and Democracy*, Collier-Macmillan, London (1970).
BEER, S.H., *Britain Against Itself: The Political Contradictions of Collectivism*, Faber and Faber, London (1982).
BENN, A., *The New Politics: A Socialist Reconnaissance*, Fabian Society, Fabian Tract 402, London (1970).
HEATH, A.F., JOWELL, R. and CURTICE, J., *How Britain Votes*, Pergamon Press, Oxford (1985).
HIMMELWEIT, H.T., HUMPHREYS, P. and JAEGER, M., *How Voters Decide*, revised edition, Open University Press, Milton Keynes (1985).
KAVANAGH, D., 'The deferential English: a comparative critique', *Government and Opposition*, vol. 6, no. 3 (1971), pp.333-360.
KAVANAGH, D., *British Politics: Continuities and Change*, OUP, Oxford (1985).
MARSH, A., *Protest and Political Consciousness*, Sage, London (1977).
MARSHALL, G., 'Some remarks on the study of working-class consciousness', *Politics and Society*, vol. 12, (1983), pp.263-301.
ROSE, R., and McALLISTER, I., *Voters Begin To Choose: From Closed-Class to Open Elections In Britain*, Sage, London (1986).

3.1 POWER OF GOVERNMENT/BUSINESS AND INDUSTRY AND WORKER PARTICIPATION (B211, B210, B233F) by 'egalitarianism' and 'moral traditionalism' (see Chapter 3, Notes 6 and 7)

	TOTAL	EGALITARIANISM		
		Left	Centre	Right
	%	%	%	%
DOES THE GOVERNMENT HAVE TOO MUCH OR TOO LITTLE POWER?				
Far too much/too much power	50	76	52	20
About the right amount of power	45	21	44	74
Too little/far too little power	5	3	4	7
DO BUSINESS AND INDUSTRY HAVE TOO MUCH OR TOO LITTLE POWER?				
Far too much/too much power	27	50	25	9
About the right amount of power	58	37	62	68
Too little/far too little power	15	13	13	23
SHOULD THE GOVERNMENT GIVE WORKERS MORE SAY IN RUNNING THE PLACES WHERE THEY WORK?				
Definitely/probably should	80	93	82	63
Probably/definitely should not	17	6	15	32
BASE: B RESPONDENTS				
Weighted	1315	302	717	296
Unweighted	1321	300	722	299

	TOTAL	MORAL TRADITIONALISM		
		Authoritarians	Conformists	Libertarians
	%	%	%	%
DOES THE GOVERNMENT HAVE TOO MUCH OR TOO LITTLE POWER?				
Far too much/too much power	50	44	49	59
About the right amount of power	45	50	46	38
Too little/far too little power	5	6	5	3
DO BUSINESS AND INDUSTRY HAVE TOO MUCH OR TOO LITTLE POWER?				
Far too much/too much power	27	27	24	34
About the right amount of power	58	55	60	54
Too little/far too little power	15	19	16	12
SHOULD THE GOVERNMENT GIVE WORKERS MORE SAY IN RUNNING THE PLACES WHERE THEY WORK?				
Definitely/probably should	80	80	80	82
Probably/definitely should not	17	15	17	17
BASE: B RESPONDENTS				
Weighted	1315	266	747	303
Unweighted	1321	271	753	297

3.2 'PROTEST' AGAINST A GOVERNMENT ACTION (B202) by 'egalitarianism' and 'moral traditionalism' (see Chapter 3, Notes 6 and 7)

	EGALITARIANISM				MORAL TRADITIONALISM			
	TOTAL	Left	Centre	Right	TOTAL	Authoritarians	Conformists	Libertarians
	%	%	%	%	%	%	%	%
ORGANISING PUBLIC MEETINGS TO PROTEST AGAINST THE GOVERNMENT								
Should definitely/probably allow	83	84	81	86	83	71	84	89
Should probably/definitely not allow	12	11	13	11	12	23	11	6
PUBLISHING PAMPHLETS TO PROTECT AGAINST THE GOVERNMENT								
Should definitely/probably allow	78	84	77	74	78	68	78	88
Should probably/definitely not allow	17	11	18	22	17	24	18	8
ORGANISING PROTEST MARCHES AND DEMONSTRATIONS								
Should definitely/probably allow	58	65	56	54	58	42	56	74
Should probably/definitely not allow	39	31	40	44	39	55	40	21
OCCUPYING A GOVERNMENT OFFICE AND STOPPING WORK THERE FOR A COUPLE OF DAYS								
Should definitely/probably allow	10	17	9	5	10	6	9	18
Should probably/definitely not allow	86	78	87	93	86	88	88	78
SERIOUSLY DAMAGING GOVERNMENT BUILDINGS								
Should definitely/probably allow	2	4	2	1	2	3	1	3
Should probably/definitely not allow	95	93	95	98	95	94	96	94
ORGANISING A NATIONWIDE STRIKE OF ALL WORKERS AGAINST THE GOVERNMENT								
Should definitely/probably allow	28	44	27	14	28	20	22	49
Should probably/definitely not allow	68	53	68	83	68	77	74	45
BASE: B RESPONDENTS								
Weighted	1315	302	717	296	1315	266	747	303
Unweighted	1321	300	722	299	1321	271	753	297

4 Nuclear reactions

Ken Young*

April 1986 was a momentous month for Britain, Europe and the Western Alliance. The disaster at the Chernobyl nuclear plant in the Ukraine in the early hours of April 26 followed only about ten days after the United States' launch of a long-distance air attack on Libya from bases in Britain. Both events received wide media coverage, were the subject of anxious and sometimes heated debate inside and outside Parliament and, on the evidence of the polls carried out in the immediate aftermath, had a sharp effect on public opinion.

Interviewing on this round of the *British Social Attitudes* series had barely started when the attack on Tripoli was launched; several hundred interviews had been completed by the time news of the Chernobyl accident reached Britain, allowing us to make some limited before-and-after comparisons. We begin this chapter by looking at attitudes towards nuclear *energy*, at its perceived risks and at the level of public support for nuclear power generation. We then investigate public attitudes towards the related question of nuclear waste disposal, an issue that also received widespread publicity during 1986. In the second part of the chapter, we re-examine attitudes towards defence and nuclear arms – to see in particular if views about the two superpowers, and about the American nuclear presence in Britain, changed in a year which saw the attack on Libya and renewed efforts to reach a strategic arms agreement.

It is on issues such as these – some dramatic, others less so – that this survey series enables us to see the direction and speed with which attitudes are changing. In particular, it enables us to isolate population subgroups among whom views on these issues are becoming more sharply polarised.

---

* Professor of Local Government Studies, University of Birmingham.

Nuclear energy after Chernobyl

This is the fourth successive *British Social Attitudes* survey in which we have explored public attitudes to nuclear power generation and its associated risks. Earlier studies in the US on these issues have indicated that public concern over what might be thought of as remote but severe threats is generally episodic: a single incident can push concern to high levels from which it subsides over time. But the evidence also suggests that incidents of sufficient magnitude can push the level of public anxiety on to a new and critically higher plateau. Such was the case with the accident at Three Mile Island in New Jersey, where a major radiation threat led to a dramatic change in American public opinion on nuclear power. Formerly sanguine – even enthusiastic – about nuclear power generation, ordinary Americans became highly critical, with women, and young women in particular, displaying particularly vociferous opposition (Nealy, Melber and Rankin, 1983).

Our findings last year, reported in full in Chapter 4 of *The 1986 Report*, suggested that a previously steady increase in concern about environmental issues (possibly diffused from the United States) appeared to have been somewhat stemmed. Indeed, we went so far as to suggest that during 1984–85 the nuclear energy industry had "had the better of the argument" about safety (p.69). Since that Report was published, the Soviet reactor at Chernobyl became the site of the most serious accident in the history of nuclear power generation. For that reason alone the 1986 results take on a new and urgent interest. Not only was Chernobyl likely to be important in forming public attitudes to future energy policy, it was also likely to have an influence on such issues as nuclear waste disposal. And our data immediately suggest that this is how it has turned out. In any event, the more favourable view of nuclear power taken by our respondents in 1985 now looks like a mere fluctuation in a trend towards increasing concern, rather than a reversal of it.

Risks of a nuclear accident

As in each of the four years of the survey, we have asked the following question, in identical format, in the self-completion questionnaire:

As far as nuclear power stations are concerned, which of these statements comes closest to your own feelings?

	1983 %	1984 %	1985 %	1986 %
They create very serious risks for the future	35	37	30	49
They create quite serious risks for the future	28	30	31	29
They create only slight risks for the future	26	23	26	17
They create hardly any risks for the future	9	8	9	4

The proportion of respondents expressing even qualified confidence in the safety of nuclear power generation has thus fallen from 35% in 1983 to 21% in 1986. However, almost half those questioned in 1986 selected the most pessimistic statement offered about the potential dangers of nuclear reactors.

The fact that our interviewers were already in the field at the time of Chernobyl allowed us to make some limited before-and-after measurements. These analyses must, however, be treated with some caution, for – as we have noted – the great majority of respondents were questioned *after* news of the disaster had reached Britain.[1] Against expectations, perhaps, the results suggest that the most substantial increase during 1985–86 in the perception of the risks posed by nuclear power stations had occurred *before* Chernobyl, but that it was carried forward and somewhat intensified among those interviewed in the following weeks.

	Nuclear power stations create 'very' or 'quite' serious risks for the future	Nuclear power stations create 'slight' or 'hardly any' risks for the future
Total	% 78	20
Responded:		
before Chernobyl accident	% 75	24
in the immediate aftermath	% 77	21
in the following weeks	% 79	19

In previous years, we have noted that women, and younger women in particular, show greater levels of anxiety about nuclear issues than do men in the same age groups. We also noted that there was a "general slackening of concern about nuclear waste" in 1985, especially among women aged under 35 and among men aged 35–54. Is the considerable surge in concern about nuclear energy, revealed in these later figures, shared by both sexes and all age groups?

Too few people were interviewed before the Chernobyl disaster to permit any analysis of changes in subgroup opinion before and after, but comparisons between years are still instructive, and can help us to identify just where the greater part of the increase in concern has taken place.

Nuclear power stations create 'very' or 'quite' serious risks for the future

	1984	1985	1986	% change 1985–1986
Men:				
18–34	61%	61%	75%	+14
25–54	67%	53%	73%	+20
55+	59%	57%	67%	+10
Women:				
18–34	76%	63%	85%	+22
35–54	69%	65%	83%	+18
55+	71%	59%	81%	+22

Clearly there has been a large increase since 1985 in the perception of risk among both sexes and in all age groups. But the overall pattern has been to *accentuate* further the differences between men and women. Among men, the increase is greatest among those aged 35–54, but even so a much higher proportion of women than men in this age group express concern about the safety of nuclear power. The crucial point is that overall seven out of ten men and more than eight out of ten women appear to be worried about the future threats posed by nuclear power stations. For full details, see **Table 4.1**.

In earlier Reports, we have shown that opinion on *all* nuclear issues also divides sharply along party lines. During 1985 nuclear energy showed signs of becoming a partisan issue, and we commented in *The 1986 Report* on the emerging party polarisation of opinion. After Chernobyl these differences persist, but the gap between the supporters of the three main political groupings in expressing worry about the future has closed:

Nuclear power stations create 'very' or 'quite' serious risks for the future

	1984	1985	1986	% change 1985–1986
Party identification:				
Conservative	56%	44%	66%	+22
Alliance	70%	61%	81%	+20
Labour	79%	75%	88%	+13

Among Labour identifiers the level of concern, already very high, has increased; but among Alliance and, most notably, Conservative identifiers it has increased considerably more. Full details appear in **Table 4.2**. With the privatisation of the electricity supply industry planned in the near future, the ownership and control of Britain's nuclear power stations is certain to be hotly debated. It must be a cause of particular concern to the government that around two thirds of its own supporters show considerable anxiety about the safety of nuclear reactors.

Energy policy options

In 1986, only 17% of UK electricity production was derived from the 35 nuclear reactors then in service.* The great bulk of the country's energy requirements are still met from coal-fired stations. As in earlier years, we asked the following question in the self-completion supplement:

> *Which one of these three possible solutions to Britain's electricity needs would you favour most?*
>
> *We should make do with the power stations we have already; OR*
> *We should build more coal-fuelled power stations; OR*
> *We should build more nuclear power stations.*

---

* Source: CEGB Annual Report (1987)

Last year we commented upon the apparent decline in resistance to the construction of more nuclear power stations. Now, however, in line with other changes, whatever revival there might have been in support for nuclear power – always a minority preference anyway – has reversed. Almost 90% – a massive majority of the population – are against increasing Britain's reliance on nuclear power to meet its energy needs.

Once again, analysis of the responses by party identification may give the present Government cause for reflection; even among its own identifiers fewer than one in five supports an increase in nuclear power generation.

Support for the construction of more nuclear power stations

	1984	1985	1986	% change 1985–1986
Total	15%	23%	11%	−12
Identifiers:				
Conservative	24%	39%	18%	−21
Alliance	14%	25%	11%	−14
Labour	8%	10%	4%	−6

Labour support for further nuclear power development could hardly be lower, but what is remarkable is the slump in Conservative support for a policy to which the present administration has given ready and unqualified endorsement. After Chernobyl, and to a large extent even before it, the nation is fairly united in its disapproval. Full breakdowns by age within sex and party identification are shown in **Table 4.3**.

Spring 1987 saw the publication of Sir Frank Layfield's Report with its recommendation that development of the proposed pressurised water reactor (PWR) at Sizewell should be approved (Layfield, 1987). Shortly afterwards, the Central Electricity Generating Board announced the development of another PWR at Hinkley Point in Somerset – this time not to be subject to a lengthy Public Enquiry. There have nonetheless also been recent signs of a reduction in the reliance upon nuclear sources of power, with the announcement by the CEGB of plans to build further coal-fired stations, despite its emphasis on nuclear energy and the sustained public relations campaign it has mounted in its favour.

Our data so far suggest clearly then that the safety issue is paramount in shaping public attitudes towards various energy options. We now offer one further piece of decisive evidence, derived from another question on respondents' assessments of the likelihood of several long-range predictions of disaster (ranging from city riots to nuclear war) coming true within the next ten years. One such prediction was that there will be a serious accident at a British nuclear power station. Here we do not have an unbroken series of figures, as the question was not included in the 1985 survey, when we might have expected a more optimistic pattern of responses consistent with the replies to the other 'nuclear' questions given in that year. The three sets of figures that we *do* have, however, suggest a trend of rising fatalism (see **Table 4.4**).

Expectations of a major accident at a British nuclear power station within the next ten years

	1983	1984	1986
	%	%	%
'Very' or 'quite' likely	45	53	59
'Not very' or 'not at all' likely	52	44	40

Detailed breakdowns for 1986 appear in **Table 4.5**. Two years earlier a clear majority expected that such a disaster would occur in Britain. After Chernobyl the majority has increased. It appears however that Chernobyl itself had no discernible effect. Our analysis of responses given before and after the disaster reveals no significant shift.*

When we cross-analyse respondents' energy policy choices by their expectations of an accident at a nuclear power station during the next ten years, we find as expected a high association between perceived risk and policy preference.

	Expectations of nuclear accident	
	'Very' or 'quite' likely	'Not very' or 'not at all' likely
	%	%
Britain should:		
make do with existing power stations	34	35
build more coal-fuelled power stations	61	41
build more nuclear power stations	3	22

Virtually no-one who reckons the chance of a major accident to be high favours the construction of more nuclear power stations. The 'perceived risk' factor is seen to be crucial.

Disposal of nuclear waste

Finally, our series of questions on environmental hazards included, as before, one on the dangers associated with the disposal of nuclear waste. This concern continues to feature prominently – it is in fact rated as more serious than any of the other seven hazards listed. "Waste from nuclear electricity stations" was named as "very serious" by almost three quarters of our respondents, above "industrial waste in the rivers and sea" (65%). This finding is consistent with those of recent surveys carried out by SCPR (Prescott-Clarke and Hedges, 1987) and by NOP (DoE, 1987). The latter indicated that nuclear waste was thought to be the most important environmental problem in Britain of a range

---

* The limitations of this analysis must be taken into account (see Note 1 at the end of this chapter).

of 18 offered, the levels of anxiety being roughly comparable with those we had found in 1985.

As with the other questions on nuclear issues, in 1985 our respondents were somewhat more sanguine about nuclear waste than those who had been questioned in earlier years. Chernobyl is unlikely to have had a *direct* influence on responses in 1986 but there may have been 'cross-infection' from one nuclear issue to another. Considerable publicity was, however, given in 1986 to the attempts by NIREX UK Ltd to conduct test bores on four sites to determine their suitability for deep burial of nuclear waste. (These plans were later abandoned, just before the 1987 general election.) Our data show a continuing high and increasing level of concern about this potential threat to the environment:

How serious an effect on our environment does waste from nuclear electricity stations have?

	1983 %	1984 %	1985 %	1986 %
'Very' or 'quite' serious	82	87	83	90
'Not very' or 'not at all' serious	15	11	15	8

In this context, the various statements issued by the CEGB and the Electricity Council, and – in particular – the technical presentations by NIREX, take too little account of the nature of public anxiety about this issue. A NIREX spokesman argues that:

> The hardest part of the road ahead rests in reassuring the public in general, and residents near the four sites under investigation in particular, of the facts that surround the search for a good safe site for the disposal of [low level wastes]. It is unfortunately true that it takes only a few moments to frighten someone with distortions and half-truths, but can take very much longer to dispel their unfounded misapprehensions. Given the substantial participation in decision-making by central and local government and members of the general public, it should be possible to achieve a high degree of consensus and confidence in the months ahead (Strange, 1987, p.27).

There could hardly be a clearer expression of the gulf between technical assessments of risk and the judgements made by the 'non-expert' public. Our findings suggest that the nuclear power industry has a much less secure base than is implied in the NIREX contention that public attitudes can be changed in "months". Indeed, a recent review of research on risk perception (Brown and White, 1987) concludes that

> the emotional connotations of nuclear power and radiation are the most powerful in influencing opinion and are most resistant to change. There is little evidence to support the view that increases in knowledge will materially influence the present adverse reactions (p.69).

Aside from attitudes *per se*, research conducted at the University of Surrey (Lee and Brown, 1983) and by SCPR for the DoE's Radioactive Waste Management Research Programme (Prescott-Clarke and Hedges, 1987) suggests that the level of *factual* knowledge of nuclear issues is not high. As Prescott-Clarke and Hedges observe:

> Most people have fragments of information [about radioactivity] which they find hard to organise into a coherent concept of the nature of radiation. Their picture of radioactivity is far from complete and is inaccurate in many of its details (p.17).

Nevertheless, of the two thirds of respondents to their survey who claimed to have some idea of what radioactivity was, almost all knew that it was potentially pernicious.

Sir Alan Cottrell (1985) argues that responses to energy policy issues are shaped by basic and uninformed predispositions and manipulated by a sensationalist press and television; and that these predispositions can be reshaped by public education. This now seems most unlikely. The findings of research commissioned by the DoE (University of Surrey, 1985) indicate that

> people are not appraising scientific 'facts' about radioactive waste as though they existed in a value-free vacuum. It is evident that beliefs about waste are inseparable from their confidence in management, worries about 'possible' harm in the future, and the relation of technological advance to their already established value systems. It is unlikely that the uncertainty surrounding waste management options now or in the future can be countered by scientific argument (p.3).

It is clear then that the nuclear energy and waste disposal industries' calculations of the likelihood of a serious incident occurring are different – and more optimistic – than those of the public.[2] There are signs, however, that this 'confidence gap' is now recognised at an official level, and that the DoE is aware of and concerned about the mismanagement of the 'risk' debate on nuclear energy issues (ESRC, 1987, pp.28-30).

Whatever steps are taken, it appears quite likely that the Chernobyl disaster will have as sustained an effect on public attitudes in this country (and in the rest of Europe) as the Three Mile Island accident had on attitudes in the United States. In Britain at any rate, it came at a time when attitudes against increased reliance on nuclear energy were already hardening.

Defence, nuclear weapons and the Western Alliance

The British government's agreement in April 1986 to the United States' launch of an air attack on Libya from Upper Heyford in Oxfordshire and Lakenheath in Suffolk provoked heated debate about the nature of the US 'special relationship' with Britain and this country's vulnerability to Arab reprisals. Polls conducted in the immediate aftermath of the raid revealed very large majorities opposing both the attack and the decision to allow Britain to be used as a base for it. Yet the domestic political effect was short-lived, with support for the Conservative Party, and for Margaret Thatcher personally, suffering no more than a mild and brief depression. 'Libya factor – what Libya factor?'

asked MORI rhetorically, in a review of the impact of the raid in its newsletter *British Public Opinion* (1986).

Our longer-term analyses would suggest, however, that the impact of the Libyan episode is more likely to be reflected in attitudes to the US military presence in Britain than in attitudes towards the British government. In *The 1986 Report* we reviewed the trends in levels of confidence in the American presence, and noted that there were signs both of a gradual erosion in public regard for the United States' contribution to world peace and in public support for US nuclear missiles on British soil. Neither question is specific to the US use of British bases in support of its own foreign policy aims – which were the subject of the questions asked in the opinion polls immediately following the raid on Libya. Nevertheless, any quickening in the loss of support for the United States revealed by our 1986 survey might plausibly be attributed, in part at least, to the hostile reception accorded by the British public to the Libyan adventure.

Changing views of the Western Alliance

We have argued in previous reports that support for NATO, which generally runs at high levels, is not affected by declining support for the US military presence, simply because NATO appears to be seen more as a *European*, than as an American-dominated, organisation (see *The 1985 Report*, p.101). In a sense, attitudes to NATO might be used as a control in measuring attitudes to the US following the Libyan episode. We also have a more general question, asked between 1984 and 1986, comparing the relative 'threats to world peace' posed by the United States and the Soviet Union. And by comparing the evaluations of the relative contributions to the safety of Britain made by *US* and *British* nuclear weapons respectively, we can isolate opposition to the presence of American missiles on British soil from more general anti-nuclear sentiment. These matched year-on-year comparisons are illuminating.

Changing views of the Western Alliance, 1983–1986

	1983 %	1984 %	1985 %	1986 %
The threat to world peace:				
America is a greater threat than Russia	N/A	11	13	17
Russia and America are equally great threats	N/A	54	55	54
Russia is a greater threat than America	N/A	26	24	18
American nuclear missiles:				
make Britain a safer place	38	36	36	29
make Britain less safe	48	51	53	60
British nuclear missiles:				
make Britain a safer place	60	56	54	52
make Britain less safe	28	33	34	37
Support for NATO:				
Britain should remain a member	79	79	74	75
Britain should withdraw	13	11	15	13

Comparisons of the responses to these three questions show a slight but progressive deterioration in the rating of the American contribution to world peace and a marked deterioration in confidence in the US nuclear presence in Britain (see **Tables 4.6** to **4.8** for detailed breakdowns). At the same time, however, support for NATO holds up well. The table thus shows both a steady trend since 1983 away from support for the US, and – in 1986 – a quickening of the pace of that shift. Such a change might well be due to 'the Libya factor', the opprobrium of which – not unexpectedly – attached less to the British government than to the United States. As the writer of an authoritative study on the agreement on US bases in the UK (Duke 1987) recently concluded, "The Libyan crisis has acted as a catalyst for debate about the future role of the American military presence in Britain" (p.*xx*). Our data broadly support that assertion.

Nuclear disarmament

The drop in support for the presence of US nuclear missiles is much greater than the drop in support for *British* nuclear weapons, despite the increasing coherence during 1985–86 in the Labour Party's non-nuclear defence stance. Has therefore the growing strength of unilateralism in Britain over recent years now reached a plateau? *The 1988 Report* will be revealing in this respect, reflecting as it will the impact of the recent debate on the issue in the run-up to the 1987 general election. Meanwhile, the movement towards unilateralism seems to have slackened – at least temporarily.

Attitudes to nuclear disarmament, 1983–86

	1983 %	1984 %	1985 %	1986 %
Britain should:				
rid itself of nuclear weapons while persuading others to do the same	19	23	27	28
keep its nuclear weapons until we persuade others to reduce theirs	77	73	68	69

The analyses of the data from previous years pointed to the significance of age and gender differences in attitudes towards nuclear disarmament; these divisions continue to be important. Support for unilateralism is strongest among the under 35s of both sexes. In particular we find that the under 25s are most sympathetic to unilateralism. As the table below shows, support for unilateralism declines very sharply with age, enjoying the support of no more than a fifth of people aged 55+. Levels of confidence in the efficacy of the US and British deterrents are similarly age-related.

Attitudes to defence issues by age within sex

	Britain should disarm unilaterally	US missiles make Britain less safe	British missiles make Britain less safe
Total	28%	60%	37%
Men:			
18–34	35%	59%	41%
35–54	26%	50%	33%
55+	20%	48%	29%
Women:			
18–34	37%	70%	44%
35–54	28%	67%	42%
55+	21%	62%	32%

Tables 4.8 and **4.9** provide further details.

However, not all those who think that British missiles make the country less safe are unilateralists: around one in ten of those who feel that the British nuclear deterrent *improves* Britain's safety are nonetheless unilateralists.[3]

Nor are all unilateralists pessimistic about the future of a world with nuclear weapons, although they are noticeably more so than multilateralists. Forty seven per cent of unilateralists think that it is "very" or "quite" likely that a nuclear bomb will be dropped somewhere in the world within the next 10 years (compared with only 29% of multilateralists); and 30% believe that a world war involving Britain and Europe is likely within the same period (compared with 19% of multilateralists).

A dramatic gap continues to exist between trust in British nuclear weapons and in American nuclear weapons on British soil. A clear majority of the ation believes that US nuclear missiles here make Britain less safe, while about one third believe the same about British nuclear missiles.

Defence and political partisanship

When we come to look at the attitudes of party identifiers we find, not surprisingly, marked cleavages on all three issues. The three main party groupings have now differentiated themselves sharply on strategic defence questions (the confusion over the substance of Alliance policy emerging only some time *after* the end of our 1986 fieldwork).

Attitudes to defence issues by party identification

	Britain should disarm unilaterally	US missiles make Britain less safe	British missiles make Britain less safe
Party identification:			
Conservative	13%	39%	20%
Alliance	27%	66%	42%
Labour	42%	75%	50%

While the divisions among those of our respondents who identified themselves
with a political party were always predictable, the *depth* of these divisions is
somewhat surprising.

Two particularly interesting features of the table above should be noted.
First, almost 40% of Conservative identifiers are unhappy about the United
States' nuclear presence in Britain. This is a lower proportion than of Alliance
identifiers (66%) and of Labour identifiers (75%), but it is still surprisingly high
(see **Table 4.8** for full details for 1986). Moreover, the greatest *increase* in
anxiety about the American presence between 1985 and 1986 occurred among
Conservative identifiers, closely followed by Alliance identifiers. Second, there
is still only minority support (42%) among Labour identifiers for their party's
policy of unilateral disarmament. Whether or not the issue of defence turned
out to be an important contribution to Labour's defeat in the 1987 general
election is still a matter for scrutiny and debate.[4] But the doubts of Labour
Party supporters, as well as the defence issues, led us to ask respondents: *Which
political party's views on defence would you say comes **closest** to your own
views?*

Alignment with party positions on defence
by party identification

| | | Party closest to own views on defence | | | |
		Conservative	Alliance	Labour	Don't know
Total	%	35	11	24	27
Party identification					
Conservative:					
partisans	%	81	4	2	11
others	%	65	3	7	23
Alliance:					
partisans	%	14	51	10	24
others	%	18	37	12	30
Labour:					
partisans	%	11	5	64	19
others	%	12	4	45	37

As we can see, no party enjoyed a majority, although the Conservatives' policy
on defence attracted by far the greatest overall support (endorsed by over a
third of our sample) while the Alliance (11%) attracted the least. Also
noteworthy is that over a quarter of the respondents were unable to give an
answer, suggesting perhaps that the respective party positions are less well
known than has been assumed. As is often the case, lack of knowledge of
political matters (or unwillingness to express opinions) is associated with
educational attainment: 83% of those with 'A' Levels or higher qualifications
nominated a party, compared with only 70% of those with lower qualifications
or none at all.

But it is the extent to which those who identify with a particular party also
identify with its defence policies that is the most interesting issue: in the table
above, we have further divided our respondents according to the strength of
their party attachment, 'partisans' being those who immediately identify

themselves as supporters of a particular party, the 'others' being those who fall short of an outright commitment of support. We can immediately see the relative strength of Conservative *identifiers'* adherence to the defence policies of their preferred party, the rather less than whole-hearted support for the distinctive policies of the Labour Party among its partisans, and only minority support for Labour's defence stance among its less committed identifiers. Even more striking perhaps is the bare majority of Alliance partisans for the defence policy advocated by their party grouping.

Conclusions

Overall, the 1986 results confirm that Britain is still far from becoming a unilateralist country. The United States' nuclear presence in Britain, made more prominent by the commitment of the Labour Party to remove American nuclear weapons, is unpopular. Indeed, a more general anti-Americanism emerges from our responses.

It is in this context that the impact of the Libyan episode ought to be seen. As Duke (1987) comments:

> Many of the questions concerning the bases have to do with wider concerns – about the state of the alliance, about the evolving European voice on defence issues, about the growing friction between more moderate European governments and the Reagan administration and, in Britain's case, about the dilemma of either being good Europeans or responding to the ties of the 'special relationship' (p.*xx*).

There seems to be little doubt that defence and related nuclear issues are now unusually prominent. When our survey was carried out in Spring 1986, the extent of the internal reforms proposed by Mikhail Gorbachev were not yet fully appreciated. Moreover, the changes in the Soviet approach to foreign policy and arms negotiation have been widely welcomed in Western Europe.

The simultaneous prominence of the issue of nuclear power, associated more with defence issues than with environmental ones in the public's mind (*The 1986 Report*, p.10), may also have contributed to the changing attitudes which our data reflect.

The deterioration of support for the American presence in Britain, and the emerging equation of Russia and America as equally great threats to world peace, may yet be stemmed or accelerated by the Gorbachev initiative on arms limitation in Europe and the US response to it. We shall have to await the results of the 1987 survey to see the direction in which attitudes are moving.

Notes

1. In our analysis of the 'Chernobyl effect' we took these three time-periods:

   Before Chernobyl accident: up to and including 28 April 1986 (when news of the disaster was just beginning to receive media coverage).

In the immediate aftermath: 29 April–11 May inclusive (when the possible effects of the radioactive fallout were causing most concern and receiving 'headline' coverage).

In the following weeks: 12 May onwards (after which media coverage began to decrease).

The dates chosen are necessarily somewhat arbitrary since, to the best of our knowledge, no organisation monitored media coverage in detail. It should also be noted that all the questions on nuclear power and waste were asked on the self-completion questionnaire, filled in *after* the main interview. While most self-completion supplements were picked up by the interviewer, or posted back, within a few days of the interview, some were undoubtedly filled in considerably later.

2. Prescott-Clarke and Hedges (1987) summarised the risk perceived by their sample as follows:

The majority (64%) of those who knew of the existence of radioactive waste felt there is a real risk of harm to the public from the way it is dealt with . . . [describing] the risk as "fairly high" . . . Radioactive waste is thought to be better controlled [than chemical waste] by "the authorities", although only 15% described it as "very well" controlled. Of the various possible triggers by which radioactive or chemical waste could harm the public, the most commonly mentioned was human error (p.11).

3. Anthony Heath writes in *The 1986 Report*: "It would, on the face of it, seem inconsistent for someone to agree that nuclear weapons make Britain safer yet that Britain should rid itself of them. On the other hand, that person might assent to the factual proposition that nuclear weapons might make Britain safer, but believe on moral, rather than on security, grounds that nuclear weapons should be eschewed. Or that person might not want Britain to be a 'safer place' to live in. The first question [on British missiles] is an 'is' question, the second [on future British nuclear defence policy] is an 'ought' question" (p.3).

4. We look forward to the results of the Oxford/SCPR *British General Election* study for confirmation or otherwise of the 'defence effect'.

References

BROWN, J.M. and WHITE, H.M., 'The Public's Understanding of Radiation and Nuclear Waste', *Journal of the Society for Radiological Protection*, vol. 7, no. 2 (1987), pp. 61-70.

COTTRELL, A., *Public Attitudes to Energy*, CEGB, London (1983).

DoE, *Digest of Environmental Protection and Water Statistics*, No. 9; Part 10. Public Attitudes to the Environment, HMSO (1987), pp. 54-61.

DUKE, S., *US Defence Bases in the United Kingdom*, Macmillan, London (1987).

ESRC, *Newsletter 59: Environmental Issues*, ESRC, London (February, 1987).

LAYFIELD, F., *Sizewell B: Public Enquiry. Summary of Conclusions and Recommendations*, HMSO, London (1987).

LEE, P. and BROWN, J., *Feasibility Study on Public Attitudes to Radioactive Waste Management*, University of Surrey, Guildford (1983).

MORI, *British Public Opinion*, vol. 8, no. 4 (April, 1986).

NEALY, S.M., MELBER, B.D. and RANKIN, W.L., *Public Opinion and Nuclear Energy*, D.C. Heath, Lexington, Mass. (1983).

PRESCOTT-CLARKE, P. and HEDGES, A., *Radioactive Waste Disposal: The Public's View,* SCPR, London (1987).
STRANGE, R.C., 'Radioactive Waste: the Facts', *Industrial Observer,* no. 9 (1987), p.27.
UNIVERSITY OF SURREY, *Public Perceptions of Aspects of Radioactive Waste Management,* University of Surrey, Guildford, (1985).

4.1 PERCEPTIONS OF RISKS FROM NUCLEAR POWER STATIONS (B219b) by age within sex, 1985 and 1986

	1985 SURVEY							1986 SURVEY								
	TOTAL	AGE+ WITHIN SEX						TOTAL	AGE+ WITHIN SEX							
		MALE			FEMALE				MALE				FEMALE			
		18-34	35-54	55+	18-34	35-54	55+		18-24	25-34	35-54	55+	18-24	25-34	35-54	55+
FEELINGS ABOUT NUCLEAR POWER STATIONS:	%	%	%	%	%	%	%	%	%	%	%	%	%	%	%	%
They create very serious risks for the future	30	29	24	24	30	28	35	49	50	46	45	40	55	56	50	50
They create quite serious risks for the future	31	32	29	33	33	37	24	29	24	30	28	27	30	29	33	31
They create only slight risks for the future	26	27	33	28	22	25	23	17	16	19	22	24	11	13	14	13
They create hardly any risks for the future	9	12	12	12	5	8	8	4	7	4	3	6	3	2	3	5
Don't know/no answer	3	1	2	3	1	3	10	2	3	1	1	2	2	2	1	3
BASE: B RESPONDENTS *Weighted*	1502	239	242	218	292	269	240	1315	96	116	222	174	115	134	255	200
Unweighted	1530	236	248	214	299	288	245	1321	89	112	228	178	108	133	264	206

4.2 PERCEPTIONS OF RISKS FROM NUCLEAR POWER STATIONS (B219b) by party identification, 1985 and 1986

| | 1985 SURVEY | | | | | 1986 SURVEY | | | | |
| | TOTAL | PARTY IDENTIFICATION[+] | | | | TOTAL | PARTY IDENTIFICATION[+] | | | |
		Conservative	Alliance	Labour	Non-aligned		Conservative	Alliance	Labour	Non-aligned
FEELINGS ABOUT NUCLEAR POWER STATIONS:	%	%	%	%	%		%	%	%	%
They create very serious risks for the future	30	17	27	45	26	49	33	51	62	45
They create quite serious risks for the future	31	27	34	30	43	29	33	30	26	33
They create only slight risks for the future	26	38	27	18	19	17	26	15	8	20
They create hardly any risks for the future	9	16	9	4	8	4	7	3	2	-
Don't know/no answer	3	3	3	3	5	2	2	2	1	2
BASE: B RESPONDENTS _Weighted_	1502	472	275	549	108	1315	451	225	468	91
Unweighted	1530	495	279	550	110	1321	452	227	471	88

4.3 POSSIBLE SOLUTIONS TO BRITAIN'S ELECTRICITY NEEDS (B219a) by age within sex and party identification

	TOTAL	AGE[+] WITHIN SEX								PARTY IDENTIFICATION[+]			
		MALE				FEMALE				Conservative	Alliance	Labour	Non-aligned
		18-24	25-34	35-54	55+	18-24	25-34	35-54	55+				
	%	%	%	%	%	%	%	%	%	%	%	%	%
WHICH ONE OF THESE THREE POSSIBLE SOLUTIONS TO BRITAIN'S ELECTRICITY NEEDS WOULD YOU FAVOUR MOST?													
We should make do with the power stations we have already	34	49	38	23	21	57	46	34	28	33	38	30	49
We should build more coal-fuelled power stations	52	32	48	60	61	36	45	54	61	46	49	63	42
We should build more nuclear power stations	11	12	12	15	14	6	6	10	8	18	11	4	7
BASE: B RESPONDENTS *Weighted*	1315	96	116	222	174	115	134	255	200	451	225	468	91
Unweighted	1321	89	112	228	178	108	133	264	206	452	227	471	88

4.4 LIKELIHOOD OF VARIOUS 'DISASTER' PREDICTIONS COMING TRUE (B225) by year 1983, 1984 and 1986

HOW LIKELY OR UNLIKELY IS IT TO COME TRUE WITHIN THE NEXT TEN YEARS?	1983 SURVEY %	1984 SURVEY %	1986 SURVEY %
Acts of political terrorism in Britain will be common events			
Very likely/quite likely	56	62	74
Not very likely/not at all likely	42	35	25
Riots and civil disturbance in our cities will be common events			
Very likely/quite likely	60	56	64
Not very likely/not at all likely	38	40	34
There will be a world war involving Britain and Europe			
Very likely/quite likely	24	21	23
Not very likely/not at all likely	73	75	76
There will be a serious accident at a British nuclear power station			
Very likely/quite likely	45	53	59
Not very likely/not at all likely	52	44	40
The police in our cities will find it impossible to protect our personal safety on the streets			
Very likely/quite likely	53	52	59
Not very likely/not at all likely	45	46	40
The government in Britain will be overthrown by revolution			
Very likely/quite likely	8	10	10
Not very likely/not at all likely	90	87	89
A nuclear bomb will be dropped somewhere in the world*			
Very likely/quite likely	N/A	35	35
Not very likely/not at all likely	N/A	62	64
Weighted	*1610*	*1522*	*1315*
Unweighted	*1650*	*1562*	*1321*

BASES: ALL RESPONDENTS (1983 and 1984)
       B RESPONDENTS (1986)

* THIS ITEM WAS NOT INCLUDED IN 1983

4.5 LIKELIHOOD OF A SERIOUS ACCIDENT AT A NUCLEAR POWER STATION (B225) by age within sex and party identification

LIKELIHOOD OF A SERIOUS ACCIDENT AT A BRITISH NUCLEAR POWER STATION WITHIN THE NEXT TEN YEARS	TOTAL	AGE+ WITHIN SEX								PARTY IDENTIFICATION+			
		MALE				FEMALE				Conservative	Alliance	Labour	Non-aligned
		18-24	25-34	35-54	55+	18-24	25-34	35-54	55+				
	%	%	%	%	%	%	%	%	%	%	%	%	%
Very likely	17	22	21	21	13	19	17	11	15	9	16	24	23
Quite likely	42	39	40	34	36	44	53	45	46	36	46	46	39
Not very likely	34	31	34	36	40	31	28	39	30	44	32	25	33
Not at all likely	6	7	4	8	9	5	2	3	7	10	5	3	4
Don't know/no answer	1	2	-	-	-	1	-	1	5	1	1	2	2
BASE: B RESPONDENTS Weighted	1315	96	116	222	174	115	134	255	200	451	225	468	91
Unweighted	1321	89	112	228	178	108	133	264	206	452	227	471	88

4.6 THREATS TO WORLD PEACE (Q9)
by age within sex, 1985 and 1986

1985 SURVEY

	TOTAL	MALE 18-34	MALE 35-54	MALE 55+	FEMALE 18-34	FEMALE 35-54	FEMALE 55+
	%	%	%	%	%	%	%
America is a greater threat to world peace than Russia	13	10	16	18	12	10	13
Russia is a greater threat to world peace than America	23	16	18	29	21	26	30
Russia and America are equally great threats to world peace	55	69	57	46	59	53	44
Neither is a threat to world peace	6	5	8	5	6	7	6
Don't know/no answer	3	1	1	2	2	4	7
Weighted	1769	287	288	245	333	308	303
Unweighted	1804	284	295	241	340	329	310

1986 SURVEY

	TOTAL	MALE 18-24	MALE 25-34	MALE 35-54	MALE 55+	FEMALE 18-24	FEMALE 25-34	FEMALE 35-54	FEMALE 55+
	%	%	%	%	%	%	%	%	%
America is a greater threat to world peace than Russia	17	18	18	16	16	20	19	19	12
Russia is a greater threat to world peace than America	18	9	13	17	22	19	14	17	27
Russia and America are equally great threats to world peace	54	62	61	56	46	55	60	55	46
Neither is a threat to world peace	9	10	8	10	14	4	5	7	9
Don't know/no answer	3	1	*	1	2	3	4	2	6
Weighted	3066	237	264	509	429	218	305	586	515
Unweighted	3100	221	262	519	443	215	305	602	530

BASE: ALL RESPONDENTS

4.7 THREATS TO WORLD PEACE (Q9) by party identification, 1985 and 1986

1985 SURVEY

| | TOTAL | PARTY IDENTIFICATION[+] | | | |
		Conservative	Alliance	Labour	Non-aligned
	%	%	%	%	%
America is a greater threat to world peace than Russia	13	7	10	19	16
Russia is a greater threat to world peace than America	23	34	20	17	21
Russia and America are equally great threats to world peace	55	56	65	56	49
Neither is a threat to world peace	6	8	3	6	6
Don't know/no answer	3	2	1	3	9
BASE: ALL RESPONDENTS Weighted	1769	545	311	645	154
Unweighted	1804	564	317	649	159

1986 SURVEY

| | TOTAL | PARTY IDENTIFICATION[+] | | | |
		Conservative	Alliance	Labour	Non-aligned
	%	%	%	%	%
America is a greater threat to world peace than Russia	17	9	17	26	13
Russia is a greater threat to world peace than America	18	29	13	12	16
Russia and America are equally great threats to world peace	54	50	61	54	54
Neither is a threat to world peace	9	10	9	7	10
Don't know/no answer	3	2	1	2	8
BASE: ALL RESPONDENTS Weighted	3066	1035	535	1072	231
Unweighted	3100	1054	542	1080	226

4.8 AMERICAN AND INDEPENDENT NUCLEAR MISSILES IN BRITAIN (Q6a, 6b) by age within sex and party identification

	TOTAL	AGE+ WITHIN SEX								PARTY IDENTIFICATION+			
		MALE				FEMALE				Conservative	Alliance	Labour	Non-aligned
		18-24	25-34	35-54	55+	18-24	25-34	35-54	55+				
	%	%	%	%	%	%	%	%	%	%	%	%	%
THE SITING OF <u>AMERICAN</u> NUCLEAR MISSILES MAKES BRITAIN:													
Safer	29	28	30	38	41	19	18	21	27	47	23	18	18
Less safe	60	60	58	50	48	72	68	67	62	39	66	75	62
No difference	3	4	5	6	3	2	1	3	1	5	4	1	2
Don't know/no answer	9	8	7	7	8	8	12	9	10	9	8	6	19
HAVING OUR <u>OWN</u> INDEPENDENT NUCLEAR MISSILES MAKES BRITAIN:													
Safer	52	46	52	58	59	45	43	47	55	69	46	42	39
Less safe	37	43	39	33	29	44	44	42	32	20	42	50	41
No difference	2	2	4	4	3	1	1	2	1	3	3	1	1
Don't know/no answer	9	10	5	5	8	11	12	10	12	8	9	7	19
BASE: ALL RESPONDENTS													
Weighted	3066	237	264	509	429	218	305	586	515	1035	535	1072	231
Unweighted	3100	221	262	519	443	215	305	602	530	1054	542	1080	226

4.9 NUCLEAR DISARMAMENT (Q7)
by age within sex, social class, highest educational qualification obtained and party identification

WHICH, IF EITHER, OF THESE TWO STATEMENTS COMES CLOSEST TO YOUR OWN OPINION OF BRITISH NUCLEAR POLICY?	TOTAL	AGE[+] WITHIN SEX								SOCIAL CLASS					HIGHEST QUALIFICATION OBTAINED[+]					PARTY IDENTIFICATION[+]			
		MALE				FEMALE				I/II	III non-manual	III manual	IV/V	Other	Degree	Pro-fessional level	'A' level	'O' level/ CSE	Foreign/ Other/ None	Conser-vative	Alliance	Labour	Non-aligned
		18-24	25-34	35-54	55+	18-24	25-34	35-54	55+														
	%	%	%	%	%	%	%	%	%	%	%	%	%	%	%	%	%	%	%	%	%	%	%
Britain should rid itself of nuclear weapons while persuading others to do the same	28	38	33	26	20	39	35	28	21	25	26	29	29	39	41	26	33	27	27	13	27	42	32
Britain should keep its nuclear weapons until we persuade others to reduce theirs	69	59	66	72	77	60	60	69	73	73	71	69	66	57	54	73	64	71	69	85	71	55	57
Neither of these	2	3	2	2	2	-	3	2	3	3	2	1	4	2	4	1	2	2	3	1	2	2	7
BASE: ALL RESPONDENTS																							
Weighted	3066	237	264	509	429	218	305	586	515	714	722	628	703	300	206	366	268	820	1398	1035	535	1072	231
Unweighted	3100	221	262	519	443	215	305	602	530	726	740	639	706	289	207	370	268	829	1421	1054	542	1080	226

5 Food values: health and diet

Aubrey Sheiham and Michael Marmot

with Don Rawson and Nicola Ruck*

Since the early 1980s, the British diet has become a matter for heated debate. Food has been the subject of front page newspaper articles, major television documentaries, radio series and best-selling books. In particular, the relationship between the food we eat and the diseases we commonly suffer has made news: health professionals have gone public in saying that our diet causes ill health. The general public has bought the books, written letters to the media and has changed some of its food habits; the food industry has responded by producing new products. All this seems to indicate an enormous change in attitudes.

Twenty years ago it was orthodoxy among nutritionists that people followed life-long habits and cared only about the taste and appearance of foods – not about their nutritional value. Now health and nutrition have become important in food choice. Some changes have been occurring gradually, such as the increasing belief in the harmful effects of high sugar intake. Others, such as the realisation of the dangers of saturated fat products, have been more rapid. The important questions now are: how widespread is concern about a healthy diet, and to what extent is this concern determining food choice?

The story so far

Looking back at the results of a survey carried out in the late 1960s (UK Margarine and Shortening Manufacturers' Association, 1969), we can see just

* Aubrey Sheiham is Professor of Community Dental Health and Dental Practice, University College London; Michael Marmot is Professor of Community Medicine, University College London; Don Rawson is Senior Lecturer in Health Education Research, Polytechnic of the South Bank; Nicola Ruck is a nutritionist.

how far the attitudes of both the public and nutritionists have changed. Then the majority of respondents believed meat, cheese, eggs and sugar (as well as fish, fruit and vegetables) to be 'healthy' or 'good'; and thought potatoes (as well as sweets, chocolates, cakes and biscuits) to be 'bad' in some way. A quarter nominated potatoes, sugar, sweets, chocolates and butter as being "not good for people with heart troubles". The great majority thought that their own diet was nutritionally 'all right'; less than one in five suggested that eating fewer 'fattening foods' would improve it. Over a third wanted to eat more meat – not necessarily to make them healthier, but certainly in the belief that this would do them good rather than harm. And the expert nutritionists' comments on the results endorsed most of these views, recommending meat and dairy products as 'good', and excess calories (in, for example, bread and potatoes) as 'bad'.

Since then, expert opinion has changed as to which components in a diet are most crucial to health. Sugar, salt, and fat (particularly saturated fat) are now widely agreed to be indicators of a 'bad' diet; a high intake of meat and dairy products is generally considered 'bad'. Fibre or complex carbohydrates are now widely agreed to be indicators of a 'good' diet; a high intake of potatoes is generally considered 'good'.

This view of a healthy diet was set out in the 'unofficial' report from NACNE, the National Advisory Committee on Nutrition Education (Health Education Council, 1983). A Sunday newspaper printed the main findings and speculated that the DHSS had refused official publication of the report because its recommendations clashed with government policies for agriculture and the food industry. All this made food and health the subject of intense public interest. The report was officially published and made available to health professionals only nine months later. A sustained media debate on the report's recommendations almost certainly made many people aware of the relationship between diet and health and of the potential of a healthy diet to prevent illness, particularly heart disease. Shortly afterwards, the Health Education Council commissioned a national survey (Research Surveys of Great Britain, 1983) which appeared to provide evidence of a major change: now a majority of the population thought that the British diet needed improving, nearly half thought that we should eat less salt, and most could correctly identify the health problems associated with high salt intake and correctly name high fibre foods.

In contrast to these findings, research commissioned by the British Nutrition Foundation (BNF, 1985) indicated that almost half of their sample was not at all worried about what they ate. Most believed in 'moderation' and 'variety' in the diet, and saw a 'proper meal' as containing cooked meat, two vegetables and a dessert. About a third said they had cut back on some foods (mainly sweets, sugar, puddings and biscuits) in the last two years, and the majority recognised the dangers of becoming overweight. The authors estimated that only about one in ten of the sample were "genuinely concerned with their food on grounds of health and nutrition". On the basis of these findings, the BNF's recommendation to the food industry was that:

> anyone hoping to increase the usage of a food, or change the balance of eating, simply by giving people more nutritional or health information is on rather shaky ground.

Statements such as this may explain the food industry's long resistance to demands from nutritionists for healthier products.

During the 1980s, then, a large amount of (sometimes conflicting) nutritional information has been published, and there is clear evidence that changes in diet have been taking place. That is why we decided to include a series of questions in *British Social Attitudes*. The results can to a limited extent be compared to those of previous surveys, but since doctors and nutritionists have changed their own views about diet in the last 20 years or so, the questions they have thought important to ask have also changed. Analysis of future trends may be more reliable, and we hope that this module will be included in future rounds of the series to provide comparable data. Our questionnaire explores both attitudes *and* eating patterns, so that we can begin to discover which attitudes are the most powerful in determining people's diets.

We begin by looking at general *attitudes* towards food, diet and health and explore in some depth certain subgroups in the population whose beliefs appear to influence their dietary habits. Second, we use the data that we have collected on eating *behaviour* to divide our sample into 'healthy' and 'unhealthy' eaters, and look at the demographic profiles of each group – investigating, for instance, age, gender and class differences in eating habits. In the third part of this chapter, we bring together the two strands and begin to investigate the relationship between attitudes and current eating habits, concentrating on those subgroups who appear, on our evidence, to be most and least resistant to the advice currently given by health professionals on what constitutes a 'healthy eating lifestyle'. Fourth, we briefly examine recent changes our respondents have made in their eating habits (substituting less healthy with more healthy food). And finally, we take a brief look at the image that our sample has of the health values of various foods, ranging from potatoes to sugar, with the purpose of seeing how far the views of the public have come to correspond with those of the majority of health professionals.

Barriers to 'healthy eating'

Past research has shown that many people would like to have a healthier diet, but have to surmount 'barriers' – some self-erected – to achieve it; others simply have misconceptions as to what constitutes 'food that is good for you', or feel that diet is unimportant to good health and that staying healthy is just a matter of luck. To tap these dimensions, we asked respondents to the self-completion supplement to say how far they agreed or disagreed with a number of statements about food, diet and health. Five of these concerned what might be termed overt barriers to buying, serving and eating 'food that is good for you' – for example, expense, inconvenience, family pressures. Two further statements were designed to find out how far people saw good health as something outside their personal control. The remaining four statements addressed the importance of exercise and weight control, 'experts'' views on diet and what constitutes a 'proper meal'.

As the table below shows, not one of these putative barriers is in fact regarded as a barrier by the majority of our respondents. Fewer than one in five think good food hard to find or that it takes too long to prepare. Substantial minorities, however, are concerned about its price and taste, and endorse the view that pressure from other members of the family could stand in the way of healthier eating habits.

Overt barriers to healthy eating

% of sample who agree or disagree with each statement Food that is good for you . . .		Agree ('strongly' or 'just')	Disagree ('strongly' or 'just')
is usually more expensive	%	49	34
generally tastes nicer than other food	%	27	37
generally takes too long to prepare	%	19	54
is easy to find in supermarkets	%	64	19
Many people would eat healthier food if the rest of their families would let them	%	42	24

Although much current health education aims to make choosing healthy food easier, it is apparent that for many people free choice is illusory. Choosing what food to buy and serve takes place in a definite social context which may exert pressures to make unhealthy selections (see Blaxter and Paterson, 1982).

When we come to look at differences between the various subgroups within the population, we begin to see patterns emerging that we shall trace during the remainder of this chapter. In particular, we note a greater awareness of 'barriers' to healthy eating among those in manual occupations (especially those in Social Classes IV and V). Manual workers are more inclined to think that healthier food costs more and takes too long to prepare. They also show a greater recognition of family resistance to healthy eating (see **Table 5.1**). Women are also more likely to be conscious of family resistance, as Charles and Kerr (1982) have observed: they reported that wives do not think it worthwhile cooking a 'proper meal' when their husbands are not there to share it, and that, in their absence, they tended to let their children decide what kind of meal should be served. It must be stressed, though, that the differences that we found are not great – certainly not great enough, at this stage of our analysis anyway – to justify concerns about 'class barriers' to healthy eating.

Two statements were designed to measure the strength of what we might call a 'fatalistic' view of diet and health. Few of our respondents subscribe to it:

		Agree ('strongly' or 'just')	Disagree ('strongly' or 'just')
Good health is just a matter of good luck	%	17	68
If heart disease is in your family, there is little you can do to reduce your chances of getting it	%	15	70

People in Social Classes IV and V tend to be more fatalistic than average, as do those with no formal educational qualifications (largely overlapping groups anyway). But we also see intergenerational differences emerging, with the over 55s noticeably more fatalistic than are younger members of the sample. Nonetheless, majorities in all population subgroups that we have examined feel that good health is, to some extent at least, within an individual's control (see **Table 5.2**).

Our last four statements were more diverse, but were still attempting to reveal possible resistance to healthy eating.

		Agree ('strongly' or 'just')	Disagree ('strongly' or 'just')
Experts contradict each other over what makes a healthy diet	%	73	11
A proper meal should include meat and vegetables	%	62	22
People worry too much about their weight	%	60	22
As long as you take enough exercise, you can eat whatever foods you want	%	31	51

Just over half of the sample thinks that exercise is no substitute for a healthy diet. Nearly three quarters, however, believe that experts give conflicting advice – reflecting perhaps the recent changes in advice (noted earlier) on which foods are important to good health. Women are more likely than men to say that experts give contradictory advice, partly perhaps as a result of their greater exposure to features on slimming in the 'women's media' (see Consumers' Association, 1986 and Thomas, Thomas and Murcott, 1984). And we should note the strength of 'traditionalist' sentiment among our sample members, about three fifths of whom think that a 'proper meal' should include meat and vegetables.

Subgroup differences are again of interest, with those in manual occupations and the less well-educated less likely than others to endorse views that are in line with contemporary health education. The Healthy Eating Study (DMB & B, 1986) compared the class divide in food habits and attitudes with what has happened to cigarette smoking: those in non-manual occupations have tended to give up and attach a stigma to it, while many manual workers have carried on smoking without feeling similar social pressures to stop. Age again comes into play: not unexpectedly, the over 55s are more inclined to hold 'traditionalist' beliefs, along with the younger men in our sample – but not younger women (see **Table 5.2**).

So the population appears largely aware of the link between diet and good health, but divided as to the importance of this link, and often unaware of, or confused about, what constitutes a healthy diet. Class and education, age and sex (but rarely region) have some bearing upon many beliefs. We go on now to look at the characteristics of healthy and unhealthy eaters and then to examine how far, if at all, *attitudes* towards food and health are carried over into eating *habits*.

Healthy and unhealthy eaters

Definitions

Any categorisation of people into those with healthy and unhealthy diets must inevitably be imprecise, not least because there is no agreed definition of what makes for a healthy pattern of eating. In any case, we would need to have collected much more detailed information (preferably in diary form) about quantities of food consumed, frequency of eating and cooking methods than space in our (primarily attitudinal) questionnaire allowed. So we were forced to adopt a less ambitious and more pragmatic categorisation.

We attempted vainly to divide our respondents into 'healthy' and 'unhealthy' eaters on the basis of whether or not they had made recent changes (largely as recommended in the NACNE Report) towards healthier eating habits. It turned out, however, that no 'naturally occurring' groups emerged on this criterion, as indeed on others we tried. We could not separate recent converts to healthy eating habits, and those who had largely failed to change, into relatively homogeneous and easily-definable groups. Rather, respondents seemed to spread themselves evenly along a continuum.

So, following advice from nutritionists, we divided the sample into two or three groups on the basis of their *current* eating habits. A healthy diet, we decided heroically, included fresh fruit and vegetables (including potatoes) and fish. An unhealthy diet included a lot of meat (processed and unprocessed), eggs, and sugar in hot drinks.*

The 732 respondents who 'scored' on six or seven definitions of eating healthily (or not eating *un*healthily) formed our group of *healthy eaters*; the 367 who 'scored' on four or fewer we defined as *unhealthy eaters*. An *intermediate group* of 418 respondents scored on five items and proved to be somewhat heterogeneous in their attitudes and characteristics: later in this chapter we have added them to the 'unhealthy eaters'; in this section we show them separately.

We looked first at whether current healthy eating patterns were the result of recent changes in diet that our respondents had made. Surprisingly, perhaps, the link was not marked. Current healthy eaters (by our definition) had averaged just under three changes towards healthier eating in the last two or three years, while unhealthy eaters averaged just under two out of the five changes we offered. That the discrepancy is not greater may be explained in part by an earlier conversion to a better diet among our current healthy eaters. And it must be emphasised, of course, that *reported* eating behaviour may not accurately reflect actual food consumption.

Characteristics of healthy and unhealthy eaters

When we looked earlier at general attitudes, we found noticeable differences according to class, education, age and gender, but almost no regional

---

* At the end of the chapter we give the precise definitions of our 'healthy' and 'unhealthy' eaters and of the 'intermediate' group.

differences. We now look at patterns of behaviour, to see if our sample also divides and if so, in similar ways.

		Healthy eaters	Intermediate	Unhealthy eaters
Total	%	48	28	24
Social Class:				
I/II	%	60	26	14
III Non-manual	%	58	25	18
III Manual	%	37	30	32
IV/V	%	39	32	30
Highest educational qualification:				
Degree/Professional	%	59	26	15
'A' level/'O' level	%	47	29	24
CSE/Foreign/Other/None	%	45	27	27

The differences in *attitudes* glimpsed earlier are put into sharper relief when we come to look at *eating patterns*. 'Traditionalism', 'fatalism' and the perception of barriers to healthy eating among manual workers and the less highly educated seem to be translated into behaviour. The class divide is particularly marked, with over twice as many respondents in manual occupations as in professional and managerial ones classified by our definition as unhealthy eaters.

We have seen that older people tend to be traditional in their views of a 'proper meal', weight and exercise, and that a substantial minority feels that a person's health is outside his or her control. And we have also seen that these views are to some extent shared by younger men. Do these differences carry over into eating habits?

		Healthy eaters	Intermediate	Unhealthy eaters
Total	%	48	28	24
Men:				
18–34	%	23	30	47
35–54	%	43	33	24
55+	%	47	28	26
Women:				
18–34	%	48	28	25
35–54	%	60	26	14
55+	%	66	22	13

Age and gender differences are even more marked than those of class and education, with women in all age groups being much more likely than men to eat healthily; healthy eating also increases with age. At opposite ends of the spectrum are women aged 55 or over (two thirds of whom fulfil our definition of a healthy eater) and men aged 18–34, only 23% of whom do so. So we are faced with something of a paradox: older people, especially older women, are especially likely to have more 'traditional' attitudes towards food and health, to think that good health is a matter of luck, and to claim that experts give conflicting advice over what makes for a healthy diet. Yet they report a healthier diet than do their younger counterparts. One explanation might be that many of them, as pensioners, simply cannot afford to eat foods (such as meat) against which nutritional opinion is hardening. Further analysis of the data is needed to investigate this hypothesis.

Interestingly, respondents from households where there are children are more likely to be unhealthy eaters. Clearly the presence of children is related to the respondent's age, but it could also be a reflection of the family pressures against healthy eating, recognised by over two fifths of our respondents. In fact the *Lean Lifestyle Report* (Findus, 1986) found that almost half of the women interviewed believed they would eat more healthily if they did not have to cater for their families; and Charles and Kerr (1982) reported that the composition of the main family meal each day was usually determined by the man's tastes.

Regional differences in this survey must, as usual, be interpreted cautiously, all the more so since they may simply reflect the differing social class profiles of the North and South. But in so far as they exist, they do show signs of a North–South division:

		Healthy eaters	Intermediate	Unhealthy eaters
Total	%	48	28	24
Region:				
Scotland	%	42	26	33
North	%	43	29	28
Midlands and Wales	%	50	30	20
South	%	52	26	22

That there are regional differences in food consumption is confirmed by data from recent National Food Surveys (*Regional Trends*, 1987). However, the pattern is by no means clear-cut:

> Households in the North consumed more eggs, meat, flour and cakes and biscuits and less milk and cheese than those in other regions, while those in the South East and East Anglia consumed most fruit and coffee per head and least potatoes, bread and sugar and preserves (p. 112 and Table 9.11).

Whilst some dietary habits prevalent among those living in the north of England would not be commended by health professionals, others (such as a lower intake of high-fat dairy produce) would meet with their approval. Similarly lower consumption of high-fibre foods by southerners runs counter to current orthodoxy.

Attitudes and habits

We wanted to group our respondents into clusters according to the coherence and direction of their attitudes towards food, diet and health. So we first took each respondent's answers to all eleven general attitudinal questions we had asked, and computed a matrix of correlations between them. (In general, the correlations were not high, the average being 0.15 and the maximum being 0.47.)

Next we carried out a cluster analysis* on the 1416 respondents to the self-completion questionnaire and, after inspection, divided the sample into four attitudinal clusters (with about 300–500 in each):

Group 1: 'The diehards'. The predominant characteristic of people in this group is their fatalism about health; they believe it to be a matter of luck, or heredity, or both. In common with Groups 2 and 3, they are 'traditionalist' in their views about a 'proper meal', weight control and exercise as a substitute for a healthy diet. Moreover they are likely to see various barriers – such as expense and long preparation time – against healthy eating.

Group 2: 'The phlegmatic'. These people are almost as traditionalist in their views of a proper meal, exercise and weight as are the diehards, but are distinguished from those in Group 1 in that they do not tend to believe that good or bad health is simply bestowed upon us. Nor do they tend to see many barriers against healthy eating – except, perhaps crucially, taste. The overall impression that they convey is of a lack of concern about the issues of food and health.

Group 3: 'The ambivalent'. The main barrier that these people see to healthy eating is its expense. Other barriers exist, but they are not particularly high. In common with Groups 1 and 2, they are also 'traditionalists' but they are emphatically not fatalistic about health – a characteristic that they share with Group 2.

Group 3: 'The health-conscious' is the only 'non-traditionalist' Group. These people are also least likely to see (or erect) barriers against healthy eating, and overall tend to accept that a healthy diet is a good way of improving health.

If there were a perfect correspondence between attitudes and behaviour (which there almost never is), then these four attitudinal groups would vary predictably in their eating *habits*. Still, an obvious hypothesis is that the diehards have the least healthy diets, followed by the phlegmatic and the ambivalent, and that the health-conscious would have the healthiest eating habits, even though factors apart from attitudes towards food will almost certainly interfere with such neat relationships. In any case, we wished to investigate what relationship, if any, exists between attitudes and behaviour.

We had, of course, already divided our sample according to their eating *behaviour*. We then collapsed our three behavioural groups into two by including the 'intermediate' group with the unhealthy eaters, leaving the healthy eaters (with 6 or 7 good eating habits) and the remainder. We were then in a position to compare attitudes and behaviour. As can be seen from the table below, attitudes were associated positively with behaviour, but far from perfectly.

---

* Using FASTCLUS with 8 iterations.

		Healthy eaters	Unhealthy eaters
Diehards	%	39	61
Phlegmatic	%	41	59
Ambivalent	%	50	50
Health-conscious	%	66	34

On the face of it, it is rather surprising that about two fifths of those we have termed diehards are nonetheless, by our definition, 'healthy' eaters, and that (conversely) a third of those whose attitudes to diet conform to current orthodoxy appear to be 'unhealthy' eaters. We have already acknowledged that our definition of 'healthy' and 'unhealthy' eaters is necessarily flawed; more precise behavioural data might reduce these apparent anomalies. As always, however, for at least a substantial minority of respondents there is a clear contradiction between their attitudes and behaviour.

In order to explore further the differences between subgroups of the population, we then decided to classify people into four categories according to their *combined* behavioural and attitudinal characteristics:

Combination A: healthy eaters with positive attitudes. This group consists of people with 6 or 7 'good' eating habits whose attitudes *on the whole* predispose them to healthy eating (Groups 3 and 4).

Combination B: healthy eaters with negative attitudes. This group consists of people with 6 or 7 'good' eating habits, but who are phlegmatic or diehard in attitude.

Combination C: unhealthy eaters with positive attitudes. This group consists of people with 5 or fewer 'good' eating habits, but whose attitudes (Group 3 and 4) predispose them to healthy eating.

Combination D: unhealthy eaters with negative attitudes. This group consists of people with 5 or fewer 'good' eating habits and who are phlegmatic or diehard in attitude.

Each of these combinations contains workable numbers of respondents for analysis purposes (see **Tables 5.3** and **5.4**). Combinations A and D consist of people whose attitudes and behaviour tend to conform, while combinations B and C consist of people with contradictory attitudes and behaviour – according to our definitions at any rate.

If we assume that people in Combination A are the least resistant to healthy eating and those in combination D the most resistant, then we can classify various subgroups of the population according to their propensity or otherwise to adopt healthy diets. We look first at men and women of different ages.

Higher proportions of women than of men in all age groups have positive attitudes *and* behaviour. Men of all ages, but in particular those aged 18–34, are more resistant to healthy eating. Younger men are markedly more likely than older men to believe that 'healthy' food is less tasty than other food (see **Table 5.1**); so this may account for their resistance, whereas their older counterparts have other barriers – such as 'fatalism' to overcome.

		Aged 18–34		Aged 35–54		Aged 55+	
		Men	**Women**	**Men**	**Women**	**Men**	**Women**
		%	%	%	%	%	%
A:	Healthy eaters, positive attitudes	15	39	31	44	26	30
B:	Healthy eaters, negative attitudes	10	9	12	17	22	36
C:	Unhealthy eaters, positive attitudes	34	31	28	19	24	11
D:	Unhealthy eaters, negative attitudes	42	20	28	20	28	22

Striking differences also emerge when we look at our four combinations by Social Class:

		Social Class			
		I/II	**III NM**	**III M**	**IV/V**
		%	%	%	%
A:	Healthy eaters, positive attitudes	44	40	19	21
B:	Healthy eaters, negative attitudes	16	18	19	19
C:	Unhealthy eaters, positive attitudes	24	21	25	25
D:	Unhealthy eaters, negative attitudes	16	20	37	35

Whereas fewer than one in five of those in professional and managerial jobs are in the group most resistant to healthy eating, the proportion more than doubles among the semi- and unskilled. Evidence from other studies also suggests that the new orthodoxy of what constitutes a good diet, and its importance to health, is not accepted universally. They show that in lower income groups, healthy dietary changes which also save money tend to be more readily accepted and, more generally, that new orthodoxies about eating are accepted or rejected mainly according to economic imperatives, or according to whether they coincide with existing beliefs (Co-operative Wholesale Society, 1986).

Analysis of our four groups by highest educational qualification also reveals differences, with 46% of those with a degree or with professional qualifications falling into combination A as opposed to only 24% of those with CSE or no formal qualifications (see **Table 5.4**).

The table below shows regional similarities and differences.

		Region			
		Scotland	**North**	**Midlands/ Wales**	**South**
		%	%	%	%
A:	Healthy eaters, positive attitudes	23	30	27	36
B:	Healthy eaters, negative attitudes	20	13	25	17
C:	Unhealthy eaters, positive attitudes	27	25	24	23
D:	Unhealthy eaters, negative attitudes	30	33	24	23

There is no evidence here of a clear-cut North–South divide, although there is a tendency for people to be more receptive to healthy eating habits the further south they live. Two recent studies lend support to our findings. Charles and Kerr (1985) found that people in the north of England are more likely to believe that their present diet is healthy, that a 'good' diet should include a cooked meal of meat and vegetables once a day, and that this is the important message to teach their children. People living in the north have also been found to be less likely than those living in the south to agree with current nutritionists' concerns, or to buy special high-fibre and low-fat foods for their health (DMB & B, 1986). If any region stands out it is Scotland, where less than a quarter of respondents are in Combination A. Re-examining the attitudinal data, we find an explanation in the Scots' particularly traditionalist attitudes towards what constitutes a 'proper meal'. These apparent regional differences may, however, be explained largely in terms of the social class differences that we have already identified. Unfortunately our sample sizes are not large enough to enable us to draw firm conclusions.

New healthy eaters

In recent years there have been many signs of a movement towards what is sometimes called a 'new eating lifestyle'. Some people's changes in diet anticipated the recommendations in the NACNE Report of 1983; others may have been stimulated by its publication and the widespread publicity it attracted. In an attempt to identify these 'new healthy eaters', we asked respondents a series of questions about any dietary changes they had made within the previous two or three years. The questions were chosen to identify changes towards foods or methods of preparation which the NACNE Report had specifically recommended, and which most nutritionists currently endorse as healthy. The table below shows the nature of the recent changes made:

Compared with two or three years ago, would you say you are now . . .	% answering 'yes'
eating more grilled food instead of fried food?	56
eating more wholemeal bread instead of white bread?	56
using more low-fat spreads or soft margarine instead of butter?	54
eating more fish and poultry instead of red meat?	44
drinking or using more semi-skimmed or skimmed milk instead of full cream milk?	33

Thus over half the sample report changes in line with three of the NACNE recommendations; even the least popular change has recently been adopted by a third of respondents. This evidence suggests overwhelmingly that medical advice nowadays to eat fewer saturated fats and to increase the intake of fibre is certainly getting through to a substantial proportion of the population. (**Table 5.5** shows the extent to which various subgroups of the population have heeded the nutritionists' advice.)

A sizeable number of people in our sample claimed to have made several changes, and a startling 86% said that they had made at least one change towards healthier eating in the last two or three years.

Changes towards healthier eating

Number of changes made within the previous two or three years	% of respondents changing %
None	14
One	18
Two	20
Three	18
Four	18
Five	11

For the sample as a whole, the average number of changes was 2.4. We then calculated the average number of changes for each of the main population subgroups as a way of identifying the characteristics of 'new healthy eaters'. It must be remembered, however, that groups with lower than average scores are not necessarily eating 'unhealthily': they may have been converted to the new eating lifestyle many years ago. Our scores reflect only *recent* change.

The *range* in the number of changes registered by the various population subgroups is not wide: the smallest for any subgroup we calculated was 2.0 and the largest was 2.8 (see **Table 5.5**). There is thus no evidence that a particular section of the population is leading a post-NACNE revolution in eating habits. We have an impression of *selectivity* in the changes made, with a small group of people recently converted to generally healthier eating, a slightly larger group showing general resistance to the idea, and a large middle group making very selective alterations in dietary habits.

Recent converts to the new eating lifestyle tend to be women (who average 2.6 changes), as opposed to men (who average 2.3). People in the middle-age range (35–54), of both sexes are particularly likely to have changed, while older men (aged 65+) and younger men (18–24) are particularly unlikely to have done so. Differences according to social class and educational attainment also emerge, with manual workers and those with only CSE or no qualifications averaging 2.2, against an average of 2.8 among those in professional and managerial jobs and 2.7 among those with 'O' levels or higher qualifications.

How far are attitudes associated with propensity to change? We looked at the average number of changes registered by the four attitudinal clusters we identified earlier. Not surprisingly, the diehards report the fewest average changes and the health-conscious the most. Even the ambivalent score relatively highly. This evidence on changes in diet contributes further to our portrayal of a population that is highly selective in the extent to which it adopts current orthodoxy.

	Average change score
Health-conscious	3.0
Ambivalent	2.7
Phlegmatic	2.1
Diehards	1.9

Changes in eating patterns

We have so far referred only to general measures of change in eating habits, and to those broad groups of respondents we have called 'healthy' and 'unhealthy' eaters for analysis purposes. Now let us be more specific about the images of various foods, and about the changes that have actually been taking place.

Health properties of foods

We show below, for each of the seven foods which earlier formed part of our classification into 'good' and 'bad' eating habits (according to the quantity of each consumed), what changes in consumption have been made. We have not separated out here recent changes from earlier ones, as the vast majority of changing has reportedly taken place in the last two to three years. The crude measure in the table of a *healthy* or *unhealthy* change is whether or not the direction of change conforms to current orthodoxy. The basis of the categorisation is shown in each case.

		'Healthy' change	'Unhealthy' change	No change
Sugar in hot drinks	%	57 (less now)	2	41
Processed meat, such as sausages, ham and tinned meat	%	37 (less now)	7	56
Fresh fruit and vegetables	%	26 (more now)	7	67
Beef, pork or lamb	%	27 (less now)	7	66
Eggs	%	24 (less now)	10	67
Fish	%	20 (more now)	18	62
Potatoes	%	6 (more now)	22	72

NB. All percentages above are based on those saying they have 'ever eaten' that food.

The unmistakable message of the table above is that such changes as there have been have tended to conform with nutritional orthodoxy. The notable exception is the reported consumption of potatoes which has clearly gone in the wrong direction – for reasons we will come to. In addition, almost as many people report eating less fish now as report eating more.

We also asked about changes in bread consumption but have left it out of the table here (and of our earlier classifications) because it is too difficult to slot into a category of 'healthy' or 'unhealthy' eating. We asked about bread for other reasons; if we had wished to classify it according to nutritional standards, we would have had to ask for more details than we could pursue in this survey about the type of bread normally eaten. Although the same is partly true about potatoes (chips versus jacket, for instance) we did not feel that the difficulty was as great. According to our sample, bread consumption, like potato consumption, has fallen (26%) rather than risen (9%), with the remaining two thirds or so of respondents reporting no change at all. Even so, bread consumption is still high: only one person in ten has a slice of bread less than daily, and 56% have three or more slices per day. Similarly potatoes are still very popular, with almost three quarters of the sample saying that they eat potatoes on four or more days a week. So, although consumption of these two carbohydrates, as reported by our sample, is falling, it remains at a very high level.

We later went on to ask those people who had changed their eating patterns *why* they had changed. But we also wanted to know whether or not the 'non-changers' were aware of the nutritional messages about each of the foods on the list, or perhaps resistant to these messages. We did this by asking respondents reporting no change on a particular food whether they thought that food was 'good for one', 'bad for one', or 'neither'.

	Good for one %	Neither %	Bad for one %
Fresh fruit and vegetables	95	3	*
Fish	91	8	*
Eggs	73	23	4
Bread	70	26	3
Beef, pork or lamb	66	30	3
Potatoes	64	30	5
Sugar in hot drinks	26	28	45
Processed meat	23	61	15

NB. Percentages are based on those saying for each food that they eat 'about the same amount' as they did two or three years earlier.

Fresh fruit and vegetables and fish receive a massive vote for having good health properties, with virtually no-one dissenting. Eggs, bread, red meat, and potatoes have very similar images, being seen mostly as 'good for one'. At the opposite end, processed meat is seen by less than a quarter of the sample as 'healthy'. Only sugar is popularly seen to be 'bad for one', but even so by a minority.

Reasons for change

We now return to those who reported having changed their eating habits in relation to one or more of the eight listed foods. In each case we asked them why, presenting a card with a number of possible reasons, including 'none of these'. The reasons covered weight control, value for money, taste, health, and – more specifically – 'told to for medical reasons'.

Very few respondents said that they were 'told to change for medical reasons': the largest proportion (eight per cent) cited this in relation to sugar and eggs – in the latter case very possibly arising from the association between cholesterol level and heart disease. We cannot tell from these data, however, whether the medical profession is failing to advise patients to change their diets, or whether the message is not being heeded, or whether more general messages from doctors are being received about food and health, which do not get reported in this category.

Weight control features as a prominent reason for cutting down on potatoes, bread and sugar. This may well reflect older dietary guidance which emphasised high carbohydrate foods as the main cause of weight gain. If so, it underlines the tenacity of beliefs. It may take some time before the old ideas are replaced with newer thinking. Significantly, too, the link between carbohydrates and weight suggests that becoming (or remaining) slim is a more important motivation for changing diet than is staying healthy.

Another barrier to change is cost, though this factor works in both directions. As **Figure 4.1** shows, cost (or at any rate poor value for money) works against red meat and processed meat more than against fish. But good value for money seems to work in favour of eggs.

Figure 4.1

Cost factor

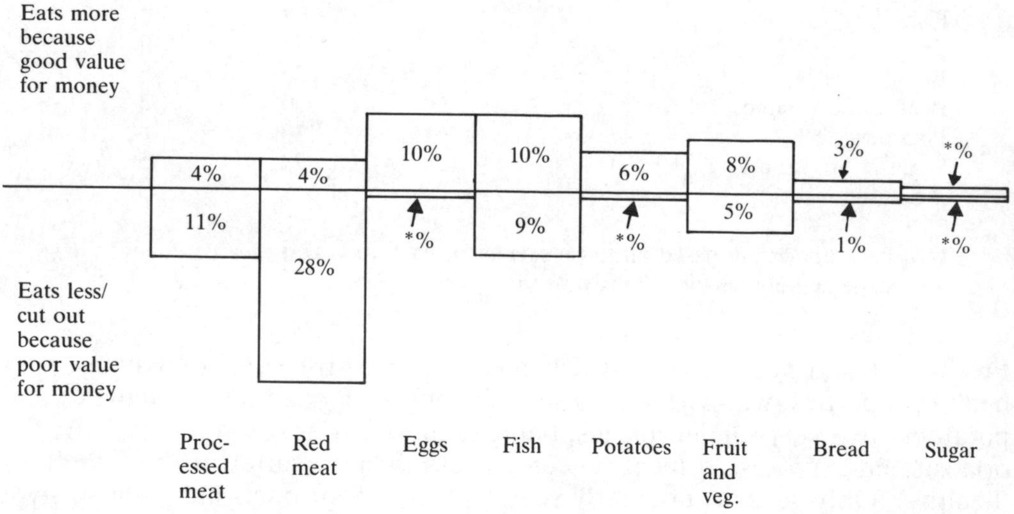

Compare the distribution in **Figure 4.1** with that in **Figure 4.2**, which shows the proportions who have changed their eating habits of each food for reasons of *health*, rather than medical reasons *per se*. For processed meat and red meat, the health message and the cost barrier appear to be mutually reinforcing; less encouragingly, for fish they appear to be in opposition to each other.

Figure 4.2

Health factor

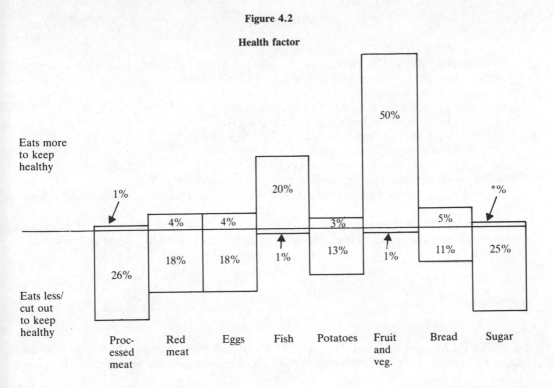

For further details about reasons for changing diet, in particular in relation to the factor of taste, see **Table 5.6**.

Conclusions

Encouragingly for health promoters, trends in dietary attitudes and behaviour are clearly in the direction recommended by health professionals and health educators. Many people are eating less meat, sugar and eggs, more fruit and vegetables, grilling rather than frying their food, drinking more semi- or skimmed milk, and eating more wholemeal than white bread. The main reasons for changing eating habits appear to be to improve or maintain health and to keep slim. This is manifested in positive attitudes to natural foods such as fruit and vegetables, and negative attitudes to sugar and animal fats.

Women lead men in positive attitudes to healthy eating. But according to the evidence available, men are more likely than women to determine what foods are served. Moreover, traditional attitudes, fatalism, and a general resistance to healthy foods are still shared by many women and men alike. As in other domains, people's behaviour seems to be changing in advance of their attitudes, which is no bad thing in itself. At least diets *are* changing for the better. But unless attitude change follows (and there is no guarantee that it will in the absence of persuasive continuing health education), people's former eating habits could easily re-establish themselves. We hope to be able to chart such trends during the course of this series.

Note

1. For the purposes of this analysis, a 'healthy eater' has been defined as someone who fulfils all seven, or six out of the seven, following criteria:

    - eats processed meat less than twice a week
    - eats beef, lamb or pork less than once a day
    - eats eggs two or three days a week or less often
    - eats fish at least once a week
    - eats potatoes at least once a week
    - eats fresh fruit and vegetables at least four days a week
    - takes sugar in hot drinks only rarely or never (i.e. less than one teaspoon a day)

    'Unhealthy eaters' were defined as those who fulfilled four or fewer of these criteria; and the 'intermediate' group (by definition) fulfilled five of the seven.

References

BLAXTER, M. and PATERSON, E., *Mothers and Daughters: a Three-generational Study of Health Attitudes and Behaviour*, Heinemann Educational Books, London (1982).
BRITISH NUTRITION FOUNDATION, *Eating in the Early 1980s*, BNF, London (1985).
CHARLES, N. and KERR, M., *Attitudes towards the Feeding and Nutrition of Young Children*, HEC Research Project, no. 4, London (1985).
CONSUMERS' ASSOCIATION, 'Report on Healthy Eating Survey', *Which?*, London (January, 1986).
CO-OPERATIVE WHOLESALE SOCIETY, 'Food Labelling Research [October 1986]', Reported in *Nutrition and Food Science*, (Jan.–Feb. 1987).
D'ARCY, MASIUS, BENTON AND BOWLES, *The Healthy Eating Survey*, DMB & B, London (1986).
FINDUS, *The Lean Lifestyle Report*, Findus, London (1986).
HEALTH EDUCATION COUNCIL, *A Discussion Paper on Proposals for Nutritional Guidelines for Health Education in Britain*, HEC, London (1983).
Regional Trends, 22, HMSO, London (1987).
RESEARCH SURVEYS OF GREAT BRITAIN, LTD., *Healthy Eating*, RSGB, London (1983).
THOMAS, M., THOMAS, V. and MURCOTT, A., *Initial Research on the Food/ Nutrition Book*, HEC, London (1984).
UK MARGARINE AND SHORTENING MANUFACTURERS' ASSOCIATION, *Food Facts and Fallacies*, London (1969).

Acknowledgements

We are grateful to the Health Education Council for its financial support to the questionnaire module on attitudes to food, diet and health, and our particular thanks are due to Deborah Leonard, formerly Research Officer at the HEC, for her help and advice in deciding upon appropriate topic areas. SCPR and the authors must, however, accept the final responsibility for question wording and the interpretation of the findings.

5.1 ATTITUDES TO FOOD, HEALTH AND DIET (A222 A-E)
by age within sex, social class, highest educational qualification obtained and region

	TOTAL	AGE+ WITHIN SEX MALE 18-34	35-54	55+	FEMALE 18-34	35-54	55+	SOCIAL CLASS I/II	III non-manual	III manual	IV/V	Other	HIGHEST QUALIFICATION OBTAINED+ Degree/Prof.	A' level/'O' level	CSE/Foreign/Other/None	REGION Scotland	North	Midlands/Wales	South
	%	%	%	%	%	%	%	%	%	%	%	%	%	%	%	%	%	%	%
FOOD THAT IS GOOD FOR YOU USUALLY TASTES NICER THAN OTHER FOOD																			
Agree strongly/just agree	27	19	22	38	29	23	34	22	22	29	35	28	23	18	33	32	26	30	25
Neither agree nor disagree	34	40	38	33	31	33	31	37	39	34	27	35	36	39	31	35	37	34	33
Just disagree/disagree strongly	37	41	39	25	39	42	34	41	38	37	35	34	39	42	34	26	36	34	41
FOOD THAT IS GOOD FOR YOU IS USUALLY MORE EXPENSIVE																			
Agree strongly/just agree	49	45	48	47	51	52	48	39	44	53	62	46	41	42	55	55	48	51	47
Neither agree nor disagree	16	25	20	21	11	10	12	19	14	19	14	15	18	16	15	18	17	16	16
Just disagree/disagree strongly	34	29	31	29	37	37	39	42	42	27	23	37	39	42	28	26	34	32	37
FOOD THAT IS GOOD FOR YOU GENERALLY TAKES TOO LONG TO PREPARE																			
Agree strongly/just agree	19	19	20	20	16	17	24	14	14	23	28	20	14	13	24	20	18	23	18
Neither agree nor disagree	25	38	22	30	27	19	17	27	23	27	25	23	25	29	23	23	27	25	25
Just disagree/disagree strongly	54	42	57	48	56	62	58	59	62	49	45	53	59	56	51	56	54	50	56
IT IS EASY TO FIND FOOD THAT IS GOOD FOR YOU IN SUPER-MARKETS																			
Agree strongly/just agree	64	56	57	64	59	70	77	63	66	60	67	66	65	57	68	68	61	61	68
Neither agree nor disagree	15	20	22	13	17	10	8	16	15	17	13	11	14	20	13	14	13	14	17
Just disagree/disagree strongly	19	23	21	19	22	18	12	20	18	21	17	19	20	22	17	16	24	22	15
MANY PEOPLE WOULD EAT HEALTHIER FOOD IF THE REST OF THEIR FAMILIES WOULD LET THEM																			
Agree strongly/just agree	42	34	38	40	46	45	50	36	44	40	50	41	39	42	44	43	44	42	41
Neither agree nor disagree	32	39	38	32	28	31	24	38	30	32	28	30	38	32	30	30	33	30	32
Just disagree/disagree strongly	24	26	23	25	24	21	23	25	25	26	18	26	22	26	23	23	21	26	24
BASE: Weighted	1387	232	236	190	214	266	250	318	341	290	315	123	259	395	731	141	375	295	576
RESPONDENTS Unweighted	1416	228	240	197	222	272	257	330	351	290	321	124	265	402	748	147	385	303	581

5.2 ATTITUDES TO FOOD, HEALTH AND DIET (A222 F-K)
by age within sex, social class, highest educational qualification obtained and region

	TOTAL	AGE+ WITHIN SEX MALE 18-34	MALE 35-54	MALE 55+	FEMALE 18-34	FEMALE 35-54	FEMALE 55+	SOCIAL CLASS I/II	III non-manual	III manual	IV/V	Other	HIGHEST QUALIFICATION OBTAINED+ Degree/Prof.	'A' level/'O' level	CSE/Foreign/Other/None	REGION Scotland	North	Midlands/Wales	South
	%	%	%	%	%	%	%	%	%	%	%	%	%	%	%	%	%	%	%
AS LONG AS YOU TAKE ENOUGH EXERCISE YOU CAN EAT WHATEVER FOODS YOU WANT																			
Agree strongly/just agree	31	39	31	41	16	21	38	21	24	42	39	29	18	22	40	35	30	32	30
Neither agree nor disagree	17	19	18	12	17	18	16	13	18	18	17	17	11	18	18	20	18	18	14
Just disagree/disagree strongly	51	41	50	45	66	59	44	65	58	38	41	50	70	59	40	43	51	47	55
IF HEART DISEASE IS IN YOUR FAMILY, THERE IS LITTLE YOU CAN DO TO REDUCE YOUR CHANCES OF GETTING IT																			
Agree strongly/just agree	15	13	11	24	11	10	23	6	11	22	24	12	5	9	21	16	13	20	14
Neither agree nor disagree	13	19	11	13	10	9	14	9	12	19	14	10	7	12	15	16	15	12	11
Just disagree/disagree strongly	70	67	77	60	77	78	60	85	77	57	59	72	86	78	61	66	71	67	73
THE EXPERTS CONTRADICT EACH OTHER OVER WHAT MAKES A HEALTHY DIET																			
Agree strongly/just agree	73	65	73	76	65	74	80	72	73	74	73	67	70	74	72	62	69	76	76
Neither agree nor disagree	15	19	15	13	19	12	12	12	18	16	14	14	10	15	16	23	16	12	14
Just disagree/disagree strongly	11	14	12	7	15	11	6	14	9	9	11	15	19	9	9	14	13	11	10
PEOPLE WORRY TOO MUCH ABOUT THEIR WEIGHT																			
Agree strongly/just agree	60	53	61	68	61	57	68	53	59	61	68	61	49	56	66	62	60	65	57
Neither agree nor disagree	16	24	16	15	15	14	12	17	16	18	15	15	18	18	15	20	15	16	16
Just disagree/disagree strongly	22	22	22	17	22	27	17	30	25	20	15	20	30	26	17	17	23	17	26
GOOD HEALTH IS JUST A MATTER OF GOOD LUCK																			
Agree strongly/just agree	17	16	13	23	14	14	28	9	11	23	26	17	5	11	24	16	19	20	14
Neither agree nor disagree	13	10	14	15	12	12	15	12	15	15	10	13	12	11	14	13	13	12	13
Just disagree/disagree strongly	68	72	72	60	81	72	54	78	74	61	61	65	82	77	59	69	67	65	71
A PROPER MEAL SHOULD INCLUDE MEAT AND VEGETABLES																			
Agree strongly/just agree	62	64	58	67	57	59	67	50	57	69	72	62	48	58	68	71	59	61	61
Neither agree nor disagree	15	17	19	12	14	14	12	18	15	16	11	14	16	17	13	9	15	15	16
Just disagree/disagree strongly	22	18	23	18	28	26	20	32	27	15	14	20	36	24	17	19	23	22	22
BASE: A RESPONDENTS weighted	1387	232	236	190	214	266	250	318	341	290	315	123	259	395	731	141	375	295	576
Unweighted	1416	228	240	197	222	272	257	330	351	290	321	124	265	402	748	147	385	303	581

5.3 BEHAVIOURAL/ATTITUDINAL COMBINATIONS (derived from A89a AND A222 A-K) by age within sex and social class

| | TOTAL | AGE+ WITHIN SEX | | | | | | SOCIAL CLASS | | | | |
| | | MALE | | | FEMALE | | | I/II | III non-manual | III manual | IV/V | Other |
COMBINED BEHAVIOURAL AND ATTITUDINAL CHARACTERISTICS:	%	18-34 %	35-54 %	55+ %	18-34 %	35-54 %	55+ %	%	%	%	%	%
COMBINATION A: Healthy eaters												
- attitudinally health-conscious (n = 195)	14	7	15	10	17	18	17	25	17	5	8	14
- attitudinally ambivalent (n = 237)	17	8	16	16	22	26	14	19	23	14	13	15
- total (n = 432)	31	15	31	26	39	44	30	44	40	19	21	28
COMBINATION B: Healthy eaters												
- attitudinally phlegmatic (n = 122)	9	6	7	10	4	10	16	11	10	8	7	7
- attitudinally diehard (n = 126)	9	4	5	12	5	7	20	5	8	11	12	8
- total (n = 248)	18	10	12	22	9	17	36	16	18	19	19	15
COMBINATION C: Unhealthy eaters												
- attitudinally health-conscious (n = 98)	7	9	9	5	9	6	5	8	8	6	5	9
- attitudinally ambivalent (n = 239)	17	25	20	19	23	13	6	15	14	19	20	19
- total (n = 337)	24	34	28	24	31	19	11	24	21	25	25	28
COMBINATION D: Unhealthy eaters												
- attitudinally phlegmatic (n = 173)	12	20	15	10	12	10	8	11	13	16	11	12
- attitudinally diehard (n = 197)	14	22	14	19	9	9	14	6	7	21	24	16
- total (n = 370)	27	42	28	28	20	20	22	16	20	37	35	28
BASE: A RESPONDENTS *Weighted*	1387	232	236	190	214	266	250	318	341	290	315	123
Unweighted	1416	228	240	197	222	272	257	330	351	290	321	124

5.4 BEHAVIOURAL/ATTITUDINAL COMBINATIONS (derived from A89a and A222 A-K) by highest educational qualification obtained and region

COMBINED BEHAVIOURAL AND ATTITUDINAL CHARACTERISTICS:	TOTAL	HIGHEST QUALIFICATION OBTAINED[+]			REGION			
		Degree/ Professional	'A' level/ 'O' level	CSE/Foreign/ Other/None	Scotland	North	Midlands/ Wales	South
	%	%	%	%	%	%	%	%
COMBINATION A: Healthy eaters								
- attitudinally health-conscious (n = 195)	14	24	16	10	9	14	11	16
- attitudinally ambivalent (n = 237)	17	22	19	14	14	15	15	20
- total (n = 432)	31	46	35	24	23	30	27	36
COMBINATION B: Healthy eaters								
- attitudinally phlegmatic (n = 122)	9	8	8	9	7	8	12	8
- attitudinally diehard (n = 126)	9	5	5	13	13	6	13	9
- total (n = 248)	18	13	13	22	20	13	25	17
COMBINATION C: Unhealthy eaters								
- attitudinally health-conscious (n = 98)	7	12	9	5	6	8	8	6
- attitudinally ambivalent (n = 239)	17	15	20	17	22	16	17	17
- total (n = 337)	24	26	29	21	27	25	24	23
COMBINATION D: Unhealthy eaters								
- attitudinally phlegmatic (n = 173)	12	9	16	12	15	15	9	12
- attitudinally diehard (n = 197)	14	6	8	20	14	18	15	11
- total (n = 370)	27	15	24	32	30	33	24	23
BASE: A RESPONDENTS								
Weighted	1387	259	395	731	141	375	295	576
Unweighted	1416	265	402	748	147	385	303	581

5.5 RECENT CHANGES TO HEALTHIER EATING (A90)
by age within sex, social class, highest educational qualification obtained and region

	TOTAL	AGE WITHIN SEX — MALE			FEMALE			SOCIAL CLASS				HIGHEST EDUCATIONAL QUALIFICATION[+]			REGION			
		18-34	35-54	55+	18-34	35-54	55+	I/II	III non-manual	III manual	IV/V Other	Degree/ Prof.	'A' level/ 'O' level	CSE/ Foreign/ Other/ None	Scotland	North	Midlands/ Wales	South
	%	%	%	%	%	%	%	%	%	%	%	%	%	%	%	%	%	%
COMPARED WITH TWO OR THREE YEARS AGO, WOULD YOU SAY YOU ARE NOW ...																		
... eating more grilled food instead of fried food?	56	58	59	46	66	58	50	59	63	53	54	57	63	53	57	54	60	55
... eating more wholemeal bread instead of white bread?	56	50	59	47	59	60	57	65	61	52	47	64	61	50	52	54	57	56
... using more low fat spreads or soft margarine instead of butter?	54	51	61	46	55	62	50	57	53	51	55	60	54	53	56	52	57	54
... eating more fish and poultry instead of red meat?	44	30	48	41	45	52	45	49	53	35	38	52	46	40	39	41	47	45
... drinking or using more semi-skimmed or skimmed milk instead of full cream milk?	33	27	34	20	42	42	29	41	36	25	31	43	38	27	34	35	31	31
NUMBER OF CHANGES MADE:																		
None	14	17	13	20	11	11	15	10	11	19	14	11	11	18	14	15	15	14
One	18	22	15	24	15	13	20	15	17	20	22	13	17	21	19	18	14	20
Two	20	21	17	21	19	20	19	19	16	20	19	18	20	20	20	23	18	18
Three	18	19	21	15	21	16	20	20	18	18	22	23	20	16	19	16	21	18
Four	18	14	20	12	20	23	21	23	23	14	13	22	21	16	17	16	21	19
Five	11	8	14	8	14	16	7	13	14	9	9	14	13	10	10	12	11	11
AVERAGE CHANGE SCORE	2.4	2.1	2.6	2.0	2.7	2.7	2.3	2.8	2.6	2.2	2.2	2.8	2.6	2.2	2.4	2.4	2.5	2.4
BASES: A RESPONDENTS Weighted	1518	252	256	218	232	286	273	352	367	313	138	277	424	810	149	401	336	632
Unweighted	1552	249	261	226	241	293	282	367	378	314	138	285	434	831	155	412	347	638

5.6 REASONS FOR RECENT DIETARY CHANGES (A89e)

REASONS FOR CHANGE	PROCESSED MEAT LIKE SAUSAGES, HAM, ETC.		BEEF, LAMB OR PORK		EGGS		FISH		POTATOES		FRESH FRUIT AND VEGETABLES		BREAD		SUGAR IN HOT DRINKS	
	Eating more now	Eating less now/ cut down/ cut out	Eating more now	Eating less now/ cut down/ cut out	Eating more now	Eating less now/ cut down/ cut out	Eating more now	Eating less now/ cut down/ cut out	Eating more now	Eating less now/ cut down/ cut out	Eating more now	Eating less now/ cut down/ cut out	Eating more now	Eating less now/ cut down/ cut out	Taking more now	Taking less now/ cut down/ cut out
	%	%	%	%	%	%	%	%	%	%	%	%	%	%	%	%
To help control my weight	*	12	1	4	2	3	5	1	1	35	12	1	1	32	*	29
I was told to for medical reasons	-	7	*	6	-	8	3	2	1	4	3	1	1	4	-	8
It is good value for money	4	*	4	*	10	*	10	-	6	*	8	-	3	*	*	-
It is poor value for money	-	11	*	28	-	*	*	9	-	*	*	5	-	1	-	*
I wanted to keep healthy	1	26	4	18	4	18	20	1	3	13	50	1	5	11	*	25
I just like it more	5	-	8	-	10	-	20	-	8	-	21	-	9	-	2	-
I just don't like it as much	-	25	-	14	-	27	-	18	-	12	-	7	-	15	-	22
None of these reasons	6	11	4	13	4	15	5	14	5	17	5	6	8	14	1	7
BASE: A RESPONDENTS MAKING A RECENT CHANGE Weighted	668	668	513	513	501	501	560	560	423	423	500	500	552	552	835	835
Unweighted	695	695	531	531	519	519	565	565	435	435	505	505	568	568	858	858

6 Family matters

Sheena Ashford*

"Myths about the institutions of marriage and the family are widely held . . . and seem to reflect an underlying belief that these institutions . . . are threatened" (Brown *et al*, 1985). In this chapter, we look for evidence as to whether traditional attitudes towards marriage and family are changing to such an extent that they may begin to pose a real threat to either institution. First, through a range of questions asked of our respondents, we consider what factors contribute to a happy marriage and what grounds are thought to be sufficient for divorce. Second, we ask how parents should divide their time between job and family. Third, we investigate the ways in which couples manage the money that comes into the household. Last, we look at parent–child relationships, at the ways in which these relationships have changed over the last generation and at the part played by older children in important family decisions.

Of these questions about family life, most are entirely new, some are replicated from, or based on, questions included in an international survey mounted by the European Values Systems Study Group (EVSSG) through Gallup in 1981, and a few are drawn from other surveys. On some topics, therefore, we have the opportunity to look for shifts in attitudes, but technical differences between this and earlier surveys means that direct comparisons always have to be treated with caution. A brief note on the scope and methodology of the 1981 EVSSG study appears at the end of this chapter.[1]

---

* Research Fellow, Centre for the Study of Individual and Social Values, University of Leicester.

Marriage and divorce

The past 40 years or so have seen changes in society's view of what makes for an ideal marriage. In *The Matrimonial Survey* of 1947 (published in Gorer, 1955) a happy marriage was defined as a complementary relationship in which the functions of husband and wife contrast with one another, "man as breadwinner and defender of the home, woman as housewife and mother; man as aggressive and woman as timid". By 1969, when the survey was repeated (Gorer, 1970), a more common a view of marriage was one where the partners should have more equal roles. These findings, and those from later surveys* (Young and Willmott, 1973; Gillis, 1985) have led to a change of emphasis. The complementary marriage was being replaced by a companionate one, involving compatibility and friendship between the partners, in which husband and wife no longer have such different, mutually exclusive roles.

The high divorce rate – one in three marriages nowadays is likely to break up – and the rising proportion of single-parent households (currently almost nine per cent of the total, *Social Trends*, 16, 1986), have led to fresh questions about the nature of marriage. Is marriage still highly valued and does its future look secure?

Attitudes to marriage

Responses to questions in our survey about the institution of marriage, society's responsibility for safeguarding it, the adequacy of preparation for married life and whether marriage is taken too lightly, do not appear to justify concern that 'anti-marriage' sentiments are either widespread or increasing. Rather more than two thirds of respondents support the notion that "as a society, we ought to do more to safeguard the institution of marriage", and only six per cent disagree. Similarly high levels of support were recorded in the EVSSG survey in 1981.

Support for the institution of marriage reflects itself in feelings about divorce, but much less markedly than might be expected. We return to this subject later, but it is worth noting now that around 40% believe that divorce should be made more difficult to obtain against only 27% who disagree, with the remaining third in favour of the *status quo*. But as we found in the 1983 and 1984 rounds of *British Social Attitudes*, the views of various population subgroups vary sharply: men (especially those aged under 35) are more in favour than women of a relaxation in the divorce laws, while older people (particularly older women) are less so (see **Table 6.1**). These differences probably reflect differing perceptions of the consequences of divorce.

While these results suggest continuing support for marriage as an institution, there is also a widespread feeling that others (presumably not our respondents themselves) treat marriage too frivolously. Confronted with the statement that "Most people nowadays take marriage too lightly", nearly three quarters agree, with only one in ten in disagreement. There is also a fair degree of concern

---

* See the review of survey findings by the Study Commission on the Family (1982).

about the adequacy of preparation for marriage: over half (53%) do not believe that "most young couples start their married life well prepared for its ups and downs". These findings reinforce those of a NOP survey carried out for the Study Commission on the Family, which reported majority support for couples being obliged to go through a course of marriage guidance and counselling before being allowed to marry (NOP, 1982).

By themselves, these data provide no strong evidence about *trends* in attitudes to marriage. They do however contain pointers to the direction of change, especially as the attitudes of older respondents are notably more conservative and supportive of marriage than those of younger ones (see **Table 6.1**). It may simply be that people become more conservative in their attitudes as they grow older, or it may be that these age differences suggest an underlying change between generations in attitudes to marriage. We shall have to repeat these questions in future surveys before safely drawing conclusions.

Changes in social attitudes may stem at least partly from dissonant views among small but *growing* subgroups within the population, for example, those who are separated or divorced or those who live with partners to whom they are not married. Do groups like these hold distinctive attitudes towards marriage and divorce? Inevitably, our samples of separated or divorced respondents and of cohabitees are small (73 and 39 respectively) so any conclusions must be tentative. But our results do suggest that those who have been divorced or separated are more liberal in their attitudes towards marriage and divorce than are the married (or widowed). Moreover, the group with the most distinctively liberal views is our small sample of cohabitees. As the table below shows, they are emphatically against making divorce more difficult to obtain and markedly less sympathetic to the notion that society ought to do more to protect marriage.

Attitudes to marriage

	Married/ widowed %	Not married %	Separated/ divorced %	Cohabitees %
Divorce should be made more difficult to obtain:				
Agree	41	36	26	19
Disagree	25	24	50	50
Society ought to do more to safeguard marriage:				
Agree	75	59	61	39
Disagree	5	9	17	22

So, with the growth of alternatives to marriage, the institution itself may come to be seen as rather less central than it has been up to now.

Features of successful and unsuccessful marriages

We next asked respondents about the factors that contribute to a successful marriage. A similar question had been asked on the 1981 EVSSG survey. Each of 13 features was read out and our respondents were asked to say how important it was, using a four-point scale ranging from "very" to "not at all". The items are shown below in the order in which they were rated as very important.

Very important to a successful marriage:	%
Faithfulness	86
Mutual respect and appreciation	77
Understanding and tolerance	69
Living apart from in-laws	55
Happy sexual relationship	50
Adequate income	34
Good housing	33
Having children	31
Sharing chores	25
Tastes and interests in common	21
Same social background	11
Shared religious beliefs	9
Agreement on politics	3

Faithfulness within marriage is as highly valued as it was five years earlier, and is still top of the list – regardless of age, sex or social class of respondent. Other "very important" features of a successful marriage are personal factors such as "mutual respect and appreciation", "understanding and tolerance" and "a happy sexual relationship", all mentioned by between half and three quarters of our respondents.

Background factors, such as "adequate income" and "good housing", are – like "having children" – seen as rather less important, being cited by about a third of respondents. Sociocultural factors – "tastes and interests in common", "same social background", "shared religious beliefs" and "agreement on politics" – are felt to be the least important to marital success of the list presented.

Not surprisingly, perhaps, the two background factors show the most marked and consistent subgroup variations in response. Those in the higher social classes, the better qualified and the young see an adequate income and good housing as less important than do those in the manual social classes, those with few or no formal qualifications and older people. The data appear to show the increasing strains that can be placed upon marriage over time by the pressures of poor housing and (to a rather lesser extent) low income – strains to which those in the higher social classes and the better qualified are less likely to be exposed and which they are possibly less able to appreciate.

Background factors thought very important to a successful marriage

	Adequate income	Good housing
Social Class:		
I/II	27%	22%
III Non-manual	29%	29%
III Manual	42%	40%
IV/V	40%	42%
Highest educational qualification:		
Degree/professional	24%	20%
'A' Level/'O' Level	29%	20%
CSE	32%	31%
None	41%	46%
Age: 18–24	28%	19%
25–34	31%	22%
35–44	33%	30%
45+	37%	42%

The importance accorded to having children also varies (but less so) by social class and education, but only among men is there a marked age difference: while only one in five 18–34 year old men regards children as very important to a successful marriage, the proportion nearly doubles among men aged 55 and over. In other respects subgroup differences are less striking, although the over 44s do tend to attribute more importance than the young to "social background", "tastes and interests in common" and "shared religious beliefs" (but not "agreement on politics"). These and other differences are shown in **Table 6.2**.

The five years separating this survey from the EVSSG study have seen some modifications in the public's views about these features. The earlier question was slightly different, but the responses are broadly comparable with ours.[2] Fidelity apart, fewer people nowadays seem to endorse *any* of the factors as very important. "Tastes and interests in common", "a happy sexual relationship" and "having children" show the greatest falls. Virtually no-one, however, regards a happy sexual relationship as *unimportant* to a happy marriage. The lesser importance accorded to having children is consistent with the shift in emphasis (noted earlier) towards a more companionate type of marriage – less dependent on mutually exclusive and complementary roles.

Attitudes to divorce

We then asked respondents to tell us whether each of ten reasons was felt to be sufficient grounds for divorce.* Hardly surprisingly, responses suggest that attitudes to divorce are associated quite strongly with beliefs about what makes marriages successful.

Reasons sufficient for divorce

	%
Consistent unfaithfulness	94
Violence	92
Ceasing to love the other	75
Consistent over-drinking	59
Personalities don't match	42
Sexual relationship not satisfactory	28
Can't have children	7
Can't get along with relatives	4
Financially broke	4
Long-term illness	3

We have seen that 86% of respondents look upon fidelity as very important to a successful marriage; and we also find that consistent unfaithfulness is most commonly mentioned as a sufficient reason for ending a marriage. Other factors most often mentioned are those which touch most directly on the personal side of relations between husband and wife: marital violence and lack of love; and – less often – a personality mismatch and an unsatisfactory sexual relationship. We have already noted the relatively limited importance that respondents attach to background factors in making a marriage successful; and only very few people indeed regard similar factors – inability to have children, being broke and one or other partner ill for a long time – as grounds for divorce. Problems such as these may make a successful marriage harder to achieve but, for our respondents at least, they do not constitute adequate grounds for ending it.

Six of the ten grounds for divorce we presented were endorsed by so many or so few respondents that there is scarcely room for subgroup differences to emerge. Of the remaining four, drinking too much is (not surprisingly) more likely to be cited by women than by men. With that exception, men and women do not differ. When we come to look at personal factors – absence of love and personality differences – we find that age comes into play, younger people seeing them as rather more of a threat to marriage than those aged over 44 do.

	Total	Age		
		18–34	35–54	55+
	%	%	%	%
It is a sufficient reason for divorce				
when either partner has ceased to love the other	75	82	76	66
when their personalities don't match	42	48	41	37
when the sexual relationship is not satisfactory	28	24	26	33

* This question was also included in the 1981 EVSSG study.

But, as we can see, unsatisfactory sexual relations within marriage is cited rather *more* often by older than by younger respondents as a justification for divorce.

We have already noted that between 1981 and 1986 there appears to have been a fall in the proportions regarding *any* of 13 features we presented, ranging from faithfulness to agreement on politics, as very important to a successful marriage. In contrast, there has been a rise (by between one per cent and 15%) in the number who believe that *each* of the 10 items we presented constitutes sufficient grounds for divorce.

It has been suggested that an unsatisfactory marriage is more likely to result in divorce when one or both partners have ready access to an alternative relationship or at least to an acceptable alternative life-style. This 'marital alternatives' view (Udry, 1981) would predict that working women, those with no dependent children, and those (mainly in the younger age groups) with greater prospects of alternative relationships or life-styles would be more inclined towards divorce than those who have little or no access to alternative sources of income, resources and emotional support.

The attitudes expressed by our respondents do not tend to bear out this theory. Working women and couples without young children are no more likely than other respondents to regard any of the factors we cited as sufficient grounds for divorce. There is some evidence noted earlier, that younger people (especially younger men) are more liberal than older people in their attitudes towards divorce, but younger people tend to hold such views about most moral issues.

Home and work – a woman's place?

The increase in the number of women in employment, and in the number of working mothers in particular, raises questions about the changing nature of the woman's role and about the relationship between family life and work. Forty eight per cent of mothers with dependent children are now out at work.* Does this combination of parenthood and work result predominantly from choice or necessity? Financial need would seem to be the main reason why many women go out to work: one study estimates that the number of families in poverty would be between three and four times as great without wives' earnings (Central Policy Review Staff, 1980, para. 6.4). For many wives, the price paid for working is high. Guilt, stress and physical tiredness are common complaints (Rapoport and Rapoport, 1982; Sharpe, 1984; Yeandle, 1984). And although husbands often 'help out' by undertaking a few extra domestic tasks, households in which domestic work is shared equally are very much in the minority (*Women and Employment Survey,* Martin and Roberts, 1984; *The 1985 Report,* pp. 56-59). There are however benefits apart from money. Paid employment means greater financial and, often, social independence and

---

* *OPCS Social Survey Division. 1986 General Household Survey,* 1984, London, HMSO Series GHS No. 14 (Table 6.5).

provides at least a temporary escape from domestic drudgery (Cragg and Dawson, 1984). So, even in households where there is little or no financial stress, women may feel on balance that having a job is preferable to staying at home.

To find out our respondents' views, we asked them which of six work arrangements they thought was best for a family with children under five and for a family with children in their early teens. We distinguished these two types of household because survey evidence has shown that women's work patterns are closely related to the age of the children in their care, with mothers of pre-school children most likely to be at home full-time (Martin and Roberts, 1984). Aside from any practical constraints which may make it difficult for mothers of young children to work, partial or complete withdrawal from the labour market during the period when childrearing demands are heaviest may reflect a preferred solution as much as an imposed one.

For convenience we have grouped the different work arrangements under the four headings: 'traditional', 'compromise', 'equality' and 'role-reversal'.*

Preferred working arrangements for parents . . .

	. . . with children under 5 years old %	. . . with children in their early teens %
'Traditional' father working full-time and mother at home	76	19
'Compromise' father working full-time and mother working part-time	17	60
'Equality' both parents working full-time or both working part-time	3	17
'Role-reversal' mother works full-time and father works part-time or stays at home	*	1

The arrangements preferred by the great majority of respondents are highly conventional, particularly for families with a pre-school child for whom only 21% want to see the mother go out to work at all. The 'traditional' solution gives way to a 'compromise' arrangement for households with children in their early teens. When children are older a mother's place is apparently no longer in the home – at least not all the time. Most people would still prefer to see women straddling the domains of work and home while men are committed to full-time employment. The notion that both partners should play symmetrical or equal roles is still rather alien. So while, by a margin of four to one, respondents would prefer women with teenage children to have some form of

---

* These terms are intended as a convenient shorthand: no evaluation should be inferred.

employment outside the home, by far the most popular arrangement is for the father to work full-time and the mother part-time.

Surprisingly, perhaps, there is broad agreement among subgroups in our sample as to the best arrangements for families with pre-school children. Women are no more likely than men to favour mothers of young children going out to work. Different social class and income groups also share similar views, although there is a tendency for the less well off to favour a 'compromise' solution, presumably to alleviate financial stress. Opinions are rather more divergent about arrangements for families with teenagers, women being somewhat less keen on the 'traditional' arrangement than are men. For full details, see **Table 6.3**.

It is age and marital status however, that most differentiates respondents. Younger people (especially the 18–24 year olds) are less keen on 'traditional' working arrangements for either type of household, and are particularly resistant to the 'full-time housewife' solution in a household with teenage children.

	Age			
	18–24	25–34	35–44	45+
	%	%	%	%
Preferred working arrangements for parents with children under 5 years old:				
'Traditional'	52	71	78	84
'Compromise'	36	19	12	13
'Equality'	10	7	3	1
Preferred working arrangements for parents with children in their early teens:				
'Traditional'	8	11	12	28
'Compromise'	49	63	66	60
'Equality'	42	23	15	9

Indeed, over a third of 18–24 year olds favoured the mother of an under-five having a job, only a bare majority thinking that she should stay at home. And they are almost evenly divided between the 'equality' and 'compromise' solution for a teenage household.

We must, however, sound a note of caution. In *The 1985 Report* we found that "ideas [on the domestic division of labour] were clearly tempered by experience, as married men and women were less egalitarian (even prescriptively) than either the formerly married or the never married" (p. 58). And so it proves here too. The married members of the two younger age groups in our sample (the 18–34 year olds) are noticeably less egalitarian than are the unmarried ones, especially over working arrangements in a teenage household. Experience apparently tempers both partners' idealistic views of marriage.

	All aged 18–34	Aged 18–34 Unmarried	Married
	%	%	%
Preferred working arrangements for parents with children under 5 years old:			
'Traditional'	63	55	70
'Compromise'	26	30	21
'Equality'	8	10	7
Preferred working arrangements for parents with children in their early teens:			
'Traditional'	10	9	10
'Compromise'	57	47	64
'Equality'	31	40	23

We also examined the relationship between the *actual* and *ideal* division of labour inside and outside the home. Of married people under pensionable age, around half (52%) form part of a dual earner household where both partners work at least ten hours per week,* and just over a third (36%) followed the 'traditional' (male breadwinner, female homemaker) pattern. Only five per cent (48) were from 'role-reversal' households (with a female breadwinner and a male homemaker) and only seven per cent (68) formed part of 'no earner' households, so we omit these latter two groups from the table below.[3]

	Actual working arrangements among married respondents*		
	'Traditional'	'Compromise'	'Equality'
	%	%	%
Preferred working arrangements for parents with children under 5 years old:			
'Traditional'	83	75	71
'Compromise'	13	20	20
'Equality'	2	2	4
Preferred working arrangements for parents with children in their early teens:			
'Traditional'	21	10	9
'Compromise'	63	78	61
'Equality'	11	11	24

* *Note:* those over pensionable age are not included in this table

What is particularly striking is the wide gulf between what people would

---

* Note that the dual earner group includes individuals from 'compromise' households and from households operating 'equality' and 'role-reveral' systems.

ideally like to happen and what they actually do. People from dual earner households emerge as only a little more unconventional than the 'traditionalists', despite expectations to the contrary. As many as 70% of those from households with full-time working wives believe that mothers of young children should stay at home. And only just over a quarter of them opt for the 'equality' solution for families with young teenagers. By a large majority, then, our respondents are unsympathetic to a more egalitarian division of domestic tasks, or to any radical change in the role of women outside the home – whatever their *own* household arrangements may be.

Family size

With methods of birth control widely available these days, family size is a matter of choice for most couples. Large families of five or more children are now much rarer than they used to be. Women no longer have to spend a large part of their adult years either pregnant or caring for small children or both. We wanted to know whether or not our respondents saw changes such as these as desirable, and asked them both about ideal family size *and* about whose responsibility it should be to decide how many children to have.

The great majority of people (71%) regards two children as ideal. A small minority (13%) feels that three children are ideal, but hardly anybody would choose to have more than three. Only two per cent regard one child as ideal and less than one per cent say 'none at all'. Age, sex, marital status, social class and education make little difference to notions of ideal family size; but, not unexpectedly, Roman Catholics tend to prefer larger families. Comparable British data on ideal family size in the recent past are not available, but survey results from the US show that there has been a dramatic change in opinion over the last 25 years or so. In 1962, 81% of respondents to a national survey said that three or more children was "ideal": by 1980 the proportion had fallen to 34%.[4]

Should the decision to have a child be left to the father, to the mother, should it be a joint decision, or 'left to nature'? The vast majority (90%) believes that the decision should be taken jointly. In those few instances where the decision is seen as belonging to just one partner, it is much more often the mother who is felt to have the right to decide. 'Leaving it to nature' to determine final family size is a decidedly unpopular choice – even among Roman Catholics.

Manual workers and people without formal qualifications are rather more likely than their counterparts to leave the decision to the mother. With these exceptions, the consensus on this question is so wide that subgroup differences hardly have room to emerge. Jointly deciding on family size is as popular among women as among men, and is virtually as popular among older respondents as among younger. Similarly older people are as reluctant as younger people are to let 'nature' determine family size, suggesting that contraception is generally accepted even among those to whom it was not widely available in the past.

Family finance arrangements

Married men and women are not financially equal. Although married women have had the legal right to control and manage their own financial affairs since the early years of this century (Gillis, 1985), in practice this has seldom been accompanied by real financial independence. The higher average wage earned by men, and the more restricted employment opportunities available to women, together with their heavier domestic responsibilities, mean that most married women are dependent on their husbands' earning power for a large part of their lives. The extent of this dependence is highlighted by the heavier long-term financial burden borne by divorcing wives than by divorcing husbands, and by the relatively poor living standards of mothers who bring up their children single-handed.

Women who go out to work while their children are young may also experience other difficulties – for example the guilt sometimes felt by working mothers of young children and the absence of suitable childcare (Martin and Roberts, 1984). As a result, many women must be either very eager or very needy to take up paid jobs while their children are still young. Even now only a small minority of women do in fact work continuously throughout their lives (Dex, 1984). Yet taking even a short break from work often means coming back with divided loyalties to poorer prospects, so reinforcing financial dependence on men and marriage.

Past studies, for example Edwards (1982) and Stamp (1985), have shown that the way in which husbands and wives manage the money that comes into the household is related to their earning power. So we asked our married and cohabiting respondents how they and their partner organised their family finance, and then analysed their responses to see if households of different types – high income, dual earner and so on – managed in different ways. Lastly we asked if their parents had organised things in the same way or differently.

Family finance arrangements

	%
'Common pot'	
partners pool all the money and each takes out what he/she needs	51
'Allowance'	
one partner manages all the money and gives the other his/her share	33
'Partial pool'	
partners pool some of the money and keep the rest separate	10
'Independent'	
partners keep their own money separate	5

Completely free access to household income by both partners is thus the single most common arrangement, followed by a system of restricted access for one or other partner. And comparatively few respondents (15%) report using a system which involves separating some or all of the household income into mutually exclusive 'pots'.

In small scale studies, it has been shown that access varies according to level of income (Edwards, 1982). In lower income families, most or all of the husband's wage is handed over to the wife; in middle income families, husbands are often responsible for bills and give their wives an allowance; in high-earning (mostly two-income) households, earnings are more often (at least partly) pooled. As the sources and size of household income vary over the family life cycle, so a family's approach to money management tends to alter (Pahl, 1984). Families also change their strategy according to changing circumstances: for example, in households where the male earner becomes unemployed, the wife often has to take over the burden of managing scarce resources (Morris, 1983).

As the table below shows, although the 'common pot' system is still the most popular arrangement among households of almost every type, the 'allowance' system is markedly more prevalent among manual workers and lower income families than among non-manual workers and higher income families. Among the unemployed, it is even more popular than the 'common pot'.

Family finance arrangements

		'Common pot'	'Allowance'	'Partial pool'	'Independent'
Total	%	51	33	10	5
Social class:					
I/II	%	52	26	12	9
III Non-manual	%	53	29	12	5
III Manual	%	48	39	7	4
IV/V	%	48	39	9	3
Income:					
Less than £5,000 p.a.	%	50	40	7	3
£5,000–£7,999 p.a.	%	44	39	11	6
£8,000–£11,999 p.a.	%	50	38	8	4
£12,000–£17,999 p.a.	%	60	24	11	5
£18,000 p.a. or more	%	48	25	15	10
Employment status:					
In paid work	%	51	29	12	7
Unemployed	%	41	49	5	5
Actual working arrangements:					
'Traditional'	%	47	46	3	4
'Compromise'	%	52	27	15	5
'Equality'	%	57	18	14	9

More surprising, perhaps, is that one in four of the highest-earning households (£18,000+ p.a.) operates a system that involves one partner having limited access, or no access at all, to the other's money. Many of these high income households are of course 'dual earner' ones and there is a striking contrast between the arrangements made by 'dual earner' and 'traditional' households with one (male) earner. For full details, see **Tables 6.4** and **6.5**.

Nearly 90% of respondents remembered how their parents organised their family finances, and just over half arranged things differently.

| | | Parents' arrangements were . . . | | |
		. . . the same	. . . different	Don't remember
Respondent's arrangements are:				
'Common pot'	%	31	57	10
'Allowance'	%	48	38	13
'Partial pool'	%	14	68	16
'Independent'	%	11	69	17

So the present generation has apparently moved away from giving (or accepting) an allowance, and towards other arrangements – mainly to the 'common pot' system whereby all household income is pooled. This change suggests that, in this aspect of marriage as well as others, there has been a movement in recent years towards a more 'sharing' partnership and greater equality within it.

Children's needs and parents' obligations

Most earlier research into the changing nature of the family has focused on relations between husband and wife. As a result, subjects such as parental attitudes and behaviour towards children, and the role of children in the family, have been neglected. We know very little about changes in parent–child relationships over time, although there are suggestions that they have become progressively much more relaxed and open during the course of the present century (Hoggart, 1957; Young and Willmott, 1957; Newson and Newson, 1963; Klein, 1965). In Young and Willmott's view, the new companionship between a man and a woman reflects not only a rise in the status of the wife but also a rise in the status of children.

Recently the Study Commission on the Family (1982) voiced its concern that the power of the family as a major socialising force may be weakening. With more women out at work, there might be a growing disengagement from home life and a deterioration of parent–child relationships. On the other hand, it could be argued that the opportunities provided for the mother to escape from what may be reluctant domesticity may help to promote closer personal relationships and make the sharing of values between generations more likely.

We asked respondents to the self-completion supplement to say how much they agreed or disagreed with the statement that "to grow up happily, children need a home with both their own father and mother". Over three quarters of respondents agreed, 61% of them strongly.* Despite the fact that divorce is increasingly common, the great majority of people still believe that a home needs two parents for children to be happy. This broad consensus conceals some interesting subgroup differences. Younger people (aged 18–34), especially younger women, are less strongly in agreement, as are the highly educated, the separated and the divorced, and our small sample of cohabitees. Men and those in manual occupations, on the other hand, are rather more likely to believe that an undivided family is essential to children's happiness (see **Table 6.6**).

In the interview questionnaire, we asked whether parents' or children's interests should be paramount. Respondents were asked to say which of these two statements best described their views:

> *Parents' duty is to do their best for their children, even at the expense of their own well-being; OR*
> *Parents have a life of their own and should not be asked to sacrifice their own well-being for the sake of their children*

An overwhelming majority (84%) thinks that the children's interests should come first, an even higher proportion than in 1981 when respondents to the EVSSG survey were asked exactly the same question. Again a rather lower proportion of younger women and the highly educated (especially graduates) endorse this view, but still a substantial majority accept the general consensus in placing the children's interests above those of parents (see **Table 6.6**).

Changes in parent-child relationships

Do today's parents believe they are bringing up their children differently from the way in which *they* were brought up? Is there any evidence from our data that relationships between parents and children are more relaxed and open than a generation or two ago, as Hoggart (1957) and others have claimed? In an attempt to answer questions such as these, we first asked *parents* in our sample if they were stricter, franker and so on with their children than their parents were with them. We then went on to ask *all* respondents to what extent they felt their parents had tried to influence their attitudes and beliefs – and to ask the *parents* in our sample how far they try (or tried) to influence *their* children. It must be noted, however, that our respondents spanned two and a half generations. The youngest were talking about growing up in the 1970s and early 1980s, the oldest about a childhood in Edwardian Britain.

In all but two respects, the majority of contemporary parents report changes. Children appear to have gained in status within the family – to be given more independence by, and to enjoy more respect from, their parents than was the case a generation earlier.

---

* Respondents to the 1981 EVSSG study were asked: "if someone says a child needs a home with both a father and mother to grow up happily, would you tend to agree or disagree?" Sixty seven per cent agreed.

Parents' perceptions of changes in parent–child relationships

	I with my children %	My parents with me %	No difference %
Who would be *more likely* to . . .			
let the child have a say in decisions?	66	1	30
allow the child to express itself freely?	65	1	33
treat the child as a friend?	56	2	41
show interest in the child's activities?	55	2	42
allow the child privacy?	44	3	52
show affection to the child?	39	2	58
take a strong line on behaviour?	24	31	44

Only in allowing privacy and showing affection is there a majority view among parents that things are much the same as when *they* were children.

Finding out whether people *believe* that they act differently from the way their parents did is not, of course, the same as measuring *actual* changes in behaviour. But by comparing the answers given by older and younger parents, we may be able to pick up hints of intergenerational differences in attitudes. On the evidence of our data, such differences appear to be slight but consistent: towards allowing children more freedom of expression, a greater say in decisions and more privacy (the latter possibly as a result of the general post-war improvement in housing conditions and smaller family size). Interestingly, the younger the parents the more likely they are to say that they take a stronger line on behaviour with their children than their parents did with them. Could it be that the generation which grew up in the 1950s and 1960s is taking a tougher line on discipline than their parents are often thought to have adopted? Is there, after all, a movement towards 'Victorian values' at least in this respect?

The second topic we touched upon was the extent to which parents today actually try to get their children to share their own attitudes and beliefs, compared with parents of earlier generations. According to our respondents, earlier generations of parents clearly were less frank about some issues than others. For instance, almost all our respondents' parents had discussed their religious beliefs and moral views with their children and the vast majority had made their political opinions known, but more than a third had never discussed sex. Today's parents claim to be about as willing as their own parents were to talk about morality and politics, and more willing especially to talk about sex (see **Tables 6.7** and **6.8**).

Except in matters of right and wrong, the great majority of respondents do not remember their parents' trying hard to influence their views. Today's parents seem to show considerably more concern to impart their views about sexual behaviour, but are less active than their parents were in trying to get their children to share their religious beliefs.

Influencing children's views*

To get children to share own	My parents tried 'very' or 'quite' hard	I try/tried/ will try 'very' or 'quite hard'
attitudes towards right and wrong	86%	91%
religious beliefs	28%	19%
views about sexual behaviour	16%	47%
political point of view	11%	8%

* *Note:* percentages are based on parents only

What we do not know, of course, is the *nature* of the beliefs and views that parents – yesterday's and today's – tried or are trying to impart. For instance, the present generation *may* be more permissive than their parents were in their views about sex, but the data here can tell us only that they are more willing to talk about their views and more concerned that their children should share them. But other data (for example *The 1984* and *1986 Reports*) show that intergenerational differences in attitudes toward sexual permissiveness are both large and widespread.

Surprisingly, perhaps, education and social class do not divide the sample as they do on some other aspects of family life. Men and women, too, share much the same views, but it is noticeable that more women than men claim that their parents had never talked about sex at home, indicating another possible intergenerational change. Roman Catholics are more likely than others to feel that their parents had tried to influence their religious beliefs, *and* they are in turn a little more likely than others to try to influence their own children's religious beliefs.

Yet again, though, it is age that differentiates our sample most. In general, the older the person, the more likely they are to report that their parents tried hard to influence their views. For example, twice as many older (45+) respondents as 18–24 year olds say that their parents tried very or quite hard to get them to share their religious beliefs. Similarly, while 37% of 18–24 year olds say that their parents had tried very hard to shape their attitudes to right and wrong, among those aged 45 or over the proportion rises to 54%.

There are traces of similar age differences nowadays: younger parents today are less likely to want their children necessarily to share their views on religion and right and wrong. However the age group keenest to influence their children on sexual matters is the 35–44 year olds – perhaps because many are themselves parents of children reaching puberty.

Qualities that parents should try to teach children

We presented respondents with a list of 'qualities' (drawn from the 1981

EVSSG survey) and asked them to choose those which they thought most important to try to teach children.*

Three qualities – honesty, good manners, and respect for others – stand out as by far the most popular, each being valued by more than half of the sample. In contrast, religious faith, patience, imagination and leadership are seldom chosen – each receiving less than 10% endorsement.

Qualities that parents should try to teach children

	%
Honesty	86
Good manners	72
Respect for other people	67
Cleanness and neatness	42
To act responsibly	35
Independence	24
Hard work	24
Unselfishness	23
Loyalty	22
Being careful with money	22
Determination and perseverance	20
Self-control	19
Obedience	12
Religious faith	9
Patience	8
Imagination	6
Leadership	2

Men and women largely agree in their view of what children should be taught. Also, the absence of any marked age differences would suggest that these values have changed little over the past generation or so, and that they stem from beliefs, deeply embedded in our national culture, as to which personal qualities are desirable and should be passed on.

The importance of social class to child-rearing attitudes and practices is, by contrast, well known from several small-scale studies (for example Klein, 1965 and Newson and Newson, 1963). Our data support these findings. Social class has a marked influence on the popularity of five items – neatness and cleanness, acting responsibly, care over money, determination and self-control. While the middle classes more frequently value qualities associated with self-motivation and independence – such as acting responsibly, determination and self-control – working class people are keener on those associated with discipline – neatness

---

* The list of qualities was presented in the self-completion supplement. Of the 17 included, respondents were asked to choose up to five.

and cleanness, being careful with money and, to a lesser extent, obedience. These findings have much in common with Kohn's (1977) extensive survey in America of personal and parental values. He found that, in line with their greater exercise of autonomy at work, the middle classes tend to value such 'self-direction' qualities as acting responsibly, determination and self-control in their children; the working classes on the other hand, who tend to have much less freedom to direct their work activities, are more likely to value qualities – such as neatness, cleanness and obedience – which are associated with conformity. Qualities may also be more highly valued when they are more difficult to achieve. Both Newson and Newson (1963) and Kohn (1977) have suggested that keeping children clean and neat may be more difficult for poorer parents and so may be a source of greater concern to them. Similarly, emphasising the need to be careful with money would certainly make more sense to families where there is little money to spend.

Another of Kohn's findings is borne out by ours. If the middle classes place weight on 'self-direction', the more highly educated among them admire this quality even more. The small number of graduates in our sample, in particular, have markedly different priorities than have those with lower or no qualifications, placing greater weight on independence, unselfishness and imagination, in preference to good manners, hard work and obedience. Further details are given in **Table 6.9**.

A comparable but not identical question was asked in the 1981 EVSSG study, and for 13 of the 17 items the results of the two surveys are much the same. However, there appears to have been a substantial drop (of between 14% and 25%) in the proportions endorsing four of the qualities – self-control, loyalty, unselfishness and obedience.*

The role of children in family decision making

Since the literature on family relations largely excludes the possible influence of children, and indeed other relatives within the household, on family decision making, we decided to include an exploratory question on this topic, asked of all respondents with past or present responsibility for bringing up a child. Supposing, we asked, a big decision was being made, say, over going on holiday, or having someone to live in the household for a while, how would or should that decision be made? We presented four options on a card.

---

* Such apparent shifts must be treated warily, particularly since in 1981 the question was asked during a personal interview and not on a self-completion questionnaire, and so it is possible that the differences are entirely artefactual.

Children's role in decision making

	All ever responsible for bringing up child(ren)	Child(ren) in household but none aged 10 or over	Child(ren) aged 10 or over in household	Others responsible for bringing up child(ren) in the past
	%	%	%	%
Parents and children decide together	44	34	47	46
Parents discuss with children but decide alone	28	30	31	24
Parents decide alone	25	32	21	26
Children decide	1	1	1	*

As can be seen, although decision making power rests *ultimately* with parents for at least half of respondents, for nearly three quarters children's views are taken into account in some way. Men, especially younger men, are more likely to favour family decisions being made by the parents alone. Those in Social Classes I and II and the highly educated are particularly likely to associate themselves with the 'consultation only' approach, and less likely to favour a joint decision. For further details, see **Table 6.10**.

We are conscious, however, that definitions here are extremely important. Consultation can be either full-hearted or token, and it is not altogether clear which definition respondents had in mind. Similarly, the respondent's present (or past) experience of childrearing makes a difference to response. Even so, the tendency towards a greater openness and equality in parent–child relationships, discussed by Young and Willmott (1973), is strongly supported by our data. It is the general direction of views about family decision making that this question was designed to elicit, rather than the precise proportions who favour certain approaches; and the lack of authoritarianism and *dirigisme* expressed by parents, especially women, is striking.

Conclusions

In their attitudes towards marriage and other family matters, the British emerge as highly and consistently conventional. The ideal household consists of a breadwinner father, a homemaker mother and two children. The notion of a working wife who maintains a domesticated husband at home is emphatically rejected. Yet contemporary marriage emerges nonetheless as a companionate partnership. A successful marriage is seen to be sustained above all by good personal relations between the spouses, rather than, say, by a comfortable life-style or having children. Thus divorce is most often felt to be justified when personal relations are poor, rather than when times get bad. The view of an ideal marriage includes sharing a wide range of decisions from money management to planning a family.

This emphasis on personal relationships extends to children too. Nowadays they appear generally to enjoy greater autonomy, and to have a more relaxed and open relationship with their parents, than children in earlier generations did. Yet informality in parent–child relations should not be taken as a sign of parental disengagement: parents nowadays feel strongly that they should try to influence the moral and sexual views of their children and are, if anything, more prepared to take a firm line on discipline than were parents a generation ago. The most important qualities that children should be taught are thought to be the highly conventional ones of honesty, good manners and respect for others.

Whether or not these parental ideals will survive the reality of increasing social and economic pressures placed on family life nowadays remains an open question. These pressures, together with the discrepancy we have observed between ideals and reality – for instance, in relation to the division of labour inside and outside the home – warn us against undue optimism.

Notes

1. The European Value Systems Study Group (EVSSG) was established in 1978 to conduct a cross-national survey of the social and moral values held by citizens of 10 Western European countries. The British Study used a nationally representative two-stage probability sample, stratified by region and town size, which produced a total of 1031 achieved interviews (excluding a booster sample of 200 young adults aged 18–24, selected by quota sampling methods). Fieldwork was carried out by Gallup between April and June 1981. The British EVSSG data referred to in this chapter do not include the booster sample, so that the 1981 sample and ours are broadly comparable in demographic terms.

    Reports of the overall European results of the survey appear in Harding and Phillips (1986). The British results are reported in Abrams *et al* (1985). The questionnaires, data tapes and code book for the ten-country survey are lodged at the ESRC's Data Archive at the University of Essex.
2. Some of the apparent changes which have taken place over the five years separating the two surveys may be due to a change in question wording. We offered respondents here a fourth response category, "not at all important", in addition to the three options offered in 1981. This may have resulted in fewer endorsements of the "very important" option, although it does not explain why changes on some items are much greater than on others.
3. One cautious observation can perhaps be made. Against expectations, 'role-reversers' are strongly in favour of the mother staying at home to look after pre-school children; so those few respondents in our sample who form part of households where the wife financially supports the husband would appear to be reluctant 'role-reversers', in circumstances not of their choosing, but dictated by need. See Martin and Wallace (1984), who note the ambivalence of many married women about their 'entitlement' to work when high levels of unemployment deny men jobs and the opportunity to support their families.
4. Sources: Gallup, AIPO 655 and 164G, in a personal communication from Tom W. Smith, Senior Study Director and Co-Principal Investigator, General Social Survey, NORC, University of Chicago.

References

ABRAMS, M., GERARD, D. and TIMMS, N. (eds.), *Values and Social Change in Britain*, Macmillan, London (1985).
BROWN, J., COMBER, M., GIBSON, K. and HOWARD, S., 'Marriage and the Family' in Abrams, M. *et al* (see above).
CENTRAL POLICY REVIEW STAFF, *People and their Families*, HMSO, London (1980).
CRAGG, A. and DAWSON, T., *Unemployed Women: a Study of Attitudes and Experiences*, Research Paper No. 47, Department of Employment, London (1984).
DEX, S., *Women's Work Histories: an Analysis of the Women and Employment Survey*, Research Paper No. 46, Department of Employment, London (1984).
EDWARDS, M., 'Financial Arrangements made by Husbands and Wives', *Australian and New Zealand Journal of Sociology*, vol. 18, (1982), pp. 320-338.
GILLIS, J., *For Better, for Worse: British Marriages, 1600 to the Present*, OUP, Oxford (1985).
GORER, G., *Exploring English Character*, Cresset Press, London (1955).
GORER, G., *Sex and Marriage in England Today*, Cresset Press, London, (1970).
HARDING, S., and PHILLIPS, D. with FOGARTY, M., *Contrasting Values in Western Europe*, Macmillan, London (1986).
HOGGART, R., *The Uses of Literacy*, Chatto and Windus, London (1957).
KLEIN, J., *Samples from English Cultures, Volume II*, Routledge & Kegan Paul, London (1965).
KOHN, M. L., *Class and Conformity*, University of Chicago Press, Chicago (1977).
MARTIN, J. and ROBERTS, C., *Women and Employment – a Lifetime Perspective*, HMSO, London (1984).
MARTIN, R. and WALLACE, J., *The Working Woman in Recession*, OUP, Oxford (1984).
MORRIS, L., *Redundancy and Patterns of Household Finance* (Steel Project), University College of Swansea, Swansea (1983).
NEWSON, J., and NEWSON, E. M., *Patterns of Infant Care in an Urban Community*, Penguin, Harmondsworth (1963).
NOP MARKET RESEARCH LTD. (1982) [Report in] STUDY COMMISSION ON THE FAMILY (see below).
PAHL, R. E., *Divisions of Labour*, Basil Blackwell, Oxford (1984).
RAPOPORT, R. and RAPOPORT, R., *Families in Transition*, Routledge & Kegan Paul, London (1982).
SHARPE, S., *Double Identity: the Lives of Working Mothers*, Penguin, Harmondsworth (1984).
STAMP, P., 'Balance of Financial Power in Marriage: an Exploratory Study of Breadwinning Wives', *Sociological Review*, vol. 33, (1985), pp. 546-557.
STUDY COMMISSION ON THE FAMILY, *Values and the Changing Family*, Study Commission on the Family, London (1982).
UDRY, J. R., 'Marital Alternatives and Marital Disruption', *Journal of Marriage and the Family*, vol. 43, no. 4, (1981), pp. 889-897.
YEANDLE, S., *Women's Working Lives*, Tavistock, London (1984).
YOUNG, M. and WILLMOTT, P., *Family and Kinship in East London*, Routledge & Kegan Paul, London (1957).
YOUNG, M. and WILLMOTT, P., *The Symmetrical Family*, Routledge & Kegan Paul, London (1973).

6.1 ATTITUDES TO MARRIAGE AND DIVORCE (A217a, 217b, 217c, 217e) by sex, age within sex, compressed social class, marital status and religion

	TOTAL	SEX		AGE+ WITHIN SEX						COMPRESSED SOCIAL CLASS			MARITAL STATUS+				RELIGION+				
				MALE			FEMALE														
		Male	Fe-male	18-34	35-54	55+	18-34	35-54	55+	Non-manual	Man-ual	Other	Married now	Living as married	Separated/divorced/widowed	Not married	Roman Cath-olic	C of E/Anglican	Other Chris-tian	Non-Chris-tian	No Reli-gion
	%	%	%	%	%	%	%	%	%	%	%	%	%	%	%	%	%	%	%	%	%
DIVORCE IN BRITAIN SHOULD BE MADE MORE DIFFICULT TO OBTAIN THAN IT IS NOW																					
Agree strongly/just agree	39	31	46	27	29	39	38	41	59	39	39	39	40	(19)	44	36	49	40	49	(81)	29
Neither agree nor disagree	33	37	29	39	42	29	35	33	21	32	34	36	34	(31)	22	38	25	33	30	(19)	37
Just disagree/disagree strongly	27	31	23	34	29	29	27	26	18	29	26	22	26	(50)	32	24	24	26	20	(-)	33
MOST YOUNG COUPLES START THEIR MARRIED LIFE WELL PREPARED FOR ITS UPS AND DOWNS																					
Agree strongly/just agree	29	26	33	25	25	27	32	29	38	23	37	26	28	(22)	36	30	35	29	27	(50)	29
Neither agree nor disagree	17	18	16	22	17	15	19	15	15	17	16	20	17	(17)	15	22	20	15	16	(13)	19
Just disagree/disagree strongly	52	55	51	52	58	54	49	55	46	59	45	51	54	(61)	47	47	43	56	54	(35)	52
AS A SOCIETY, WE OUGHT TO DO MORE TO SAFEGUARD THE INSTITUTION OF MARRIAGE																					
Agree strongly/just agree	71	67	75	49	71	83	62	73	88	71	71	76	74	(39)	77	59	74	81	78	(94)	56
Neither agree nor disagree	21	24	19	36	22	11	29	21	9	22	22	15	20	(37)	13	31	21	15	16	(-)	32
Just disagree/disagree strongly	6	8	5	13	6	3	8	5	2	7	6	7	5	(22)	7	9	4	3	4	(6)	11
MOST PEOPLE NOWADAYS TAKE MARRIAGE TOO LIGHTLY																					
Agree strongly/just agree	74	72	77	62	75	80	68	79	82	71	79	72	77	(64)	76	62	70	80	79	(94)	67
Neither agree nor disagree	15	18	14	28	14	9	20	12	10	17	12	20	13	(24)	11	29	18	12	13	(6)	20
Just disagree/disagree strongly	9	9	9	13	9	8	13	9	7	11	8	7	9	(11)	10	8	11	7	8	(-)	12
BASE: A Weighted	1387	658	729	232	236	190	214	266	250	659	605	123	956	(36)	184	204	152	505	220	(16)	494
RESPONDENTS Unweighted	1416	665	751	228	240	197	222	272	257	681	611	124	966	(34)	199	209	159	522	225	(16)	493

6.2 IMPORTANT FACTORS IN A SUCCESSFUL MARRIAGE (A77)
by sex, age, social class, marital status and highest educational qualification obtained

HOW IMPORTANT IS EACH ONE TO A SUCCESSFUL MARRIAGE?	TOTAL	SEX		AGE+				SOCIAL CLASS					MARITAL STATUS+				HIGHEST QUALIFICATION OBTAINED+			
		MALE	FE-MALE	18-24	25-34	35-44	45+	I/II	III non-manual	III manual	IV/V	Other	Married now	Living as married	Separated/ divorced/ widowed	Not married	Degree	Pro-fessional	'A'/'O' level/ CSE	Foreign/ other/ none
	%	%	%	%	%	%	%	%	%	%	%	%	%	%	%	%	%	%	%	%
Faithfulness	86	85	87	86	84	86	88	83	87	86	89	89	87	(82)	85	84	75	88	87	87
Mutual respect and appreciation	77	75	78	74	74	82	76	81	81	74	72	73	78	(88)	73	74	94	81	80	71
Understanding and tolerance	69	65	72	64	59	74	72	74	75	63	65	65	68	(72)	72	67	89	68	71	65
Living apart from in-laws	55	53	57	53	62	60	51	51	60	58	54	47	56	(74)	55	47	43	55	57	56
Happy sexual relationship	50	50	51	58	48	46	51	50	49	50	51	54	48	(77)	52	56	54	49	49	51
An adequate income	34	33	35	28	31	33	37	27	29	42	40	32	35	(29)	38	27	27	23	29	41
Good housing	33	31	35	19	22	30	42	22	29	40	42	33	34	(23)	43	22	21	19	22	46
Having children	31	29	33	29	26	29	34	26	32	32	35	30	34	(32)	24	25	19	26	31	34
Sharing household chores	25	26	25	32	22	24	25	22	21	30	29	25	24	(41)	27	27	30	22	21	29
Tastes and interests in common	21	20	21	17	17	16	25	23	18	19	22	25	19	(37)	25	19	28	17	18	23
Same social background	11	10	13	4	11	6	16	11	9	12	16	8	11	(10)	18	7	9	11	6	16
Shared religious beliefs	9	8	10	5	6	6	13	9	7	10	11	10	9	(-)	14	8	7	6	6	13
Agreement on politics	3	2	3	1	1	1	4	1	2	3	5	3	2	(-)	3	2	1	2	1	4
BASE: A RESPONDENTS																				
Weighted	1518	726	791	199	286	304	729	352	367	313	348	138	1041	(39)	206	225	89	188	536	698
Unweighted	1552	736	816	197	293	307	755	367	378	314	355	138	1053	(37)	224	230	94	191	548	717

6.3 PREFERRED FAMILY WORKING ARRANGEMENTS (A76a, 76b)
by age within sex, marital status, annual household income and household type

	TOTAL	AGE WITHIN SEX						MARITAL STATUS				ANNUAL HOUSEHOLD INCOME					HOUSEHOLD TYPE				
		MALE			FEMALE			Married now	Living as married	Separated/ divorced/ widowed	Not married	Under £5,000	£5,000-£7,999	£8,000-£11,999	£12,000-£17,999	£18,000+	Married/ male earner	Married/ dual earner	Married/ female earner	Married/ no earner	Other
		18-34	35-54	55+	18-34	35-54	55+														
	%	%	%	%	%	%	%	%	%	%	%	%	%	%	%	%	%	%	%	%	%
FOR A FAMILY WITH CHILDREN UNDER FIVE YEARS OLD, WHICH ONE OF THE ARRANGEMENTS DO YOU THINK IS BEST?																					
'Traditional'*	76	60	81	88	66	80	82	80	(56)	80	61	81	75	77	78	73	83	73	(88)	80	74
'Compromise'	17	26	13	8	26	13	15	15	(30)	16	26	15	21	20	14	14	13	20	(6)	16	18
'Equality'	3	9	2	1	6	2	-	2	(8)	2	8	2	3	3	4	5	2	3	(4)	4	4
'Role-reversal'	*	-	-	1	*	*	1	*	(-)	1	*	1	1	-	-	1	-	*	(-)	-	1
FOR A FAMILY WITH CHILDREN IN THEIR EARLY TEENS, WHICH ONE OF THE ARRANGEMENTS DO YOU THINK IS BEST?																					
'Traditional'	19	14	19	35	6	13	29	19	(12)	28	12	31	19	13	12	18	21	10	(23)	19	25
'Compromise'	60	50	60	52	65	72	59	64	(52)	56	49	52	60	71	67	53	63	69	(59)	55	51
'Equality'	17	33	17	9	28	11	8	14	(31)	13	35	15	18	16	19	20	11	18	(13)	25	21
'Role-reversal'	1	*	-	1	1	1	1	1	-	1	*	*	*	*	-	2	1	1	(-)	-	1
BASE: A RESPONDENTS																					
Weighted	1518	252	256	218	232	286	273	1041	(39)	206	225	347	238	282	258	224	329	473	(48)	68	599
Unweighted	1552	249	261	226	241	293	282	1053	(37)	224	230	368	247	282	264	224	337	475	(47)	69	624

* 'Traditional'   - father working full-time and mother at home
  'Compromise'   - father working full-time and mother working part-time
  'Equality'   - both parents working full-time or both working part-time
  'Role-reversal' - mother works full-time and father works part-time or stays at home.

6.4 FAMILY FINANCE ARRANGEMENTS (A78b)
by age within sex, social class and marital status

HOW DO YOU AND YOUR PARTNER ORGANISE THE MONEY THAT COMES INTO YOUR HOUSEHOLD?

	TOTAL	AGE+ WITHIN SEX						SOCIAL CLASS				MARITAL STATUS+	
		MALE			FEMALE			I/II	III non-manual	III manual	IV/V Other	Married now	Living as married
		18-34	35-54	55+	18-34	35-54	55+						
	%	%	%	%	%	%	%	%	%	%	%	%	%
'Common pot' - partners pool all the money and each takes out what he/she needs	51	46	49	47	59	50	53	52	53	48	52	51	(33)
'Allowance' - one partner manages all the money and gives the other his/her share	33	41	32	35	20	33	35	26	29	39	41	34	(10)
'Partial pool' - partners pool some of the money and keep the rest separate	10	4	10	10	14	10	8	12	12	7	1	9	(38)
'Independent' - partners keep their own money separate	5	7	7	6	6	4	2	9	5	4	4	5	(10)
BASE: A RESPONDENTS - MARRIED/LIVING AS MARRIED *Weighted*	1086	124	238	176	145	248	155	281	276	220	239	1041	(39)
Unweighted	1097	120	241	181	147	251	157	290	281	219	241	1053	(37)

6.5 FAMILY FINANCE ARRANGEMENTS (A78b)
by annual household income and household type

	TOTAL	ANNUAL HOUSEHOLD INCOME+					HOUSEHOLD TYPE				
		Under £5,000	£5,000–£7,999	£8,000–£11,999	£12,000–£17,999	£18,000+	Married/ male earner	Married/ dual earner	Married/ female earner	Married/ no earner	Other
HOW DO YOU AND YOUR PARTNER ORGANISE THE MONEY THAT COMES INTO YOUR HOUSEHOLD?	%	%	%	%	%	%	%	%	%	%	%
'Common pot' – partners pool all the money and each takes out what he/she needs	51	50	44	50	60	48	47	54	(54)	43	53
'Allowance' – one partner manages all the money and gives the other his/her share	33	40	39	38	24	25	46	22	(29)	47	34
'Partial pool' – partners pool some of the money and keep the rest separate	10	7	11	8	11	15	3	15	(13)	8	9
'Independent' – partners keep their own money separate	5	3	6	4	5	10	4	7	(4)	2	4
BASE: A RESPONDENTS – MARRIED/LIVING AS MARRIED Weighted	1086	171	179	240	224	179	329	473	(48)	68	161
Unweighted	1097	175	183	239	228	179	337	475	(47)	69	162

6.6 ATTITUDES TO PARENTING (A217D, A72)
by age within sex, social class and highest educational qualification obtained

	TOTAL	AGE+ WITHIN SEX						SOCIAL CLASS					HIGHEST QUALIFICATION OBTAINED+			
		MALE			FEMALE			I/II	III non manual	III manual	IV/V	Other	Degree	Professional	'A'/'O' level/CSE	Foreign/Other/None
		18-34	35-54	55+	18-34	35-54	55+									
TO GROW UP HAPPILY, CHILDREN NEED A HOME WITH BOTH THEIR OWN FATHER AND MOTHER	%	%	%	%	%	%	%	%	%	%	%	%	%	%	%	%
Agree strongly/just agree	78	73	81	93	61	73	89	74	77	82	82	78	62	70	78	83
Neither agree nor disagree	9	11	10	3	12	12	4	12	9	7	7	9	20	11	9	6
Just disagree/disagree strongly	12	15	8	2	27	15	6	14	14	10	11	12	16	19	13	10
BASE: A RESPONDENTS Weighted	1387	232	236	190	214	266	250	318	341	290	315	123	81	178	502	624
Unweighted	1416	228	240	197	222	272	257	330	351	290	321	124	85	180	510	640

WHICH BEST DESCRIBES YOUR VIEWS?

	TOTAL	MALE 18-34	MALE 35-54	MALE 55+	FEMALE 18-34	FEMALE 35-54	FEMALE 55+	I/II	III non manual	III manual	IV/V	Other	Degree	Professional	'A'/'O' level/CSE	Foreign/Other/None
	%	%	%	%	%	%	%	%	%	%	%	%	%	%	%	%
Parents' duty is to do their best for their children, even at the expense of their own well-being	84	84	83	88	77	82	91	78	85	86	85	86	70	78	85	87
OR																
Parents have a life of their own and should not be asked to sacrifice their own well-being for the sake of their children	11	11	11	9	17	11	6	13	10	9	12	7	19	13	10	9
BASE: A RESPONDENTS Weighted	1518	252	256	218	232	286	273	352	367	313	348	138	89	188	536	698
Unweighted	1552	249	261	226	241	293	282	367	378	314	355	138	94	191	548	717

6.7 PARENTAL INFLUENCE ON CHILDREN (A75a)
by sex, age, social class and parents' social class

DO YOU REMEMBER HOW HARD YOUR PARENTS TRIED TO GET YOU TO SHARE THEIR OWN ...	TOTAL	SEX		AGE+				SOCIAL CLASS					PARENTS' SOCIAL CLASS+			
		Male	Female	18-24	25-34	35-44	45+	I/II	III non manual	III manual	IV/V	Other	Upper middle/middle	Upper working/working	Working	Poor
	%	%	%	%	%	%	%	%	%	%	%	%	%	%	%	%
... RELIGIOUS BELIEFS?																
very hard/quite hard	27	27	28	15	24	26	33	28	26	27	30	27	25	29	27	32
not very hard/not at all hard	70	72	69	84	74	74	64	70	71	71	69	70	71	68	71	66
(Never talked about)	1	*	2	1	1	-	2	1	2	*	1	1	2	1	1	-
... VIEWS ABOUT SEXUAL BEHAVIOUR?																
very hard/quite hard	17	12	22	20	19	18	16	21	21	10	18	14	21	23	15	14
not very hard/not at all hard	47	59	36	71	63	55	30	49	44	54	44	39	47	47	49	35
(Never talked about)	35	28	40	8	18	25	52	29	34	35	37	44	31	27	35	49
... ATTITUDES TOWARDS RIGHT AND WRONG?																
very hard/quite hard	87	88	86	87	83	90	87	90	88	86	85	85	86	87	88	85
not very hard/not at all hard	11	11	11	12	16	9	9	8	10	13	12	13	13	9	10	13
(Never talked about)	1	1	1	1	-	-	1	1	1	1	1	-	1	-	1	1
... POLITICAL POINT OF VIEW?																
very hard/quite hard	10	10	11	8	7	12	12	10	10	10	13	9	12	9	10	13
not very hard/not at all hard	78	81	75	88	86	80	72	82	79	77	74	78	78	82	78	73
(Never talked about)	10	8	11	3	7	7	14	6	9	12	11	11	8	5	10	13
BASE: A RESPONDENTS																
Weighted	1518	726	791	199	286	304	729	352	367	313	348	138	265	183	917	128
Unweighted	1552	736	816	197	293	307	755	367	378	314	355	138	272	187	937	131

6.8 PARENTAL INFLUENCE ON CHILDREN (A75b)
by sex, age, social class and parents' social class

	TOTAL	SEX		AGE[+]				SOCIAL CLASS					PARENTS' SOCIAL CLASS[+]			
		Male	Female	18-24	25-34	35-44	45+	I/II	III non manual	III manual	IV/V	Other	Upper middle/ middle	Upper/ working	Working	Poor
	%	%	%	%	%	%	%	%	%	%	%	%	%	%	%	%
HOW HARD (DID)/(DO)/(WILL) YOU TRY TO SHARE YOUR OWN ...																
... RELIGIOUS BELIEFS?																
very hard/quite hard	19	14	23	(3)	10	15	24	15	24	14	22	20	23	20	18	21
not very hard/not at all hard	79	84	76	(97)	88	85	74	83	75	85	77	76	76	79	80	78
(Never talked about)	1	1	1	(-)	1	*	1	*	1	*	1	3	2	2	1	-
... VIEWS ABOUT SEXUAL BEHAVIOUR?																
very hard/quite hard	47	39	53	(46)	53	58	40	48	54	40	47	42	51	43	46	45
not very hard/not at all hard	43	50	37	(51)	44	36	45	45	39	49	38	45	41	49	42	48
(Never talked about)	9	10	9	(-)	3	6	13	5	7	10	13	13	8	7	11	6
... ATTITUDES TOWARDS RIGHT AND WRONG?																
very hard/quite hard	91	93	91	(89)	92	96	90	93	93	91	91	87	90	90	92	91
not very hard/not at all hard	7	6	8	(11)	7	4	9	6	6	7	9	12	9	10	7	8
(Never talked about)	*	*	*	(-)	-	-	1	-	1	1	-	-	-	-	1	-
... POLITICAL POINT OF VIEW?																
very hard/quite hard	8	8	9	(-)	5	5	11	6	5	7	15	10	11	10	7	11
not very hard/not at all hard	87	88	86	(97)	93	91	83	90	90	88	81	85	85	89	88	84
(Never talked about)	4	3	5	(3)	2	4	5	2	5	5	4	4	3	1	5	3
BASE: A RESPONDENTS EVER RESPONSIBLE FOR BRINGING UP A CHILD																
Weighted	1142	511	630	(37)	181	279	645	255	268	243	286	89	180	130	694	117
Unweighted	1172	520	652	(36)	184	281	671	269	277	246	292	88	186	135	711	120

6.9 QUALITIES DESIRED IN CHILDREN (A216)
by age within sex, social class, highest educational qualification obtained and household composition

FIVE MOST IMPORTANT QUAL-ITIES WHICH PARENTS CAN TRY TO TEACH THEIR CHILDREN	TOTAL	AGE+ WITHIN SEX						SOCIAL CLASS					HIGHEST QUALIFICATION OBTAINED+				HOUSEHOLD COMPOSITION+		
		MALE			FEMALE			I/II	III non manual	III manual	IV/V	Other	Degree	Pro-fessional	'A'/'O' level/CSE	Foreign/ other/ none	Youngest person under 5	Youngest person 5-17	Other
		18-34	35-54	55+	18-34	35-54	55+												
	%	%	%	%	%	%	%	%	%	%	%	%	%	%	%	%	%	%	%
Honesty	86	78	89	87	89	88	83	90	85	85	85	78	80	89	86	85	86	88	84
Good manners	72	70	74	77	81	67	69	63	77	76	75	66	37	65	76	76	77	75	70
Respect for other people	67	61	66	61	69	72	70	66	67	65	69	66	75	62	62	71	66	69	66
Cleanness and neatness	42	49	42	46	47	37	33	26	41	51	52	41	15	28	46	46	43	45	41
To act responsibly	35	35	37	29	34	41	35	43	37	32	25	46	61	39	37	30	33	38	35
Independence	24	23	21	17	26	31	23	24	23	27	23	20	34	26	23	22	19	25	25
Hard work	24	29	24	33	9	24	25	27	21	28	24	17	18	19	22	28	13	24	26
Unselfishness	23	22	21	17	33	23	20	23	28	15	21	25	34	23	25	19	34	21	21
Loyalty	22	16	21	23	22	23	27	19	22	20	24	27	13	25	19	25	25	18	23
Being careful with money	22	24	20	23	18	22	22	15	22	24	27	20	8	19	21	24	19	22	21
Determination and per-severance	20	21	25	22	19	19	16	35	18	15	11	22	45	34	18	14	23	20	20
Self-control	19	19	20	25	19	19	23	25	19	15	17	21	31	25	17	18	19	13	22
Obedience	12	13	10	14	19	8	12	8	9	17	17	11	4	7	14	13	20	11	11
Religious faith	9	5	9	10	8	10	15	8	12	9	8	11	8	11	11	8	7	9	10
Patience	8	6	10	11	7	7	7	8	8	8	10	6	3	7	8	9	6	8	8
Imagination	6	13	6	1	7	5	2	9	6	8	2	5	20	8	7	3	11	4	6
Leadership	2	5	4	1	*	1	1	4	1	2	-	4	1	6	2	1	3	2	2
BASE: A RESPONDENTS																			
Weighted	1387	232	236	190	214	266	250	318	341	290	315	123	81	178	502	624	188	391	800
Unweighted	1416	228	240	197	222	272	257	330	351	290	321	124	85	180	510	640	184	402	820

6.10 CHILDREN AND FAMILY DECISIONS (A73c)
by age within sex, social class, highest educational qualification obtained and household composition

	TOTAL	AGE[+] WITHIN SEX						SOCIAL CLASS					HIGHEST QUALIFICATION OBTAINED[+]				HOUSEHOLD COMPOSITION[+]		
		MALE			FEMALE			I/II	III non manual	III manual	IV/V	Other	Degree	Pro-fessional	'A'/'O' level/ CSE	Foreign/ other/ none	Youngest person under 5	Youngest person 5-17	Other
		18-34	35-54	55+	18-34	35-54	55+												
SUPPOSE THERE IS/(WAS) A BIG DECISION BEING MADE IN YOUR HOUSEHOLD, WHAT DO YOU THINK (SHOULD HAPPEN)/(USED TO HAPPEN)/ (USUALLY HAPPENS)?	%	%	%	%	%	%	%	%	%	%	%	%	%	%	%	%	%	%	%
The parent(s) decide and tell the child(ren) afterwards	25	38	31	23	25	16	28	24	22	29	26	28	24	25	28	24	30	22	26
The parent(s) decide after discussing it with the child(ren)	28	32	32	24	22	29	26	40	29	24	22	15	44	37	31	22	29	32	24
Everyone discusses it and the family decides together	44	27	34	46	48	53	45	31	45	44	50	55	25	36	38	51	37	44	46
The children have the final say	1	-	*	2	1	1	-	*	1	1	1	-	-	-	-	1	1	1	1
BASE: A RESPONDENTS EVER RESPONSIBLE FOR BRINGING UP A CHILD																			
Weighted	1142	85	228	197	132	268	230	255	268	243	286	89	58	148	339	591	200	372	564
Unweighted	1172	82	233	205	138	276	238	269	277	246	292	88	61	152	348	609	197	383	584

7 Interim report: The countryside

*Ken Young**

In *The 1986 Report*, we discussed the findings of a series of questions, asked for the first time in 1985, on attitudes towards the countryside. We explored respondents' perceptions of the extent to which the countryside was changing, asking what those changes were and examining the extent to which they were seen to threaten the countryside. In 1986 we repeated some of these questions, and introduced others designed to gauge the level of concern about specific threats to the countryside. We also asked our respondents how likely they would be to translate this concern into action. In view of recent proposals for alternative land uses in rural areas, responses to all these questions are timely.

Concern for the countryside

Each year since 1983, we have asked a question designed to measure the level of concern felt about a range of environmental hazards. In a sense, this question places concern for the countryside in context. The slight but consistent changes that have occurred, taken with others which are reported later in this chapter, suggest that anxiety about a number of environmental threats is slowly but more or less consistently rising. Our data support the view that there is a gradual 'greening' of the electorate, a movement to which all political parties have to some extent responded. (See **Table 7.1** for full details.)

---

* Professor of Local Government Studies, University of Birmingham.

	% regarding each of these environmental hazards as 'very' or 'quite' serious	
	1983	1986
	%	%
Industrial waste in rivers or sea	91	94
Waste from nuclear electricity stations	82	90
Industrial fumes in the air	83	89
Lead from petrol	84	85
Noise and dirt from traffic	66	73
Noise from aircraft	30	42
Acid rain	N/A	86

The changing countryside

In 1986 we repeated a number of questions, first asked in 1985, about broad agricultural policy, the main sources of threat to the countryside and the balance of responsibility between government and the farming community for conserving the environment. The responses to these questions showed little change over the year, with the exception of a small (four per cent) rise in the number of people willing to tolerate higher prices as a possible cost of preserving the countryside against industrial development.

We also asked in both years a set of questions designed to explore people's general sense of, and reactions to, change in the countryside. Not unexpectedly, perhaps, *perceptions* of change were similar to those expressed the year before (see **Tables 7.2** and **7.3** for further details). Yet the degree of *concern* about the countryside has increased markedly, and apparently independently of perceived change. As many as 40% of respondents are now "very concerned" about the countryside, which suggests a potential political issue that warrants closer inspection.

Perceptions and evaluations of countryside change, 1985–1986

	1985	1986
	%	%
The countryside:		
is much the same	20	22
has changed a bit	23	25
has changed a lot	49	48
The countryside has changed:		
for the better	11	13
for the worse	49	51
better in some ways/worse in others	11	8
Respondent is:		
very concerned	31	40
a bit concerned	37	35
not particularly concerned	32	25

Is this rising level of concern confined largely to particular subgroups of the population, or is it shared by all? This year, as last, we find that concern is associated with political commitment – partisans of all parties generally expressing greater anxiety (as indeed they tend to do about most other issues). Details are shown in **Tables 7.4** and **7.5**.

But this year we also find a more marked association between concern and age, suggesting that a mobilisation of opinion among those in the middle age group (35–54) may be taking place.

Concern about countryside by age within sex

	% "very concerned"		
	1985	1986	% change
Men:			
18–34	29%	38%	+9
35–54	38%	52%	+14
55+	33%	45%	+12
Women:			
18–34	23%	26%	+3
35–54	31%	41%	+10
55+	34%	39%	+5

This movement of opinion is consistent with other indications of a particularly active and socially concerned group of people in this age range. It seems that age and gender divisions may well become as relevant to countryside issues as they are, for instance, on nuclear issues (see Chapter 4 of this Report). We shall monitor these movements in future surveys.

Enjoyment of the countryside

Concern for the countryside – which may be rather arms-length – is not the same as *caring* for the countryside, a feeling derived from personal enjoyment. We tried to tap this dimension this time by asking respondents in the self-completion questionnaire: *Which one of these three statements comes closest to your own views?*

I care about what happens to the countryside and I get a lot of **personal** *enjoyment from it;*

I care about what happens to the countryside but I don't get a lot of **personal** *enjoyment from it; and*

I don't care much what happens to the countryside – I'm just not that bothered.

Seventy-two per cent chose the first option and three per cent chose the third. Overwhelmingly then, our respondents claim to care about the countryside, although about a quarter do not themselves get much or any pleasure from it. Not unexpectedly, care for the countryside *and* personal enjoyment of it is greatest among those who live there (84%), although two thirds of those living in big cities or the suburbs also expressed these feelings. On the face of it then, there is no sharp conflict of interests between urban and rural communities on this issue, as there is on more specific questions about perceived threats to the countryside (see below).

The replies to the questions about care and enjoyment also show an association with age. As we have seen, fewer under-35s (and under-25s in particular) express *concern* about the countryside than do older people, and fewer of them derive *personal enjoyment* from the countryside. This may well be a reflection partly of demographic differences between urban and rural areas and partly of the fact that older respondents have simply had more time to visit and appreciate the countryside. Full details are shown in **Table 7.6**.

We compared the responses of men and women of different ages to these questions: while women apparently care about the countryside as much as men do (and indeed somewhat more in the younger age group), they are less likely to be concerned about *changes* to the countryside. It is not that their perception of change is any different from that of men. Rather, women are less likely to see the changes as necessarily harmful.

Threats to the countryside

Expressions of concern are one thing: registering that concern is quite another. So in 1986 we asked respondents whether or not they would be concerned about three hypothetical threats to the countryside and, if so, which if any of a number of courses of political action, they would be likely to choose. The three threats posed were:

> *A protected site where wild flowers grew was going to be ploughed for farmland;*
>
> *A housing development was being planned in a part of the countryside you knew and liked;*
>
> *Forests in Britain were in danger of being damaged by acid rain.*

Our purpose in asking respondents about their propensity to act, either individually or collectively, was not to predict exactly what kinds of steps they might take, but rather to obtain a measure of strength of feeling. In other words, we wanted to see whether or not concern was so strongly felt that it might potentially lead to some sort of action, and if so, for what types of issues this potential existed.

In *The 1986 Report* (pp.11–17), we discussed people's disposition to political activity – then in the context of "an unjust or harmful law being considered by Parliament." Compared with this admittedly rather extreme provocation, the three kinds of environmental threat asked about in 1986 did little to mobilise even the most concerned citizens. Even the more popular forms of personal action – contacting an MP or councillor – are not strongly favoured, and it seems that the majority would content themselves at most with signing a petition. There were, however, some differences in responses to the three issues.

Actions in response to specific threats to the countryside

	Ploughing up of wild flowers	Housing development	Damage to forests by acid rain
	%	%	%
Not concerned	40	22	12
Concerned but likely to take no action	12	14	18
Likely to act and . . .			
sign a petition	33	45	51
contact MP/councillor	16	23	22
join conservation group	8	8	10
give money to a campaign	8	10	13
contact a government or planning department	7	11	9
contact radio, TV or newspaper	5	7	8
volunteer to work for a campaign	5	8	8
go on a protest march or demonstration	3	6	5

In 1986, we also asked our respondents whether they had ever taken any of the actions listed above about 'a countryside issue'. A quarter had, but the great majority of these had gone no further than to sign a petition. Seven per cent had given money to a campaign; fewer than five per cent had taken any other action. As yet, then, the countryside is not seen by the overwhelming majority of the population as a cause for which they would actively crusade. Concern is relatively passive and seems likely to remain so for all but a minority of people who are already activists, such as members of clubs or organisations connected with the countryside, who are typically highly educated and in non-manual occupations (see **Table 7.7**). On the evidence of our survey, the political base of an active 'green' movement – or for the Green Party itself – is still very small.

Before turning to the more general questions of land use and the farmer's role in the countryside, we should note that, of the three threats posed, forests damaged by acid rain was the one that attracted most concern.* It may be that this threat seemed more menacing because it was less place-specific than the other two. Or it may be that the other two threats were accompanied by more obvious compensatory benefits, such as food production or providing homes (although respondents did seem less worried about losing wild flowers and keeping farmland than about losing land for housing development). Nevertheless it is surprising that the issue of acid rain seems to have caught the public's imagination in a comparatively short time, even if the majority feels reluctant or powerless as yet to do anything about it.

---

* Readers will also remember that over half the sample also named acid rain as a "very serious" environmental hazard, and a further third rated it as "quite serious".

The future of the countryside

We have seen that the great majority of people claim to care about the countryside and to derive enjoyment from it. But how do people visualise this 'cared-for' countryside of which they make little actual use? Their focus on the aesthetic rather than the functional changes which are taking place suggests an idealisation of rural Britain in which, as Newby (1979) puts it, "the urban majority shows little interest in rural change except in its most visual aspects". Our data suggest, however, that 'the urban majority' does not differ notably in its views on countryside issues from that smaller number who actually live there.

The farmer's role

In both 1985 and 1986 we asked a series of questions about the farmer's role in the countryside, inviting respondents in the self-completion questionnaire to say how much they agreed or disagreed with each of these statements:

> *Modern methods of farming have caused damage to the countryside;*

> *If farmers have to choose between producing more food and looking after the countryside, they should produce more food;*

> *All things considered, farmers do a good job in looking after the countryside;*

> *Government should withhold some subsidies from farmers and use them to protect the countryside, even if this leads to higher prices.*

In 1986, we reported that "while most people appear to be content with the farmer's record in looking after the countryside, irrespective of where they live, those who live in the country do seem to have a more critical stance towards agricultural policy" (p.66). A very similar picture emerges now. The differences between those living in urban and rural areas remain small, except in relation to the industrialisation of agriculture, about which country dwellers are more critical.

The farmer's role in the countryside

	Current residence			
	Big city %	Suburbs %	Small city or town %	Country %
% agreeing that . . .				
modern farming damages the countryside	57	62	64	67
farmers should produce more food	46	44	48	41
farmers look after the countryside well	77	78	79	78
government should withhold subsidies from farmers	46	51	48	49

Analyses by other subgroups are shown in **Table 7.8**.

New policy issues

Over the last two years or so, rural policy issues have been changing. The emphasis now is much less on the transformation of the rural landscape by 'agribusiness' and on the changing nature of the rural population, and is instead on the issue of land use – particularly in the growth areas of South-east England, East Anglia and the South-west. Pressure by land-starved volume house builders has coincided with the need to reduce agricultural production, leading to the formulation of a new, but as yet tentative, policy to free agricultural land for other forms of development.

The current proposals on alternative land use and the rural economy represent the government's response to agricultural over-production. More than one million hectares could be withdrawn from food production over the next decade, creating the risk of dereliction and land blight in the countryside as serious as that brought about by the flight of investment from the inner cities. To counter this, the government proposes to relax some of the long-standing restrictions on building on agricultural land, to encourage small-scale industries in the countryside, and to develop leisure facilities, tourism and afforestation. These proposals undercut much of the existing planning system and have led conservationist groups to predict a 'free for all'. Meanwhile many farmers have evidently already begun to recycle their land and buildings to provide alternative sources of income.

The proposals on alternative land use were not revealed until early in 1987, although the essentials of the new direction were not unexpected. We shall thus only be able fully to explore public reaction to them in *The 1988 Report*, based on new questions in the 1987 survey. However we did include a number of items in 1986 which enable us to assess the prominence of land use issues and to see whether or not there is an 'urban–rural split' on the future of the countryside.

Policy preferences

In the self-completion questionnaire we asked respondents to consider each of five policies:

 increasing the amount of countryside being farmed;

 building new housing in country areas;

 putting the needs of farmers before protection of wildlife;

 providing more roads in country areas;

 increasing the number of picnic areas and camping sites in the countryside.

The response choices we offered were: "it should be encouraged", "don't mind one way or the other", "it should be discouraged", "it should be stopped altogether". The overall pattern of preferences emerges clearly. As the table below shows, for the great majority of the population, orientations to the countryside are shaped primarily by a concern for its amenity value as against either its economic or even its residential functions.

		Should be encouraged	Don't mind	Should be discouraged	Should be stopped
Increase picnic areas and camp sites	%	54	28	14	3
Provide more roads	%	20	29	40	10
Build new housing	%	12	22	50	14
Increase farming land	%	10	35	45	8
Put farmers' needs before wildlife protection	%	9	20	54	15

Thus almost 70% of the sample opposes putting the need of farmers before the protection of wildlife and one half is opposed to giving over a greater proportion of the countryside to farming. Moreover, the only change favoured by a majority is for the benefit of visitors to the countryside, through increasing the number of picnic areas and camp sites.

We might expect views on the future of the countryside to be shaped according to where people live, with country dwellers having more definite views on land use, and town dwellers emphasising amenity and leisure aspects. And we might also expect them to be shaped by general orientations to the environment which, as we have seen, tend to be associated with age, the 35–54 year olds being rather more favourable to conservation issues. So we ought to examine whether attitudes to the future of the countryside are primarily a matter of self-interest or of ideology.

As the table below shows, on the issue of more land for farming use, people do differ according to where they live, with those who live in big cities being either more likely not to mind or to be favourable towards increasing farmland (perhaps because they associate farmland with amenity values).

		Increasing the amount of countryside being farmed			
		Should be encouraged	Don't mind	Should be discouraged	Should be stopped
Current residence:					
big city	%	14	46	33	6
suburbs	%	11	34	46	7
small city or town	%	10	33	45	9
country	%	8	34	49	8

But age-related differences are even larger, with the greater 'greenness' of the middle age group once again becoming apparent (see **Table 7.9**).

On the issue of new housing in country areas, the residential differences are even more apparent. Those who live in big cities, and who are therefore more likely to have a sense of housing stress around them, are most in favour of building housing in the countryside, although even among this group only one fifth do so. Two thirds of those who live in the countryside itself, however, and who are more likely to be adversely affected by development, oppose new housing construction, as do those who live in the suburbs.

Building new housing in country areas

		Should be encouraged	Don't mind	Should be discouraged	Should be stopped
Current residence:					
big city	%	20	25	47	7
suburbs	%	9	22	53	14
small city or town	%	12	24	46	16
country	%	12	19	54	13

The age differences noted earlier are again present, with more than 70% of the middle age group opposing further development of rural areas (see **Table 7.9**). In general it appears that rural housing needs are barely recognised as a problem in their own right.

People who live in the countryside are more 'conservationist' (but only marginally) than those who live elsewhere in respect of wildlife and farming and, like those in the suburbs, are less inclined than their urban counterparts to favour more road provision. These and other subgroup differences in respect of attitudes towards roads and leisure amenities in country areas are also shown in **Table 7.9**.

Conclusions

The overall conclusion from this scrutiny is surprising and counter-intuitive. We expected that the practical issues of future land use patterns in the countryside would divide country dwellers sharply from town dwellers, but this has hardly been the case. Nor, as we might have expected, is this because people in big cities or their suburbs have no view on these issues: the future of the countryside appears to be nearly as important to them in most aspects as it is to those who live there, and their responses are not as dissimilar as we might have expected.

Although the 'urban majority' is markedly less likely than country dwellers to say that they too derive enjoyment from the countryside, that does not stop them from adopting policy positions on most of the choices we presented. But concern about the countryside does not seem to lend itself easily to any form of action in its defence. Is it perhaps that these feelings belong to a personal domain that is not greatly influenced by more general issues of rural development policy?

In so far as there are consistent divisions of opinion on the future of the countryside – and they are not great – they are age-related with the 35–54 year olds having the most marked protective instincts. Perhaps this is the group, whose households are no longer dominated by infants and toddlers, which is the most likely to use the countryside as its playground. The 1987 survey, to be reported next year, will analyse respondents' views on the government's specific proposals for the future of the countryside.

Reference

NEWBY, H., *Green and Pleasant Land: Social Change in Rural England*, Hutchinson, London (1979).

Acknowledgements

We are grateful to the Countryside Commission both for its financial support, which has allowed us to include questions on countryside issues since 1985, and for its advice and help (also given by its sister body, the Countryside Commission for Scotland) in designing the questionnaire modules. However, the final responsibility for question topics and wording, and for the interpretation of the results, must lie with SCPR and the author.

7.1 ENVIRONMENTAL NUISANCE (B218)
by age within sex, social class, highest educational qualification obtained and party identification

	TOTAL	AGE WITHIN SEX MALE 18-34	MALE 35-54	MALE 55+	FEMALE 18-34	FEMALE 35-54	FEMALE 55+	SOCIAL CLASS I/II	III non-manual	III manual	IV/V	Other	HIGHEST QUALIFICATION OBTAINED Degree	Profess-ional	'A' level/CSE	'O' level	Foreign/Other/None	PARTY IDENTIFICATION Cons.	Alli-ance	Labour	Non-aligned
	%	% % %			% % %			%	%	%	%	%	%	%	%	%	%	%	%	%	%
NOISE FROM AIRCRAFT																					
Very serious	9	7	7	13	6	7	20	9	7	10	11	10	9	9	2	7	13	8	7	12	8
Quite serious	33	23	36	30	37	37	34	36	33	26	32	42	44	30	33	31	34	31	33	34	41
LEAD FROM PETROL																					
Very serious	42	34	43	34	42	46	53	40	41	41	45	47	50	36	39	39	45	36	41	48	47
Quite serious	43	46	42	40	45	44	37	43	44	40	42	42	31	47	47	46	40	44	45	40	44
INDUSTRIAL WASTE IN THE RIVERS AND SEA																					
Very serious	65	65	72	56	61	72	66	62	67	66	64	70	62	68	61	69	64	61	66	69	65
Quite serious	29	30	23	32	33	25	29	31	27	28	30	25	29	27	37	25	30	32	28	25	30
WASTE FROM NUCLEAR ELECTRICITY STATIONS																					
Very serious	72	71	72	63	71	78	77	65	77	72	74	77	64	72	65	75	74	61	75	80	77
Quite serious	18	18	18	22	20	16	15	22	14	20	19	14	20	19	22	16	18	24	17	13	15
INDUSTRIAL FUMES IN THE AIR																					
Very serious	46	44	52	35	42	47	52	45	47	45	45	48	44	45	42	49	45	44	45	47	44
Quite serious	43	42	39	47	48	47	35	43	41	42	45	43	39	42	49	41	44	43	42	44	50
NOISE FROM DIRT AND TRAFFIC																					
Very serious	25	18	28	28	18	20	39	22	26	29	23	22	26	20	18	20	30	22	20	29	19
Quite serious	49	45	45	45	51	57	43	53	46	40	53	48	54	48	56	49	46	47	53	47	55
ACID RAIN																					
Very serious	54	48	58	44	51	56	66	49	56	52	59	52	48	47	43	54	59	52	52	57	45
Quite serious	33	33	32	33	34	34	29	38	30	31	30	34	34	43	43	30	29	31	36	31	41
BASE: B RESPONDENTS																					
Weighted	1315	212	222	174	249	255	200	317	318	263	293	125	102	161	112	357	582	451	225	468	91
Unweighted	1381	201	228	178	241	264	206	319	323	273	292	114	100	165	113	357	585	452	227	471	88

7.2 EVALUATION OF COUNTRYSIDE CHANGES (B101a, B101b) by age within sex, 1985 and 1986

| | 1985 SURVEY | | | | | | | 1986 SURVEY | | | | | | |
| | TOTAL | MALE AGE+ WITHIN SEX | | | FEMALE | | | TOTAL | MALE AGE+ WITHIN SEX | | | FEMALE | | |
		18-34	35-54	55+	18-34	35-54	55+		18-34	35-54	55+	18-34	35-54	55+
COUNTRYSIDE:	%	%	%	%	%	%	%	%	%	%	%	%	%	%
Has not changed	27	29	22	26	33	24	27	22	28	22	24	20	17	21
Changed for the better	11	14	9	14	9	11	11	13	11	9	17	13	14	14
Changed for the worse	49	44	59	47	48	51	47	51	46	61	46	49	54	50
Better in some ways/worse in others	11	12	9	12	9	12	14	8	7	6	10	4	10	10
Don't know/no answer	1	1	1	2	1	1	1	6	8	2	3	15	4	5
BASE: B RESPONDENTS Weighted	1769	287	288	245	333	308	303	1548	249	252	211	291	299	242
Unweighted	1804	284	294	241	340	329	310	1548	234	258	217	279	309	248

7.3 EVALUATION OF COUNTRYSIDE CHANGES (B101a, B101b) by party identification, 1985 and 1986

| | 1985 SURVEY | | | | | 1986 SURVEY | | | | |
| | TOTAL | PARTY IDENTIFICATION+ | | | | TOTAL | PARTY IDENTIFICATION+ | | | |
		Conservative	Alliance	Labour	Non-aligned		Conservative	Alliance	Labour	Non-aligned
COUNTRYSIDE:	%	%	%	%	%	%	%	%	%	%
Has not changed	27	25	22	31	37	22	23	15	22	28
Changed for the better	11	11	9	14	8	13	12	13	15	6
Changed for the worse	49.	50	57	46	45	51	52	59	49	46
Better in some ways/worse in others	11	13	11	9	9	8	9	8	7	6
Don't know/no answer	1	1	1	1	2	6	5	6	7	14
BASE: B RESPONDENTS Weighted	1769	545	311	645	154	1548	505	264	553	125
Unweighted	1804	564	317	649	159	1548	508	265	552	120

7.4 CONCERN ABOUT THE COUNTRYSIDE (B102) by age within sex, 1985 and 1986

CONCERN ABOUT THINGS THAT MAY HAPPEN TO THE COUNTRYSIDE	1985 SURVEY							1986 SURVEY						
	TOTAL	AGE[+] WITHIN SEX						TOTAL	AGE[+] WITHIN SEX					
		MALE			FEMALE				MALE			FEMALE		
		18-34	35-54	55+	18-34	35-54	55+		18-34	35-54	55+	18-34	35-54	55+
	%	%	%	%	%	%	%	%	%	%	%	%	%	%
Very concerned	31	29	38	33	23	31	34	40	38	52	45	27	41	39
A bit concerned	37	37	38	29	44	42	29	35	33	34	26	42	35	34
Does not concern me particularly	32	34	25	39	33	27	37	25	29	14	29	30	24	26
No answer	*	*	*	-	-	*	-	*	-	-	*	*	-	2
BASE: B RESPONDENTS														
Weighted	1769	287	288	245	333	308	303	1548	249	252	211	291	299	242
Unweighted	1804	284	295	241	340	329	310	1548	234	258	217	279	309	248

7.5 CONCERN ABOUT THE COUNTRYSIDE (B102) by party identification, 1985 and 1986

CONCERN ABOUT THINGS THAT MAY HAPPEN TO THE COUNTRYSIDE	1985 SURVEY					1986 SURVEY				
	TOTAL	PARTY IDENTIFICATION[+]				TOTAL	PARTY IDENTIFICATION[+]			
		Conservative	Alliance	Labour	Non-aligned		Conservative	Alliance	Labour	Non-aligned
	%	%	%	%	%	%	%	%	%	%
Very concerned	31	34	36	29	17	40	44	43	37	30
A bit concerned	37	43	38	32	32	35	35	38	33	33
Does not concern me particularly	32	23	26	38	49	25	20	18	30	36
No answer	*	-	*	*	1	*	*	*	1	-
BASE: B RESPONDENTS										
Weighted	1769	545	311	645	154	1548	505	264	553	125
Unweighted	1804	564	317	649	159	1548	508	265	552	120

7.6 CARE ABOUT AND ENJOYMENT OF THE COUNTRYSIDE (B224)
by age within sex and current residence

| | TOTAL | AGE+ WITHIN SEX | | | | | | CURRENT RESIDENCE | | | |
| | | MALE | | | FEMALE | | | Big city | Suburbs | Small city or town | Country |
		18-34	35-54	55+	18-34	35-54	55+				
WHICH OF THESE THREE STATEMENTS COMES CLOSEST TO YOUR OWN VIEWS?	%	%	%	%	%	%	%	%	%	%	%
I care about what happens to the countryside, and I get a lot of _personal enjoyment_ from it	72	63	79	75	68	74	75	66	67	72	84
I care about what happens to the countryside, but I don't get a lot of _personal enjoyment_ from it	24	33	20	21	24	22	23	28	29	24	15
I don't care much what happens to the countryside - I'm just not that bothered	3	4	1	2	6	2	2	4	3	4	2
BASE: B RESPONDENTS Weighted	1315	212	222	174	249	255	200	134	438	450	293
Unweighted	1321	201	228	178	241	264	206	119	443	457	302

7.7 ACTIVISM OVER COUNTRYSIDE ISSUES (B106a, B106b)
by age within sex, social class, highest educational qualification obtained and current residence

	TOTAL	AGE WITHIN SEX — MALE 18-34	MALE 35-54	MALE 55+	FEMALE 18-34	FEMALE 35-54	FEMALE 55+	SOCIAL CLASS I/II	III non-manual	III manual	IV/V	Other	HIGHEST QUALIFICATION — Degree	Professional	'A' level	'O' level CSE	Foreign/Other/None	CURRENT RESIDENCE Big city	Suburbs city	Small city or town	Country
	%	%	%	%	%	%	%	%	%	%	%	%	%	%	%	%	%	%	%	%	%
HAVE YOU EVER DONE ANY OF THE THINGS ON THIS CARD ABOUT A COUNTRYSIDE ISSUE?																					
Yes	25	23	33	18	22	29	21	36	29	19	15	23	44	40	30	26	16	24	24	23	29
No	75	76	67	82	77	71	78	64	71	80	85	77	56	60	71	74	83	76	76	77	70
WHICH ONES HAVE YOU EVER DONE? (ASKED OF ALL ANSWERING YES)																					
Signed a petition	18	19	22	11	18	22	15	25	21	15	12	17	30	28	20	20	12	19	18	17	20
Given money to a campaign	7	8	10	4	5	9	6	13	10	4	2	6	18	11	12	7	4	12	9	4	7
Contacted MP or councillor	4	3	7	6	2	5	3	8	5	3	2	2	11	8	4	4	2	8	3	3	6
Contacted a government or planning department	4	3	8	2	2	4	4	8	4	2	2	2	8	13	3	3	2	4	3	4	4
Joined a conservation group	4	4	5	1	4	4	4	6	4	2	1	4	11	8	4	4	1	7	4	2	3
Volunteered to work for a campaign	2	2	3	*	3	2	2	4	3	2	1	2	5	4	3	3	1	4	2	2	1
Contacted radio, TV or newspaper	1	1	2	-	*	1	1	1	2	-	1	1	1	2	1	1	-	1	1	1	1
Gone on a protest march or demonstration	1	1	*	*	1	1	-	1	1	1	1	3	1	1	4	*	1	*	1	1	1
BASE: B RESPONDENTS																					
Weighted	1548	249	252	211	291	299	242	362	355	314	354	162	117	177	130	422	700	162	521	517	348
Unweighted	1548	234	258	217	279	309	248	359	362	325	351	151	113	179	130	419	704	145	525	323	355

7.8 THE FARMER'S ROLE IN THE COUNTRYSIDE (B221)
by age within sex, social class and highest educational qualification obtained

| | TOTAL | AGE+ WITHIN SEX | | | | | | | | SOCIAL CLASS | | | | | HIGHEST QUALIFICATION OBTAINED+ | | | | |
| | | MALE | | | | FEMALE | | | | I/II | III non-manual | III manual | IV/V | Other | Degree | Profess-ional | 'A' level | 'O' level/ CSE | Foreign/ Other/ None |
		18-24	35-34	35-54	55+	18-24	25-34	35-54	55+										
	%	%	%	%	%	%	%	%	%	%	%	%	%	%	%	%	%	%	%
A. Modern methods of farming have caused damage to the countryside — Agree strongly/agree	63	53	62	74	68	49	65	59	64	64	63	63	62	66	77	67	66	62	60
B. If farmers have to choose between producing more food and looking after the countryside, they should produce more food — Agree strongly/agree	45	49	34	34	59	54	37	42	52	40	41	50	48	48	29	35	38	41	54
C. All things considered farmers do a good job in looking after the countryside — Agree strongly/agree	78	71	75	68	82	87	79	85	79	76	78	78	83	74	70	79	69	75	84
D. Government should withhold some subsidies from farmers and ask them to protect the countryside even if it leads to higher prices — Agree strongly/agree	49	41	59	59	51	38	47	45	49	56	46	46	46	54	58	54	56	47	47
BASE: B RESPONDENTS Weighted	1315	96	116	222	174	115	134	255	200	317	318	263	293	125	102	161	112	357	582
Unweighted	1321	89	112	228	178	108	133	264	200	319	323	273	292	114	100	165	113	357	585

7.9 POLICY PREFERENCES FOR THE COUNTRYSIDE (B223)
by age within sex, social class, highest educational qualification obtained and current residence

All figures are percentages (%).

	TOTAL	MALE 18-34	MALE 35-54	MALE 55+	FEMALE 18-34	FEMALE 35-54	FEMALE 55+	I/II	III non-manual	III manual	IV/V	Other	Degree	Professional	'A' level/CSE	'O' level/CSE	Foreign/Other/None	Big City	Suburbs	Small town or city	Country
INCREASING THE AMOUNT OF COUNTRYSIDE BEING FARMED																					
It should be encouraged	10	8	8	17	7	8	17	11	10	9	13	8	9	11	9	9	11	14	11	10	8
Don't mind	35	36	23	33	49	35	32	31	35	35	36	42	38	31	33	35	36	46	34	33	34
It should be discouraged	45	43	57	39	39	49	42	47	47	44	41	42	46	51	46	46	42	33	46	45	49
It should be stopped altogether	8	13	10	8	5	5	8	10	6	10	7	8	7	6	12	8	8	6	7	9	8
BUILDING NEW HOUSES IN COUNTRY AREAS																					
It should be encouraged	12	12	9	13	12	7	7	11	13	17	12	16	12	13	8	8	15	20	9	12	12
Don't mind	22	25	14	21	26	24	23	19	24	26	27	23	11	17	28	23	24	25	22	24	19
It should be discouraged	50	50	56	47	47	56	45	53	53	46	48	41	62	58	51	53	44	47	53	46	54
It should be stopped altogether	14	11	19	14	15	11	14	15	13	11	13	14	15	13	12	15	14	7	14	16	13
PUTTING THE NEEDS OF FARMERS BEFORE PROTECTION OF WILDLIFE																					
It should be encouraged	9	7	8	16	8	9	11	10	10	10	7	11	10	6	9	8	11	16	10	9	6
Don't mind	20	16	15	18	27	18	25	18	19	19	24	24	14	16	15	18	24	17	19	21	22
It should be discouraged	54	56	56	45	48	61	54	59	54	46	55	53	65	64	54	57	47	56	54	54	53
It should be stopped altogether	15	20	20	17	16	12	8	12	15	24	12	14	11	13	22	15	15	11	16	15	17
PROVIDING MORE ROADS IN COUNTRY AREAS																					
It should be encouraged	20	17	14	30	16	16	30	20	18	18	21	24	15	17	12	20	23	26	16	22	18
Don't mind	29	33	25	24	33	29	27	25	27	32	29	34	29	25	37	29	27	32	28	30	26
It should be discouraged	40	37	49	33	40	46	34	44	43	35	41	34	46	48	43	38	38	37	43	37	44
It should be stopped altogether	10	12	11	11	10	8	8	10	10	13	8	6	10	10	8	10	10	5	11	10	10
INCREASING THE NUMBER OF PICNIC AREAS AND CAMPING SITES IN THE COUNTRYSIDE																					
It should be encouraged	54	50	59	58	50	53	55	56	48	56	55	55	56	57	48	56	53	52	51	59	52
Don't mind	28	31	27	24	34	29	25	24	31	29	32	26	25	23	34	27	30	30	28	27	30
It should be discouraged	14	17	12	10	12	16	16	18	16	11	9	14	19	19	13	13	12	13	16	12	14
It should be stopped altogether	3	1	3	5	2	2	4	2	4	2	3	3	-	1	4	2	4	3	4	2	3
BASE: B RESPONDENTS Weighted	1315	212	222	174	249	255	200	317	318	263	293	125	102	161	112	357	582	134	438	450	293
Unweighted	1321	207	228	178	241	264	206	319	323	273	292	114	100	165	113	357	585	119	443	457	302

Column group headings: AGE[+] WITHIN SEX (MALE, FEMALE); SOCIAL CLASS; HIGHEST QUALIFICATION OBTAINED[+]; CURRENT RESIDENCE.

8 Interim report: Party politics

*John Curtice**

Mrs Thatcher's government has been trying to change the social and economic structure of Britain. In pursuit of an entrepreneurial, individualistic society it has curbed the power of trade unions, reduced government intervention in the economy, sold off council houses and widened the base of share ownership. The aim has been not simply to depart from Butskellite policies, but also to change public attitudes and so to shift the centre-ground of British politics to the right. Such changes would outlive Mrs Thatcher's government; any successor administration would have to operate, at least initially, within a public opinion defined by these new Thatcherite parameters.

Mrs Thatcher's re-election to a third term in office appears to suggest that she is succeeding in that aim. Her victory in June 1987 is surely ample proof that the British electorate has shifted decisively to the right. Or is it?

In last year's Report we suggested that the very opposite was happening (see Chapter 3; and also Chapters 4 and 6). We noted that on those issues which most sharply discriminate between Conservative and Labour supporters, the British public had shifted away from the position adopted by the Conservative Party. We also noted that between 1984 and 1985 there had been an eight per cent fall in the level of Conservative party identification. How do we square these findings with the result of the 1987 election?

That task must in part lie beyond the remit of this chapter, since the survey being reported here was conducted in the spring of 1986, around twelve months *before* the general election. But we can look for possible clues. For instance, between 1985 and 1986 the level of Conservative identification rose a little. Might this have been the forerunner of a more marked trend towards Conservatism?

---

* Lecturer in the Department of Political Theory and Institutions, University of Liverpool.

Party identification

We should note first that we are referring here to party *identification*, not voting behaviour or intention. This is meant to be a more enduring form of attachment to a party than a mere cross on a ballot or an indication of likely voting behaviour in a poll during a non-election period. Party identification is more like the relationship between football supporters and their club – an affective attachment or loyalty that survives the occasional disagreement over team selection or club policy, or even the failure of the team to fulfil expectations.

The strength of attachment people have to a party, if any, varies. In this survey, respondents are asked each year: *Generally speaking, do you think of yourself as a supporter of any one party?* Respondents who name a party in response to this question are those we take to have the strongest party identification and are called *partisans*. Those who do not name a party are asked further: *Do you think of yourself as a little closer to one political party than the others?* Those who name a party at this point are called *sympathisers*. Finally, those who do not indicate either partisan support or sympathy for a party we ask: *If there were a general election tomorrow, which party do you think you would be most likely to support?* Respondents who choose a party at this point have a weak sense of attachment, possibly amounting to little more than a current electoral preference: we call them *residual identifiers*. And those respondents who resist all three invitations to nominate a party are called *non-aligned*.

The fall in the level of Conservative identification that we reported between 1984 and 1985 can clearly be seen in the table below. So also can the possible start of a revival in 1986. Conservative identification increased in all social classes, not only in one section of society (see **Tables 8.1** and **8.2** for the 1986 figures). Still, the rise was not sufficient at that stage to reverse even half the fall of the previous year. Conservative identification was still well short of the level it was at around the time of the 1983 general election, a level which was sustained for at least a year afterwards. So the 12% Conservative lead over Labour in the 1987 general election could not have been anticipated on the basis of the underlying sympathies of the electorate twelve months earlier.

	1983 %	1984 %	1985 %	1986 %
Party identification:				
Conservative	38	39	31	34
Labour	33	35	37	35
Alliance	15	13	18	17
Other Party	1	2	1	2
Non-aligned	8	6	9	8

One other important point should be noted. We reported in 1986 (p.43) that the proportion of respondents who did not identify with *any* party had risen to nine per cent, and suggested this might be evidence supporting the thesis of an electoral cycle of partisanship. According to this thesis, at each election the stimulus of the campaign and the act of voting itself intensifies partisanship, an effect that diminishes as the experience of the election recedes (see, for example, Butler and Stokes, 1975, pp.58-62). However, the proportion of non-aligned in our sample remained more or less stable at eight per cent in 1986. Further, the distribution of identifiers between partisans, sympathisers and residual identifiers hardly changed between 1983 and 1986. So the claim that partisanship wanes outside election periods seems on this evidence to be dubious.

	1983	1984	1985	1986
	%	%	%	%
Partisans	46	47	46	46
Sympathisers	24	26	25	26
Residual identifiers	15	15	15	15

Party identification and values

The scale of the 1987 Conservative election victory was improbable a year earlier, not merely because of the distribution of party identification at that time but also because, as we noted earlier, there had been a shift to the left in public attitudes between 1983 and 1985. It was this shift, and not simply disillusionment with government performance, which apparently occasioned at least some of the decline in Conservative identification between 1984 and 1985. Indeed, in this context, even the small rise in Conservative identification between 1985 and 1986 is rather surprising. Moreover, the issues which most divided the supporters of each party in 1986 were much the same as in 1985. Conservative and Labour identifiers are most sharply divided by their belief or otherwise in the need for greater equality in society and how far they accept that governmental and other forms of collective action are desirable in its pursuit.

The following 13 attitudinal items, derived from an analysis of all those included in the 1986 survey, were the ones that discriminated most sharply between Conservative and Labour identifiers according to the 'index of dissimilarity'.* We see in the table below that the items which most sharply distinguished Conservatives from Labour supporters last year, such as employees' need for strong trade unions and whether or not a nationwide strike of all workers should be allowed, appear again this year. But a number of new items, not included in last year's survey, now also appear in the list. Two in particular are worth noting: attitudes towards stricter trade union laws and attitudes towards the abolition of private education. Both these items were included in the 1983 *British General Election* study and in that survey too

---

* The index of dissimilarity, a technique used in *The 1986 Report*, is the sum of the differences (of the same sign) between the percentage of Party A supporters in each response category and the percentage of Party B supporters in each category. It tells us nothing about the *level* of support for each attitudinal item, merely about the extent to which Conservative and Labour supporters *differ* on that item. The index can be as high as 100 and as low as 0.

	Index of dissimilarity between Conservative and Labour
Agree/disagree employees need strong trade unions	49
Government should/should not introduce stricter trade union laws	46
Government should/should not spend more money to get rid of poverty	44
Agree/disagree government should redistribute income from better-off to worse-off	43
Agree/disagree one law for rich, one law for poor	42
Organising nationwide strike of all workers should/should not be allowed	41
Agree/disagree ordinary people do not get fair share of nation's wealth	41
Agree/disagree more socialist planning best way to solve economic problems	41
Agree/disagree private enterprise best way to solve economic problems	41
Government should/should not get rid of private education	40
Agree/disagree that it is the government's responsibility to reduce the differences in income between rich and poor	39
Benefits for unemployed too low/high	39
Favour nationalisation/privatisation of companies by government	39

proved to be among the very strongest discriminators between Conservative and Labour voters (Heath, Jowell and Curtice, 1985). Their importance is thus confirmed. Other new items in the list were included in this survey as part of a new scale designed to measure the underlying values separating Conservative and Labour supporters, a theme we return to later in this chapter.

In the table below, we show those items which discriminated well between Conservative and Labour identifiers in both 1985 and 1986. The distribution of support was remarkably constant, but as can be seen from the indices of dissimilarity, the gap between Conservative and Labour identifiers generally closed. There was no overall shift back to the right; nor was there any further significant movement to the left, except on the question of American nuclear missiles (see Chapter 4 of this Report). Equally, as **Table 8.3** shows, there has been no systematic movement on issues which distinguish Conservative from Alliance identifiers. So the increase in Conservative identification cannot be accounted for by changes in these attitudes. The Thatcher policy revolution has simply *not* so far been accompanied by an equivalent revolution in public attitudes.

	% adopting 'right-wing' position		Index of dissimilarity	
	1985	1986	1985	1986
	%	%	%	%
Disagree/agree employees need strong trade unions	27	29	49	49
Organising a nationwide strike of all workers should not/should be allowed	66	68	46	41
Should not/should be government's responsibility to reduce the difference in incomes between rich and poor	24	23	44	39
Benefits for the unemployed are not/are too low	34	33	43	39
Siting of American nuclear weapons in Britain makes Britain a safer/less safe place to live	36	29	43	36
Should not/should be government's responsibility to provide a decent standard of living for the unemployed	14	13	40	34
Having our own independent nuclear missiles makes Britain a safer/less safe place to live	54	52	36	29
Like to see less/more state ownership of industry	31	30	34	30
Britain should keep/rid itself of nuclear weapons	68	69	32	30
Oppose/support reducing government spending on defence	42	41	31	28
Government should give higher priority to keeping down inflation/keeping down unemployment	22	20	30	26

Economic evaluations and expectations

Clearly then, if we are to account for the rise in Conservative identification between 1985 and 1986, we need to look at something *other* than these underlying values. Perhaps the most obvious consideration is people's judgement of the government's economic performance – in general and in relation to their own sense of prosperity. If people have confidence in the overall prospects for the economy, and especially if there has been an improvement in their own standard of living, then, it is argued, they are more likely to be sympathetic to the governing party and to vote for it. In last year's Report (p.45) we noted that there had been a sharp decline in respondents' economic optimism and suggested this was a possible factor in the decline of Conservative support. How then did our respondents view the economic situation in 1986?

As the following table shows, there was in fact a sharp improvement in the electorate's evaluation of the economic situation between 1985 and 1986. People have become much more optimistic about inflation, unemployment and their own household incomes. Only in their expectations of Britain's general

	1983 %	1984 %	1985 %	1986 %
Expect prices to go up a lot	24	31	40	26
Expect unemployment to go up a lot	31	25	33	29
Expect general industrial performance to decline	17	15	21	23
Expect own household income to fall behind prices	N/A	43	49	44
Own household's income *has* fallen behind prices	N/A	46	55	47

industrial performance, something of less immediate relevance to most people's lives than the other evaluations, was there no increased optimism.

Responses to a cross-sectional survey such as this cannot demonstrate that greater optimism in economic evaluations actually *caused* the rise in Conservative identification; we cannot show that those individuals who had become more economically optimistic between 1985 and 1986 were the ones who became Conservative identifiers. A panel survey, which interviewed the same individuals in both years, is much better suited to this purpose. Unfortunately, the *British Social Attitudes* panel, in which we reinterviewed the same people in 1985 and 1986, was based on too small a sample to illuminate this kind of issue. We must, then, look for clues in the cross-sectional survey to see whether a rise in economic optimism is a likely explanation for at least part of the rise in Conservative identification.

Consider first the following two tables. Each examines the extent to which Conservative identification varies according to people's attitudes *and* their economic evaluations. The *attitude items* on trade unions and redistribution of income are the two which most sharply discriminate between Conservative and Labour identifiers; the *economic evaluations* cover expectations about prices and unemployment. These choices are more or less arbitrary: the tables are designed to illustrate the pattern of response to virtually any of the key attitude items, dividing Conservative and Labour identifiers and any of the economic evaluations.

Both the tables below show precisely the same pattern. As we go *down* each column we can see that the level of Conservative identification rises as the answers become more 'right-wing'. This is as expected. Equally, however, as we move *across* each row of the tables, so we find that the more optimistic people are about the economy the more likely they are to be Conservative identifiers. The crucial point about this is that the association between economic evaluations and partisanship is independent of attitudes. Even among those who adopt clearly 'left-wing' positions on trade unions and redistribution – the top row in each of the two tables – support for the Conservatives rises as evaluations of the economic situation become more favourable.

This evidence makes it less surprising that support for the Conservatives rose between 1985 and 1986. As long as economic evaluations affect party identification independently of values, economic optimism may produce an increase in support for a Conservative government, despite a drift to the left in political attitudes. That respondents can change their party identification,

**% of each cell who
are Conservative identifiers**

| | Expect prices to: | | | |
	Go up a lot	Go up a little	Stay the same	Go down
Employees need strong trade unions				
Agree	10%	15%	27%	38%
Neither agree nor disagree	18%	39%	54%	73%
Disagree	28%	65%	67%	68%

| | Expect unemployment to: | | | |
	Go up a lot	Go up a little	Stay the same	Go down
Government's responsibility to reduce income differences				
Definitely should be	10%	18%	37%	40%
Probably should be	15%	36%	50%	60%
Probably should not be	39%	54%	65%	63%
Definitely should not be	61%	62%	70%	92%

irrespective of the values they hold, is clear if we analyse change in the level of Conservative identification among people with differing views on the three questions which best discriminate between Conservative and Labour. A rise in Conservative identification appears to have occurred among people of *all* shades of opinion (see also **Table 8.4**).

| | % Conservative Identifiers | | |
	1985 %	1986 %	Change
Employees need strong trade unions:			
Agree	16	16	0
Neither agree nor disagree	33	39	+6
Disagree	56	58	+2
Nationwide strike of all workers should be:			
Definitely allowed	5	9	+4
Probably allowed	12	14	+2
Probably not allowed	27	29	+2
Definitely not allowed	46	48	+2
Government's responsibility to reduce income differences:			
Definitely should be	16	20	+4
Probably should be	30	35	+5
Probably should not be	57	57	0
Definitely should not be	67	68	+1

What we appear to have found here is further evidence to support the claim of

Heath *et al* (1985) that elections are not just "won and lost in the centre-ground. They are won and lost in the heartlands as well" (p.159). Heath *et al* showed that even among people with consistently Conservative or Labour values, the level of support for their 'natural' parties varied sharply from one election to another. Here we confirm that a governing party can appeal successfully to voters whose values are different from their own, on the basis of improving economic indications. Changes in evaluations of the economy can apparently produce a rise or fall in the level of support for a party from those of *all* ideological persuasions. We thus may have a clue as to why the Conservative Party won the June 1987 election even when the electorate had been moving away from it ideologically.

But this is not the whole story. It is at best one of several explanations for the rise in Conservative identification. There is evidence in the survey which suggests that Conservative identification rose to a limited extent even *independently* of the level of economic optimism. Increased economic optimism was one, but only one, of the factors that boosted Conservative prospects in 1986.

Egalitarianism and party identification

We have shown in both this year's and last year's Reports that beliefs about equality and about the proper role of government and trade unions in its pursuit, is central to the Conservative-Labour divide. We included in the 1986 survey a set of five items designed specifically to tap the dimension of egalitarianism and to test its discriminatory power. These items were originally devised and tested in methodological work we conducted to enhance the questionnaire design of both the *British Social Attitudes* series and the *British General Election* studies (Heath *et al*, 1986).* The five items, which form a scale, are:

> *Government should redistribute income from the better-off to those who are less well-off*
>
> *Big business benefits owners at the expense of workers*
>
> *Ordinary people do not get their fair share of the nation's wealth*
>
> *There is one law for the rich and one for the poor*
>
> *Management will always try to get the better of employees if it gets the chance*

Respondents were asked whether they agreed or disagreed with these items on a simple additive or Likert five-point scale, ranging from "Agree strongly" to "Disagree strongly". By giving a score of 1 to strong agreement with an item, and 5 to strong disagreement, we have at one end of the continuum those who strongly agree with each of the five items. They have a score of five (committed egalitarians). At the other end are those who strongly disagree with each item

---

* This work was financially supported by the ESRC through a methodological enhancement grant.

and have a score of 25 (committed anti-egalitarians). Collapsing the scale to five points by dividing each respondent's score by the number of items then gives us an 'average' score for each respondent.

There are two important points about such a scale. In the first place, our five items refer to broad beliefs about inequality and exploitation in society. They do not deal with specific policy proposals, such as nationalisation or trade union legislation. Attitudes to such issues also certainly divide Conservative and Labour supporters, but they relate more to the preferred *means* by which inequalities might be reduced. Our scale attempts instead to reflect an underlying value associated with such policy positions. To the extent that it succeeds in doing so, it has the distinct advantage over specific policy batteries of being able to withstand the test of time as a device by which to measure the ideological divide between Conservative and Labour identifiers. Fundamental values of egalitarianism tend not to be as influenced by actual changes in public policy as are attitudes towards the specific policies. So, for example, if many nationalised industries are sold off, attitudes to privatisation or nationalisation might change in the light of the new *status quo*, while a good measure of underlying values remains relatively unchanged.

The second point to note about this scale is that it has very high reliability. The items on the scale are highly intercorrelated, suggesting that they are indeed all tapping the same underlying value.*

As the results below show, a majority of the British public tends towards the egalitarian end of the scale. Only one per cent of respondents are classified as strongly anti-egalitarian, meaning that they strongly disagreed with at least three of the five statements. In contrast 11% are classified as strongly egalitarian, meaning that they strongly agreed with at least three.

Egalitarian scale

		Total	Party identification		
			Conservative	Alliance	Labour
		%	%	%	%
Average Position					
Strongly egalitarian	= 1 point	11	2	10	21
	2 points	40	25	37	54
	3 points	32	40	38	20
	4 points	13	27	12	2
Strongly anti-egalitarian	= 5 points	1	3	*	–

The difference in the attitudes expressed by Conservative and Labour identifiers is clear. Three quarters of Labour identifiers score 1 or 2 points compared with just over one quarter of Conservatives. As measured by the index of dissimilarity (which was 48), the scale distinguished more sharply between Conservative and Labour supporters than all of the individual questionnaire items on our list, except for the question on strong trade unions.

---

* The reliability of the scale is very high (Cronbach's alpha = 0.87).

Egalitarianism as a value fundamentally divides Conservative and Labour identifiers. Alliance identifiers lie between the other two parties, though they are a little closer to Conservatives than to Labour. (**Table 8.5** gives further breakdowns.)

Positive and negative partisanship

The 1986 survey also included an innovation in the measurement of political partisanship. Apart from our standard series of questions which measures the direction and strength of party identification, we also asked respondents how they felt about *each* of the main parties on a seven-point scale ranging from "very strongly in favour" to "very strongly against". The question was designed to provide more information about people's emotional reactions to the parties. Unlike the question on party identification, which elicits information only about the party respondents *identify with*, this question enables us to find out what people *feel* about all of the main parties. So we can then tell, for instance, which people are antagonistic to all parties other than their own, and which have an affinity to more than one party.

The results produced a number of interesting and surprising findings. With our standard measure, we usually find that Conservative and Labour identifiers have a stronger attachment to their parties than do Liberal or SDP identifiers; there are proportionately fewer Alliance *partisans*. In 1986 we find that 61% of Conservative identifiers are partisans, compared with 55% of Labour identifiers, and only 32% of Alliance identifiers.

Yet on the new question the picture is very different. Here we find that Labour identifiers are more likely than Conservative identifiers to say they are very strongly or strongly in favour of their party. But most strikingly, while the attachment of SDP identifiers is indeed the weakest, that of Liberal identifiers is the strongest of any of the parties. On this measure, then, Alliance identifiers *overall* appear to be no weaker than other party identifiers in their attachment.

	% of identifiers 'very strongly' or 'strongly' in favour of their party %
Liberal	41
Labour	36
Conservative	29
SDP	25

The importance of this finding will, however, turn on what it tells us about voting behaviour. It is generally believed that strong supporters of a party are less likely than weak supporters to be electorally volatile. If this new question is tapping the affinities that produce loyalty to a party, then it would suggest that Liberal voters – so notoriously fickle towards their party in the past – may now be developing a firmer loyalty. We shall be exploring these issues further in future work, notably in the 1987 Oxford/SCPR *British General Election* survey.

By asking respondents about any negative feelings they may have towards all of the main parties, as well as about their positive feelings, our new measure enables us to examine the psychological distance between parties. How far is affinity towards one party associated with antipathy towards another? Does this vary between parties? Knowing the answers to questions such as these may help to explain the pattern of electoral movement between the parties. For example, if respondents are not actively opposed to a party, they may find it relatively easy to switch to that party.

	Party identification		
	Conservative	Labour	Liberal or SDP or Alliance
	%	%	%
'Very strongly' or 'strongly' against:			
Conservative Party	–	57	26
Labour Party	32	–	13
Liberal Party	9	7	–
SDP Party	11	8	–

Here a rather more familiar picture emerges. Very few Conservative or Labour identifiers are strongly *against* either the SDP or the Liberal Parties. The acrimony at *élite* level between the Labour Party and the SDP is not reflected in the wider electorate. Similarly, as expected, Alliance identifiers are less antagonistic towards either the Conservative or the Labour Party than are identifiers with those two parties towards each other. It may be then that the volatility of Alliance voting derives less from the weakness of their supporters' attachments *per se* than from their supporters' relative lack of antagonism towards the other main parties.

But so far as the Conservative and Labour Parties are concerned, a strong attachment to one is associated with a strong antagonism to the other. Fully 80% of those who were very strongly in favour of the Labour Party were also very strongly opposed to the Conservatives. Similarly, 50% of very strong Conservative supporters were very strongly opposed to Labour. Conversely, those only weakly in favour of either Conservatives or Labour were generally not strongly opposed to the other Party (10% and 28% respectively). This pattern may help to explain why, despite the considerable attention given to it beforehand, new tactical voting by Labour voters was not widespread in the 1987 general election. Tactical voters are most likely to be people who both strongly dislike the party against which they might vote tactically *and* who are unattached enough to their preferred party to feel able to abandon it, at least temporarily. That combination of attributes is relatively rare.

In view of the post-election tensions within the Alliance, we looked for evidence in our data of any pre-existing antagonism between supporters of the two parties. We found very little. Just four per cent of SDP identifiers and 12%

of Liberal identifiers were against the other party. In 1986 at least, the Alliance was a reasonably affable one.

Conclusion

For many politicians and political activists, winning an election is assumed to give the government a mandate to implement the policies in its manifesto. For the defeated parties, on the other hand, it is a sign of the need to re-examine their platforms. But elections are not just about policies; they are also about management. The evidence presented in this chapter reminds us that a perception that the economy is improving may well bring electoral support to a governing party even when the government's other policies are unpopular. The 1980s may be the decade of Mrs Thatcher but it has not so far been a decade of popular 'Thatcherism'.

References

BUTLER, D. and STOKES, D., *Political Change in Britain,* 2nd edn, Macmillan, London (1974).
HEATH, A., JOWELL, R. and CURTICE, J., *How Britain Votes*, Pergamon, Oxford (1985).
HEATH, A., JOWELL, R., CURTICE, J. and WITHERSPOON, S., *End of Award Report to the ESRC: Methodological Aspects of Attitude Research,* SCPR, London (1986).

8.1 PARTY IDENTIFICATION (Q2a-e)
by social class, compressed Goldthorpe class schema and housing tenure

PARTY IDENTIFICATION:	TOTAL	SOCIAL CLASS					COMPRESSED GOLDTHORPE CLASS SCHEMA+					HOUSING TENURE+		
		I/II	III non-manual	III manual	IV/V	Other	Salariat	Routine non-manual	Petty bourgeoisie	Manual foremen	Working class	Owner occupier	Rented LA/NT	Other rented
	%	%	%	%	%	%	%	%	%	%	%	%	%	%
Conservative	34	47	41	25	24	25	47	39	52	26	23	40	18	30
Labour	35	20	27	47	45	43	20	28	20	46	48	28	54	39
Alliance	17	24	19	12	15	16	23	20	14	12	14	20	11	17
Other party	2	2	1	2	2	3	1	2	3	2	1	1	2	3
Non-aligned	8	4	7	9	11	7	4	8	8	7	10	6	11	8
Weighted	*3066*	*714*	*722*	*628*	*703*	*300*	*680*	*668*	*193*	*183*	*1051*	*2077*	*741*	*239*
Unweighted	*3100*	*726*	*740*	*639*	*706*	*289*	*694*	*684*	*194*	*185*	*1062*	*2103*	*750*	*237*

BASE: ALL RESPONDENTS

8.2 PARTY IDENTIFICATION (Q2a-e)
by housing tenure and shareownership, within compressed Goldthorpe class schema

PARTY IDENTIFICATION:	TOTAL	SALARIAT			INTERMEDIATE			WORKING CLASS		
		Owner occupier	Rented LA/NT	Other rented	Owner occupier	Rented LA/NT	Other rented	Owner occupier	Rented LA/NT	Other rented
	%	%	%	%	%	%	%	%	%	%
Conservative	34	49	30	(42)	43	24	39	28	14	23
Labour	35	18	35	(24)	25	47	28	39	61	47
Alliance	17	24	16	(21)	19	12	16	16	11	13
Other party	2	1	2	(2)	2	3	4	1	1	3
Non-aligned	8	3	10	(10)	7	12	5	10	10	12
Weighted	*3066*	*572*	*60*	*(47)*	*756*	*211*	*74*	*594*	*381*	*75*
Unweighted	*3100*	*584*	*62*	*(48)*	*773*	*211*	*76*	*597*	*388*	*76*

PARTY IDENTIFICATION:	SALARIAT		INTERMEDIATE		WORKING CLASS	
	Shareowner		Shareowner		Shareowner	
	Yes	No	Yes	No	Yes	No
	%	%	%	%	%	%
Conservative	60	42	52	36	43	21
Labour	14	23	15	33	30	49
Alliance	22	24	22	16	14	14
Other party	1	2	3	2	1	1
Non-aligned	2	4	4	8	5	10
Weighted	*214*	*461*	*182*	*851*	*87*	*960*
Unweighted	*223*	*466*	*223*	*466*	*85*	*973*

BASE: ALL RESPONDENTS

8.3 CONSERVATIVE/ALLIANCE ISSUES (Qs3a, 5, 17, 57, B202a, B202b) by party identification, 1985 and 1986

| | 1985 SURVEY | | | | | 1986 SURVEY | | | | |
| | TOTAL | PARTY IDENTIFICATION[+] | | | | TOTAL | PARTY IDENTIFICATION[+] | | | |
		Conservative	Alliance	Labour	Non-aligned		Conservative	Alliance	Labour	Non-aligned
	%	%	%	%	%	%	%	%	%	%
LOCAL COUNCILS OUGHT TO BE CONTROLLED BY CENTRAL GOVERNMENT										
... more than now	14	22	13	9	15	15	22	11	11	13
... about the same amount	39	46	30	39	36	37	46	31	33	37
... less than now	34	23	47	41	23	36	23	49	44	26
BRITAIN'S INTERESTS ARE BETTER SERVED BY										
... closer links with Western Europe	48	47	59	49	31	55	48	65	62	39
... closer links with America	18	18	10	22	18	18	21	13	17	22
(both equally)	20	28	20	14	19	17	24	16	10	16
GAP BETWEEN THOSE WITH HIGH INCOMES AND THOSE WITH LOW INCOMES IS										
... too large	77	61	87	87	69	78	65	85	86	81
... about right	17	32	10	8	19	16	30	10	8	12
... too small	4	4	3	4	6	3	3	4	4	4
GOVERNMENT SHOULD										
... reduce taxes and spend less on health, etc.	6	8	3	5	8	5	5	3	5	8
... keep taxes and spending at same level as now	43	55	40	34	44	44	54	37	36	47
... increase taxes and spend more on health etc.	45	33	50	56	37	46	36	55	55	34
BASES: ALL RESPONDENTS										
Weighted	1769	545	311	645	154	3066	1035	535	1072	231
Unweighted	1804	564	317	649	159	3100	1054	542	1080	226
	%	%	%	%	%	%	%	%	%	%
ORGANISING PUBLIC MEETINGS TO PROTEST AGAINST THE GOVERNMENT SHOULD										
... definitely/probably be allowed	85	82	91	87	67	83	77	87	87	81
... probably/definitely not be allowed	11	15	5	8	20	12	18	10	7	9
PUBLISHING PAMPHLETS TO PROTEST AGAINST THE GOVERNMENT SHOULD										
... definitely/probably be allowed	81	78	88	83	69	78	70	83	86	71
... probably/definitely not be allowed	14	18	8	11	20	17	25	12	10	18
BASES: ALL RESPONDENTS (1985)										
B RESPONDENTS (1986)										
Weighted	1502	472	275	549	108	1315	451	225	468	91
Unweighted	1530	495	279	550	110	1321	452	227	471	88

8.4 CONSERVATIVE/LABOUR ISSUES (Qs6a, B202F, B226F and B222G) by party identification, 1985 and 1986

1985 SURVEY

	TOTAL	PARTY IDENTIFICATION[+]			
		Conservative	Alliance	Labour	Non-aligned
SITING OF AMERICAN NUCLEAR MISSILES IN BRITAIN MAKES BRITAIN:	%	%	%	%	%
Safer	36	59	33	21	23
Less safe	53	28	56	71	59
BASE: ALL RESPONDENTS *Weighted*	1769	545	311	645	154
Unweighted	1804	564	317	649	159
ORGANISING A NATIONWIDE STRIKE OF ALL WORKERS AGAINST THE GOVERNMENT SHOULD ...	%	%	%	%	%
... definitely/probably be allowed	28	8	26	48	23
... probably/definitely <u>not</u> be allowed	66	88	69	44	64
DO YOU THINK IT SHOULD OR SHOULD NOT BE THE GOVERNMENT'S RESPONSIBILITY TO PROVIDE A DECENT STANDARD OF LIVING FOR THE UNEMPLOYED?					
... definitely/probably should	81	70	83	90	77
... probably/definitely should not	14	23	13	5	17
DO YOU THINK IT SHOULD OR SHOULD NOT BE THE GOVERNMENT'S RESPONSIBILITY TO REDUCE INCOME DIFFERENCES BETWEEN THE RICH AND POOR?					
... definitely/probably should	69	47	73	87	66
... probably/definitely should not	24	46	22	6	21
BASES: ALL RESPONDENTS (1985) *Weighted*	1502	472	275	549	108
B RESPONDENTS (1986) *Unweighted*	1530	495	279	550	110

1986 SURVEY

	TOTAL	PARTY IDENTIFICATION[+]			
		Conservative	Alliance	Labour	Non-aligned
SITING OF AMERICAN NUCLEAR MISSILES IN BRITAIN MAKES BRITAIN:	%	%	%	%	%
Safer	29	47	23	18	18
Less safe	60	39	66	75	62
BASE: ALL RESPONDENTS *Weighted*	3066	1035	535	1072	231
Unweighted	3100	1054	542	1080	226
ORGANISING A NATIONWIDE STRIKE OF ALL WORKERS AGAINST THE GOVERNMENT SHOULD ...	%	%	%	%	%
... definitely/probably be allowed	28	10	29	46	24
... probably/definitely <u>not</u> be allowed	68	87	67	50	65
DO YOU THINK IT SHOULD OR SHOULD NOT BE THE GOVERNMENT'S RESPONSIBILITY TO PROVIDE A DECENT STANDARD OF LIVING FOR THE UNEMPLOYED?					
... definitely/probably should	83	74	85	91	76
... probably/definitely should not	13	22	12	6	18
DO YOU THINK IT SHOULD OR SHOULD NOT BE THE GOVERNMENT'S RESPONSIBILITY TO REDUCE INCOME DIFFERENCES BETWEEN THE RICH AND POOR?					
... definitely/probably should	72	53	74	88	77
... probably/definitely should not	23	41	22	8	15
BASES: ALL RESPONDENTS (1985) *Weighted*	1315	451	225	468	91
B RESPONDENTS (1986) *Unweighted*	1321	452	227	471	88

8.5 EGALITARIAN SCALE (derived from B230D, B231D, E, F, I) by social class and compressed Goldthorpe class schema

AVERAGE POSITION:	TOTAL	SOCIAL CLASS					COMPRESSED GOLDTHORPE CLASS SCHEMA[+]				
		I/II	III non-manual	III manual	IV/V	Other	Salariat	Routine non-manual	Petty bourg-eoisie	Manual foremen class	Working class
	%	%	%	%	%	%	%	%	%	%	%
Strongly egalitarian = 1 point	11	4	6	15	19	14	4	6	6	16	18
= 2 points	40	30	38	52	42	42	30	39	37	45	47
= 3 points	32	40	37	24	27	27	39	37	38	31	25
= 4 points	13	22	17	5	10	10	23	16	15	3	8
Strongly anti-egalitarian = 5 points	1	2	2	-	-	2	3	1	1	-	-
BASE: B RESPONDENTS Weighted	1315	317	318	263	293	125	298	293	85	77	439
Unweighted	1321	319	323	273	292	114	301	298	86	81	443

Appendix I
Technical details of the survey

The generosity of the Monument Trust enabled us to increase the sample size of the 1986 Social Attitudes survey. In previous years we had interviewed between 1,700 and 1,800 respondents; in 1986 we interviewed 3,100. Because of this increase in sample size we were able to cover more topics in the questionnaire, asking core questions of all 3,100 respondents and other questions of a half-sample of about 1,550 respondents each – version A of one half, version B of the other. (The structure of the questionnaire is shown diagrammatically in Appendix III.)

Sample design

The survey was designed to yield about 3,000 interviews with a representative sample of adults aged 18 or over living in private households in Britain.

For practical reasons, the sample was confined to those living in private households whose addresses were included in the electoral registers. Thus we excluded people living in institutions (though not private households at such institutions) and those living in private households whose addresses were not on the electoral register. Fieldwork was timed so that current electoral registers (those coming into effect in February 1986) could be used.

The sampling method involved a multi-stage design, with four separate stages of selection.

Selection of parliamentary constituencies

The first task was to select 151 parliamentary constituencies from among all those in England, Scotland and Wales. (In Scotland constituencies north of the Caledonian Canal were omitted for reasons of cost.)

Prior to selection, the constituencies were stratified according to information held in SCPR's constituency datafile. This datafile is a compilation of information gathered from *OPCS Monitors,* and includes a variety of social indicators such as population density, per cent Labour vote at the last general election, per cent of those holding professional qualifications, per cent of male unemployment, etc. The stratification factors used in this survey were:

1.   Registrar General's Standard Region
2.   Population density (persons per hectare): over 10
                                                                       5–10
                                                                       under 5
3.   A ranking by percentage of homes that were owner-occupied. (This was felt to give more equal strata than, for instance, the percentages of those voting Labour at the last election.)

Constituencies were then selected systematically with probability of selection proportionate to size of electorate.

After the selection of the constituencies, alternate constituencies were allotted to the A or B half of the sample. In 75 areas interviewers were allocated version A of the questionnaire; in 76 areas, they were given version B.

Selection of polling districts

Within each of the selected constituencies, a single polling district was selected, again with probability proportionate to size of electorate.

Selection of addresses

Thirty addresses were selected in each of the 151 polling districts, using electoral registers. The sample issued to interviewers was therefore $151 \times 30 = 4,530$ addresses. The selection was made from a random starting-point and, treating the list of electors as circular, a fixed interval was applied to generate the required number of addresses for each polling district. By this means addresses were chosen with probability proportionate to their number of listed electors. At each sampled address the names of all electors given on the register were listed, and the name of the individual on which the sampling interval had landed was marked with an asterisk (this person is known as the 'starred elector').

Selection of individuals

The electoral register cannot be satisfactorily taken as a sampling frame of individuals, although it is reasonably complete as a frame of addresses. Therefore a further stage of selection is needed in order to convert the listing of addresses into a sample of individuals.

Interviewers were required to call at the address of each 'starred elector', and to list all those eligible for inclusion in the sample, that is, all persons currently aged 18 or over and resident at the selected household. Where the listing revealed a difference between the register entry and the current eligible members of the household (because there had been movement in or out of the address since the register was compiled, or because some people were not registered) the interviewer selected one respondent by means of a random selection grid (a Kish grid). In households where there had been no change, the interviewer was to interview the 'starred elector'. Where there were two or more households at the selected address, interviewers were required to identify the household of the 'starred elector', or the household occupying that part of the address where he or she used to live, before following the same procedure.

Prior to analysis, the data were weighted to take account of any differences between the number of people listed on the register and those found at the address. Such differences occurred in approximately 19% of cases, in each of which the data were weighted by the number of persons aged 18 or over living at that household divided by the number of electors listed on the register for that address. The vast majority of such weights fell within a range between 0.25 and 2.0; in only eleven cases were weights greater than 2.0 applied, ranging from 2.5 to 4.0.

In the remaining 81% of cases, the number of persons listed on the register and those found at the address matched, so the effective weight was one. Thus, the unweighted sample totals 3,100, and the weighted sample, 3,066.

Fieldwork

Interviewing was carried out largely during the months of April and May 1986, with approximately 11 per cent of interviews carried out in June and July.

The interviews were conducted by 149 interviewers drawn from SCPR's regular interviewing panel, all of whom attended a one-day briefing about the questionnaires and sampling procedures. Interview length of both versions of the questionnaire averaged about 65 minutes.

The overall response achieved is shown below:

	No.	%
Addresses issued	4,530	
Vacant, derelict, out of scope	76	
In scope	4,454	100
Interview achieved	3,100	70
Interview not achieved	1,354	30
Refused	1,008	23
Non-contact	189	4
Other non-response	157	4

The response rates of the A and B versions of the questionnaires were similar, with the A version having a 70% response rate and the B version having a 69%

response rate. Further details are available on request.

There were some regional variations in achieved response. The highest levels of response were achieved in the North (78%) and East Anglia (76%) with lowest levels in the North West (67%), the South East (68%) and Greater London (59%). Regional variations in response between the two different versions of the questionnaire were sometimes more marked, but in general, regional response rates of the two versions differed by only 2%–4%. Further information is again available on request.

The 1986 self-completion supplement (like that in 1985) was longer than in the first two years of the series, owing to the inclusion of the 'international' module. Where necessary, two postal reminders were sent to obtain the supplement, and completed questionnaires were accepted until mid-July.

In 363 instances (12% of the achieved sample), the self-completion questionnaire was not returned by the respondent, and is therefore absent from the dataset. (Ninety-one per cent of the version A respondents returned a self-completion questionnaire, as did 85% of version B respondents.) Those not returning a self-completion questionnaire included a higher proportion of those aged 65 or over, of those who worked in semi-skilled or unskilled manual occupations, and of those with no party allegiance.

Since the overall proportion returning a self-completion questionnaire was high (88%), we decided against corrective weighting of the supplement.

Analysis variables

A number of standard analyses were used in the tabulation of the data. Many of these appear in the tables included in this report.

Where appropriate the definitions used in creating these analysis groups are set out below.

Region

The Registrar General's 11 Standard Regions have been used. Sometimes these have been grouped. In addition, in some analyses we distinguish metropolitan counties (including Glasgow) from other areas.

Social Class

Respondents are classified according to their own social class, not that of a putative head of household. The main social class variable used in analyses in this report is Registrar General's Social Class, although socio-economic group (SEG) is also coded.

We have classified social class according to each respondent's current or last occupation. Thus, for all respondents classified as being in paid work at the time of the interview, *or* as waiting to take up a paid job already offered, *or* as retired, *or* as seeking work, *or* as looking after the home, the occupation (present, future or last as appropriate) was classified into Occupational Unit Groups, according to the *OPCS Classification of Occupations 1980.* (This follows the practice adopted since 1985, but differs from *The 1984 Report,* in classifying those looking after the home according to their last occupation.) The combination of occupational classification with employment status generates six social classes:

I	Professional	⎫
II	Intermediate	⎬ 'Non-manual'
III (Non-manual)	Skilled occupations	⎭
III (Manual)	Skilled occupations	⎫
IV	Partly skilled occupations	⎬ 'Manual'
V	Unskilled occupations	⎭

The remaining respondents were grouped as 'never worked/not classifiable'. In some cases responses are more sensibly analysed by current social class, which classifies according to current employment status only. Where this is the case, in addition to the six social classes listed above, the remaining respondents not currently in paid work are grouped into one of the following categories: 'not classified', 'retired', looking after the home', 'unemployed' or 'others not in paid occupations'.

In some chapters, John Goldthorpe's class schema is used. This system classifies occupations by their 'general comparability', considering such factors as sources and levels of income, economic security, promotion prospects, and level of job autonomy and authority. A programme has been developed which derives the Goldthorpe classification from the 5-digit Occupational Unit Groups combined with employment status. The full Goldthorpe schema has 11 categories but the version used in this book combines these into five classes:

Salariat (professional and managerial)
Routine non-manual workers (office and sales)
Petty bourgeoisie (the self-employed inc. farmers, with and without employees)
Manual foremen and supervisors
Working class (skilled, semi-skilled and unskilled manual workers, personal service and agricultural workers)

A residual category of those who have never had a job or who have given insufficient information may also be shown.

Industry

All respondents for whom an occupation was coded were allocated a Standard Industrial Classification (SIC) code (CSO as revised 1980). Two-digit class codes were applied. Respondents with an occupation were also divided into public sector services, public sector manufacturing and transport, private sector manufacturing, and private sector non-manufacturing. This was done by cross-analysing SIC categories with responses to a question about the type of employer worked for. As with social class, SIC may be generated on the basis of current occupation only, or the most recently classifiable occupation.

Party identification

Respondents were classified as identified with a particular political party on one of three counts: if they considered themselves supporters of the party (Q.2a, b), *or* as closer to it than to others (Q.2c, d), *or* as more likely to support it in the event of a general election (Q.2e). The three groups are described respectively in both text and tables as *partisans, sympathisers* and *residual identifiers*. The three groups combined are referred to as *identifiers*. Alliance identifiers included those nominating the Social Democratic Party or the Liberal Party or the Alliance. Those who indicated no party preference were classified as *non-aligned*.

Other analysis groupings

These groupings are taken directly from the questionnaire, and to that extent are self-explanatory.

Sex (A.106a; B.114a)
Age (A.106b; B.114b)
Household income (A.118a, B.126a)
Employment status (Q.21, 22, 23)
Religion (Q.68a)
Housing tenure (A.93, B.109)
Marital status (A.105b, B.113b)
Household type (A.106a, b, c; B.114a, b, c)
Ethnic group (Q.69)

Age of completing continuous full-time education (A.108, B.116)
Highest educational qualification (A.109; B.117)
Types of school attended (A.107; B.115)
Self-assigned social class (Q.67)
Self-rated racial prejudice (Q.70e)
Trade union membership (A.112a, b; B.120a, b)

Sampling errors

No sample reflects precisely the characteristics of the population it represents because of both sampling and non-sampling errors. As far as sampling error is concerned, if a sample were designed as a simple random sample (i.e. if every adult had an equal and independent chance of inclusion in the sample) then we could calculate the sampling error of any percentage, p, using the formula:

$$\text{s.e. (p)} = \sqrt{\frac{p\,(100-p)}{n}}$$

where n is the number of respondents on which the percentage is based. Once the sampling error had been obtained, it would be a straightforward exercise to calculate a confidence interval for the true population percentage. For example, a 95% confidence interval would be given by the formula:

$$p \pm 1.96 \times \text{s.e. (p)}$$

Clearly, for a simple random sample (srs), the sampling error depends only on the values of p and n. However, simple random sampling is almost never used in practice because of its inefficiency in terms of time and cost.

As noted above, the Social Attitudes sample, like most large-scale surveys, was clustered according to a stratified multi-stage design into 151 polling districts. With a complex design like this, the sampling error of a percentage is not simply a function of the number of respondents in the sample and the size of the percentage, but also depends on how the characteristic is spread within and between polling districts. The complex design may be assessed relative to simple random sampling by calculating a range of design factors, DEFTs, associated with it, where

$$\text{DEFT} = \sqrt{\frac{\text{Variance of estimator with complex design, sample size n}}{\text{Variance of estimator with srs design, sample size n}}}$$

and represents the multiplying factor to be applied to the simple random sampling error to produce its complex equivalent. A design factor of one means that the complex sample has achieved the same precision as a simple random sample of the same size. A design factor greater than one means the complex sample is less precise than a simple random sample of equivalent size.

If the DEFT for a particular characteristic is known, a 95% confidence interval for a percentage may be calculated using the formula:

$$p \pm 1.96 \times \text{complex sampling error (p)}$$

$$= p \pm 1.96 \times \text{DEFT} \times \sqrt{\frac{p(100 - p)}{n}}$$

Estimates of sampling error for the 1986 survey were made using a different procedure from that followed previously. Instead of using the World Fertility Survey 'Clusters' program for computing sampling errors for a single year, we used estimates from previous years' calculations in order to compute sampling error estimates for this year's data. By averaging two or three previous estimates of the degree of clustering of a variable (roh), and taking account of the increased number of sampling points, sampling errors were computed clerically. The use of two or three previous estimates of the degree of clustering, instead of an estimate from a single year, may actually lead to more precise estimates of sampling error.

The table overleaf gives examples of the DEFTs and confidence intervals calculated. The majority lie in the range 1.0–1.5. In general, classification variables have DEFTs in the range 1.0–1.5 with the important exception of housing tenure, which has a high DEFT because tenure is strongly related to area. The design factors for behavioural and attitudinal variables lie in the range 1.3–1.8, and for many attitudinal variables DEFTs are at the lower end of the range. In the case of attitudinal variables, then, the fact that DEFTs are close to 1.0 means that the use of standard statistical tests of significance (based on the assumption of simple random sampling) is unlikely to be seriously misleading. For certain variables, however, particularly those strongly associated with area, care needs to be taken in the interpretation of test statistics and the estimation of parameter values.

		% (p)	Complex standard error of p (%)	DEFT	95% confidence interval
Q.2	**Party identification**				
	Conservative	33.7	1.38	1.63	31.0–36.4
	Alliance	17.4	0.86	1.26	15.7–19.1
	Labour	35.0	1.56	1.83	31.9–38.1
A.93/	**Housing tenure**				
B.109	Own	67.7	2.16	2.57	63.5–71.9
	Rented from local authority	24.2	2.04	2.65	20.2–28.2
	Rented from housing association	1.6	0.49	2.16	0.6–2.6
	Other rented	6.2	0.64	1.48	5.0–7.5
A.108/	**Age of completing full-time**				
B.116	**education**				
	16 or under	74.9	1.37	1.75	72.2–77.6
	17 or 18	13.8	0.81	1.31	12.2–15.4
	19 or over	9.3	0.77	1.49	7.8–10.8
B.88a	People should obey the law without exception	54.9	1.42	1.12	52.1–57.7
B.88b	Circumstances exist in which respondent might break law	31.0	1.70	1.44	27.7–34.3
Q.7	Britain should rid itself of nuclear weapons	28.1	1.02	1.12	26.1–30.1
Q.57	Government should increase taxes and spend more on health, education and social benefits	46.0	1.18	1.32	43.7–48.3
Q.55b	Agree strongly that many people fail to claim benefits	48.7	1.63	1.81	45.5–51.9
Q.22	Per cent of people who are self-employed	10.6	0.63	1.15	9.4–11.8

It should be noted that these calculations are based on the total sample from the 1986 survey (n = 3,100) or the total 'B' sample (n = 1,548); sampling errors for proportions based on subgroups would be larger.

Appendix II
Notes on the tabulations

1. Tables at the end of chapters are percentaged vertically; tables within the text are percentaged as indicated.

2. In *end-of-chapter* tables, a percentage of less than 0.5 is indicated by *, and – is used to denote zero. Percentages based on fewer than 50 respondents are bracketed in the tables, as are the bases.

3. When bases of fewer than 50 respondents occur in tables *within the text*, reference is made to the small base size. Zero frequencies and percentages are denoted within these tables by –, and percentages of less than 0.5 by *.

4. Percentages equal to or greater than 0.5 have been rounded up in all tables.

5. Owing to the effects of rounding weighted data, the weighted bases shown in the tables may not always add to the expected base.

6. The self-completion questionnaire was not completed by 12% of respondents (see Appendices I and III). These non-respondents have been excluded from the appropriate bases.

7. Notes on breakdowns:

   Certain respondents have been omitted from some end-of-chapter tables because of missing data or unclassifiable responses or because there were too few of them. These omissions, indicated by the symbol +, occur in the breakdowns listed below. Unweighted figures only are shown, for the total sample, and (where relevant) separately for the A and B versions of the questionnaire; respondents to the two versions of the self-completion questionnaire are shown in brackets.

Age	Total: 3
	A: – (–)
	B: 3 (3)
Compressed Goldthorpe Class Schema	Total: 53
	A: 23
	B: 30 (18)
Party identification	Total: 198 comprising 81 'don't know', 51 'other party' (including Scottish Nationalist and Plaid Cymru), 43 did not answer and 23 'other answer.'
	A: 95
	B: 103 (83)
Annual household income	Total: 362
	A: 167
	B: 295 (138)
Share ownership	Total: 24
	B: 15
Highest educational qualification obtained*	Total: 5
	A: 2 (1)
	B: 3 (1)
Economic sector (public or private)	Total: 333
	B: 172
Marital status	Total: 10
	A: 8 (8)
Religion	Total: 1
	A: (1)
Parents' social class	Total: 67
	A: 25
Household composition	Total: 20
	A: (10)
Housing tenure	Total: 10

---

* In some tables, qualifications coded as "foreign" or "other" have been omitted, rather than being included with "none".

Appendix III
The questionnaires

Two different versions of the questionnaires were used. The diagram below shows the questionnaire structure and the topics covered (not all of which are reported in this volume).

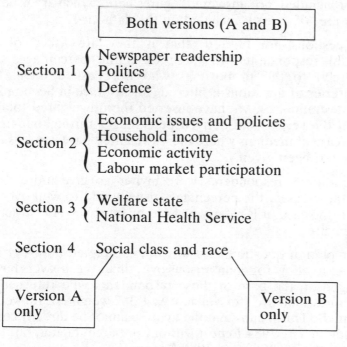

Both versions (A and B)

Section 1 { Newspaper readership
Politics
Defence

Section 2 { Economic issues and policies
Household income
Economic activity
Labour market participation

Section 3 { Welfare state
National Health Service

Section 4 Social class and race

Version A
only

Version B
only

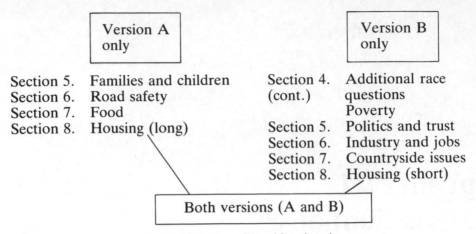

Section 9.   Classification items.

There were also two versions of the self-completion supplement, reflecting the different topics covered in the main questionnaire. The 1986 *International Social Survey* Programme (ISSP) module is in version A.

The two questionnaires (interview and self-completion) are reproduced on the following pages. We have removed the punching codes and inserted instead the percentage distribution of answers to each question. Percentages for the core questions are based on the total sample (3,066 weighted), while those for questions in version A or B are based on the appropriate subsamples (1,518 and 1,548, weighted). The pages that follow thus mirror the diagram above.

Figures do not necessarily add up to 100% because of weighting and rounding, or for one or more of the following reasons:

(i)   We have not included 'not answered' figures here, which are usually very small. They are, of course, included on the data tape.

(ii) Some subquestions are filtered, that is they are asked of only a proportion of respondents. In these cases the percentages add up (approximately) to the proportions who were asked them. Where, however, a series of questions is filtered (for instance in Section 2 of the interview questionnaire), we have inserted the unweighted total at the beginning of the series, and derived percentages throughout from that base. In the case of medians where the unweighted base was less than 50, figures have not been given.

(iii) At a few questions respondents were invited to give more than one answer. In these cases, the percentages usually add to well over 100%. Where this is the case, it is clearly marked by interviewer instructions on the questionnaire.

(iv) The self-completion questionnaire was not completed by every respondent. In order to allow for comparisons over time, the answers have been re-percentaged on the base of those respondents who returned a self-completion questionnaire (for version A: 1,387 weighted; for version B: 1,315 weighted). This means that the figures cannot be directly compared to those given in *The 1984 Report* without re-percentaging, but they are comparable with *The 1985* and *1986 Reports*.

SOCIAL AND COMMUNITY PLANNING RESEARCH

Head Office: 35 Northampton Square London EC1V 0AX Tel: 01-250 1866
Northern Field Office: Charazet House Gainford Darlington Co Durham DL2 3EG Tel: 0325 730 888

P.860

April 1986

BRITISH SOCIAL ATTITUDES:

1986 SURVEY

Serial number (202-5)

Card (206-7) 0 2

Version A = 1
B = 2 (208)

Area number

Time interview started
(24 hour clock)

- 1 -

SECTION ONE

N = 3100

1,a) Do you normally read any daily morning newspaper at least 3 times a week?

	%	Skip to
Yes	72.6	b)
No	27.4	Q.2

IF YES

b) Which one do you normally read?
IF MORE THAN ONE ASK: Which one do you read most frequently?
ONE CODE ONLY

	%
(Scottish) Daily Express	7.6
Daily Mail	8.4
Daily Mirror/Record	5.8
Daily Star	3.9
The Sun	17.1
Daily Telegraph	5.1
Financial Times	0.5
The Guardian	3.2
The Times	1.8
Today	1.1
Morning Star	0.2
Other Scottish/Welsh/regional or local daily morning paper (SPECIFY)	5.9
	0.1
Other (SPECIFY)	1.9
More than one	

ASK ALL

2,a) Generally speaking, do you think of yourself as a supporter of any one political party?

	%	Skip to
Yes	46.0	b)
No	53.1	c)

IF YES, ASK b). IF NO ASK c)
b) Which one? RECORD ANSWER BELOW AND GO TO Q.3

IF NO AT a)
c) Do you think of yourself as a little closer to one political party than to the others?

	%	
Yes	26.6	d)
No	25.3	e)

IF YES, ASK d). IF NO, ASK e)
d) Which one? RECORD ANSWER AND GO TO Q.3

IF NO AT a) AND c)
e) If there were a general election tomorrow which political party do you think you would be most likely to support?
ONE CODE ONLY

	b	d	c
Conservative	20.7	9.6	3.5
Labour	19.3	10.4	5.3
Liberal			
SDP/Social Democrat (Alliance)	5.6	5.8	6.1
Scottish Nationalist			
Plaid Cymru		1.6	
None		7.5	
Other party (SPECIFY)			
Other answer (SPECIFY)			
Don't know		4.7	

- 2 -

N = 3100

ASK ALL

3,a) Do you think that local councils ought to be controlled by central government more, less or about the same amount as now?

	%	Skip to
More	14.9	
Less	36.1	
About the same	37.2	
Don't know	11.6	

b) And do you think the level of rates should be up to the local council to decide, or should central government have the final say? RECORD IN COL b)

c) How about the level of council rents? Should that be up to the local council to decide or should central government have the final say? RECORD IN COL c)

	(b) Rates	(c) Rents
Local council	70.6	75.7
Central government	19.3	14.7
Don't know	9.1	9.2

Now a few questions about Britain's relationships with other countries.

4,a) Do you think Britain should continue to be a member of the EEC – the Common Market – or should it withdraw?

	(a) EEC	(b) NATO
Continue	61.0	75.7
Withdraw	33.1	13.0
Don't know	5.6	11.0

b) And do you think Britain should continue to be a member of NATO – the North Atlantic Treaty Organisation – or should it withdraw?

5. On the whole, do you think that Britain's interests are better served by ... READ OUT ...
... closer links with Western Europe,
or – closer links with America?

	%
... closer links with Western Europe,	55.4
or – closer links with America?	18.0
(Both equally)	16.5
(Neither)	2.6
(Don't know)	7.3

6,a) Do you think that the siting of American nuclear missiles in Britain makes Britain a safer or a less safe place to live? RECORD IN COL a)

b) And do you think that having our own independent nuclear missiles makes Britain a safer or a less safe place to live? RECORD IN COL b)

	(a) American nuclear missiles	(b) Own nuclear missiles
Safer	28.5	51.7
Less safe	59.8	37.2
No difference	3.0	2.1
Don't know	8.5	8.8

- 3 -

N = 3100

CARD A

7. Which, if either, of these two statements comes closest to your own opinion on British nuclear policy?

	%	Skip to
Britain should rid itself of nuclear weapons while persuading others to do the same	28.1	
Britain should keep its nuclear weapons until we persuade others to reduce theirs	68.7	
(Neither of these)	2.3	
Don't know	0.8	

8. Which political party's views on defence would you say comes closest to your own views?

	%	Skip to
Conservative	34.7	
Labour	24.0	
Liberal	4.5	
SDP/Social Democrat	4.5	
(Alliance)	1.7	
Other (SPECIFY) _____	0.9	
Don't know	25.7	
None	2.8	

CARD B

9. Which of the phrases on this card is closest to your opinion about threats to world peace?

	%	Skip to
America is a greater threat to world peace than Russia	16.6	
Russia is a greater threat to world peace than America	18.2	
Russia and America are equally great threats to world peace	53.9	
Neither is a threat to world peace	8.6	
(Don't know)	2.5	

10.a) Do you think the long term policy for Northern Ireland should be for it ... READ OUT ...

	%	Skip to
... to remain part of the United Kingdom,	26.5	
or - to reunify with the rest of Ireland?	56.7	
Other	8.0	
Don't know	8.3	

b) Some people think that government policy towards Northern Ireland should include a complete withdrawal of British troops. Would you personally support or oppose such a policy? Strongly or a little?

	%	Skip to
Support strongly	36.9	
Support a little	22.7	
Oppose strongly	17.4	
Oppose a little	14.6	
Other answer (SPECIFY) _____	1.9	
Withdraw in long term	1.2	
Don't know	4.8	

- 4 -

N = 3100

SECTION TWO

Now I would like to ask you about two of Britain's economic problems - inflation and unemployment.

11. First, inflation: In a year from now, do you expect prices generally to have gone up, to have stayed the same, or to have gone down?

IF GONE UP OR GONE DOWN By a lot or a little?

	%	Skip to
To have gone up by a lot	25.8	
To have gone up by a little	49.0	
To have stayed the same	17.3	
To have gone down by a little	5.8	
To have gone down by a lot	0.6	
(Don't know)	1.4	

12. Second, unemployment: In a year from now, do you expect unemployment to have gone up, to have stayed the same, or to have gone down?

IF GONE UP OR GONE DOWN By a lot or a little?

	%	Skip to
To have gone up by a lot	28.8	
To have gone up by a little	36.5	
To have stayed the same	25.0	
To have gone down by a little	6.7	
To have gone down by a lot	1.1	
(Don't know)	1.8	

13.a) If the government had to choose between keeping down inflation or keeping down unemployment, to which do you think it should give highest priority?

	%	Skip to
Keeping down inflation	20.1	
Keeping down unemployment	74.8	
Both equally	2.9	
Don't know	0.2	
Other answer (SPECIFY)	1.6	

b) Which do you think is of most concern to you and your family ... READ OUT ...

	%	Skip to
... inflation,	50.5	
or - unemployment?	44.5	
Both equally	2.0	
Neither	0.7	
Other	*	
Don't know	1.3	

14. Looking ahead over the next year, do you think Britain's general industrial performance will improve, stay much the same, or decline?

IF IMPROVE OR DECLINE By a lot or a little?

	%	Skip to
Improve a lot	3.0	
Improve a little	21.9	
Stay much the same	46.6	
Decline a little	15.9	
Decline a lot	7.0	
(Don't know)	5.5	

- 5 -

N = 3100

15. Here are a number of policies which might help Britain's economic problems. As I read them out, will you tell me whether you would support such a policy or oppose it?
READ OUT ITEMS i)-ix) AND CODE IN GRID

	Support %	Oppose %	Don't know %	Skip to
i) Control of wages by legislation %	39.5	55.6	4.6	
ii) Control of prices by legislation %	60.5	35.4	3.8	
iii) Reducing the level of Government spending on health and education %	8.6	89.8	1.4	
iv) Introducing import controls %	67.1	25.1	7.4	
v) Increasing Government subsidies for private industry %	61.0	31.2	7.2	
vi) Devaluation of the pound %	11.8	71.9	15.3	
vii) Reducing Government spending on defence %	54.9	41.0	3.6	
viii) Government incentives to encourage job sharing or splitting %	64.1	30.1	5.5	
ix) Government to set up construction projects to create more jobs %	90.6	7.0	2.1	

16. On the whole, would you like to see more or less state ownership of industry, or about the same amount as now?

	%
More	15.6
Less	30.4
About the same amount	49.4
(Don't know)	4.7

17. Thinking of income levels generally in Britain today, would you say that the gap between those with high incomes and those with low incomes is ... READ OUT ...

	%
... too large,	77.8
about right,	16.3
or - too small?	3.4
Don't know	2.2

18. CARD C
Generally, how would you describe levels of taxation in Britain today?
a) Firstly for those with high incomes? Please choose a phrase from this card. RECORD ANSWER IN COL a) BELOW
b) Next for those with middle incomes? Please choose a phrase from this card. RECORD ANSWER IN COL b) BELOW
c) And lastly for those with low incomes? Please choose a phrase from this card. RECORD ANSWER IN COL c) BELOW

Taxes are:	(a) High incomes %	(b) Middle incomes %	(c) Low incomes %
Much too high	5.2	3.8	27.7
Too high	18.0	36.4	52.9
About right	35.5	51.8	14.6
Too low	32.0	4.4	1.7
Much too low	5.4	0.3	0.6
Don't know	3.9	3.3	2.5

- 6 -

N = 3100

19.a) Among which group would you place yourself ... READ OUT ...

	%	Skip to
... high income,	2.3	
middle income,	50.7	
or - low income?	46.4	
Don't know	0.3	

b) CARD D
Which of the phrases on this card would you say comes closest to your feelings about your household's income these days?

	%
Living comfortably on present income	24.4
Coping on present income	49.4
Finding it difficult on present income	18.0
Finding it very difficult on present income	7.9
Other (SPECIFY)	0.1
Don't know	0.1

20.a) Looking back over the last year or so, would you say your household's income has ... READ OUT ...

	%
... fallen behind prices,	47.4
kept up with prices,	41.3
or - gone up by more than prices?	9.0
(Don't know)	2.1

b) And looking forward to the year ahead, do you expect your household's income will ... READ OUT ...

	%
... fall behind prices,	43.5
keep up with prices,	42.8
or - go up by more than prices?	8.9
(Don't know)	4.4

21. CARD E
Which of these descriptions applies to what you were doing last week, that is, in the seven days ending last Sunday? Any others? CODE ALL THAT APPLY IN COLUMN I
PROBE:
IF ONLY ONE CODE AT I, TRANSFER IT TO COLUMN II
IF MORE THAN ONE AT I, TRANSFER HIGHEST ON LIST TO II

	COL I	COL II ECONOMIC POSITION %	Skip to
In full-time education (not paid for by employer, including on vacation)		2.1	Q.41
On government training/employment scheme (e.g. Community Programme, Youth Training Scheme, etc)		0.6	Q.39
In paid work (or away temporarily) for at least 10 hours in the week		55.5	Q.22
Waiting to take up paid work already accepted		0.3	Q.39
Unemployed and registered at a benefit office		5.3	Q.43
Unemployed, not registered, but actively looking for a job		1.1	Q.43
Unemployed, wanting a job (of at least 10 hrs per week), but not actively looking for a job		0.9	Q.45
Permanently sick or disabled		2.3	Q.48
Wholly retired from work		14.6	Q.49
Looking after the home		17.1	Q.49
Doing something else (SPECIFY)		0.1	Q.53

FOLLOW SKIP INSTRUCTIONS TO GO TO APPROPRIATE QUESTIONS

- 7 -

N = 1718

IF IN PAID WORK OR AWAY TEMPORARILY (CODE O3 AT Q.21)

		%	Skip to
22.	In your (main) job are you ... READ OUT ...		
	... an employee,	89.4	Q-23
	or self-employed?	10.6	Q-34

ALL EMPLOYEES (CODE 1 AT Q.22) ASK Qs23-33   N = 1532

		%	
23.	How many hours a week do you normally work in your (main) job? WRITE IN: MEDIAN [39] (IF RESPONDENT CANNOT ANSWER, ASK ABOUT LAST WEEK) AND CODE:	HOURS	
	10-15 hours a week	6.5	
	16-23 hours a week	8.6	
	24-29 hours a week	3.8	
	30 or more hours a week	81.0	

		%	
24.a)	How would you describe the wages or salary you are paid for the job you do - on the low side, reasonable, or on the high side? IF 'On the low side': Very low or a bit low?		
	Very low	11.3	
	A bit low	28.9	
	Reasonable	55.1	
	On the high side	4.2	
	Other answer (SPECIFY)	0.2	
	(Don't know)	0.1	

CARD F

		%	
b)	Thinking of the highest and the lowest paid people at your place of work, how would you describe the gap between their pay, as far as you know? Please choose a phrase from this card.		
	Much too big a gap	14.2	
	Too big	24.6	
	About right	47.9	
	Too small	3.3	
	Much too small a gap	0.6	
	Other	0.3	
	(Don't know)	8.4	

		%	
25.a)	If you stay in this job would you expect your wages or salary over the coming year to ... READ OUT ...		
	... rise by more than the cost of living,	20.1	
	rise by the same as the cost of living,	44.7	
	rise by less than the cost of living,	21.9	
	or - not to rise at all?	9.6	
	(Will not stay in job)	0.9	
	(Don't know)	2.8	

		%	
b)	Over the coming year do you expect your workplace will be ... READ OUT ...		
	... increasing its number of employees,	20.5	
	reducing its number of employees,	23.3	
	stay about the same?	53.7	
	Other answer (SPECIFY)	0.1	
	Don't know	2.1	

- 8 -

N = 1532

		Col./Code	Skip to
26.a)	Thinking now about your own job. How likely or unlikely is it that you will leave this employer over the next year for any reason? Is it ... READ OUT ...		
	... very likely,	10.8	b)
	quite likely,	11.4	
	not very likely,	29.8	
	or - not at all likely?	47.7	Q-27
	Don't know	0.2	

IF VERY OR QUITE LIKELY AT a)
CARD G

b)	Why do you think you will leave? Please choose a phrase from this card or tell me what other reason there is.		

MORE THAN ONE
CODE MAY BE RINGED

	Col./Code	
Firm will close down	1.5	
I will be declared redundant	4.3	
I will reach normal retirement age	1.2	
My contract of employment will expire	0.9	
I will take early retirement	1.1	
I will decide to leave and work for another employer	9.8	
I will decide to leave and work for myself, as self-employed	2.2	
I will leave to look after home/children/relative	1.8	
Other answer (SPECIFY)	1.7	

ASK ALL EMPLOYEES

27.a)	Comparing yourself with people with the same level of education and training, would you say that your pay is ... READ OUT ...		
	... very high,	1.8	
	a little high,	10.6	
	about average,	52.7	
	a little low,	23.6	
	or - very low?	9.4	
	(Don't know)	1.7	

b)	And still comparing yourself with people with the same level of education and training, what would you say about the level of your job, that is, how quickly do you think you've got ahead ... READ OUT ...		
	... very quickly,	7.6	
	quite quickly,	20.7	
	about average,	48.8	
	not very quickly,	10.9	
	or - not at all quickly?	7.0	
	(Don't know)	4.0	

c)	And now thinking of people in similarly demanding jobs to yours, would you say that your pay is ... READ OUT ...		
	... very high,	0.7	
	a little high,	8.1	
	about average,	52.7	
	a little low,	27.1	
	or - very low?	9.5	
	(Don't know)	1.6	

- 9 -

28.a) ASK ALL EMPLOYEES [N = 1532]

Suppose you lost your job for one reason or another, would you start looking for another job, would you wait for several months or longer before you started looking, or would you decide <u>not</u> to look for another job?

	%	Skip to
Start looking	87.2	b)
Wait several months or longer	4.7	} 7.2 Q.29
Decide not to look	7.2	
Don't know	0.7	

IF START LOOKING

b) How long do you think it would take you to find an acceptable replacement job?   MEDIAN   MONTHS `0` `3` OR YEARS

	%
Never	3.9
Don't know	16.4

* **IF 3 MONTHS OR MORE, NEVER, OR DK, ASK c)- e). OTHERS GO TO Q.29.**

c) How willing do you think you would be in these circumstances to retrain for a different job ... READ OUT ...

	%
... very willing,	24.7
quite willing,	14.7
or - not very willing?	7.6
(Don't know)	0.6

d) And how willing do you think you would be to move to a different area to find an acceptable job ... READ OUT ...

	%
... very willing,	6.6
quite willing,	8.6
or - not very willing?	31.5
(Don't know)	0.9

e) And how willing do you think you would be in these circumstances to take what you now consider to be an unacceptable job ... READ OUT ...

	%
... very willing,	6.2
quite willing,	17.2
or - not very willing?	22.5
(Don't know)	1.7

29. ASK ALL EMPLOYEES

If without having to work, you had what you would regard as a reasonable living income, do you think you would still prefer to have a paid job or wouldn't you bother?

	%
Still prefer paid job	72.1
Wouldn't bother	25.9
Other answer (SPECIFY)	1.1
Don't know	0.7

30.a) During the last five years (that is since March 1981) have you been unemployed and seeking work for any period?

	%	Skip to
Yes	20.0	b)
No	79.8	Q.31

IF YES

b) For how many months in total during the last five years?   MEDIAN   MONTHS `0` `6` OR YEARS

* Filter condition changed from previous years.

- 10 -

31.a) ASK ALL EMPLOYEES [N = 1532]

For any period during the last five years have you worked as a self-employed person as your main job?

	%	Skip to
Yes	3.2	b)
No	96.7	c)

IF YES, ASK b). IF NO, ASK c)

b) In total, for how many months during the last five years have you been self-employed?   MEDIAN   MONTHS OR YEARS

NOW SKIP TO Q.32   Q.32

IF NO AT a)

c) How seriously in the last five years have you considered working as a self-employed person ... READ OUT ...

	%	Skip to
... very seriously,	6.0	d)&e)
quite seriously,	9.2	d)&e)
not very seriously,	13.7	Q.32
or - not at all seriously?	67.5	Q.32

IF VERY OR QUITE SERIOUSLY, ASK d) & e)

d) What were the main reasons you did not become self-employed? PROBE FULLY. RECORD VERBATIM.

	%
Cost/Lack of capital/Money	7.3
Risk	4.9
Recession/economic climate	.3
Other answer	4.7
Don't know	0.1

e) How likely or unlikely is it that you will work as a self-employed person as your main job in the next five years ... READ OUT ...

	%
... very likely,	1.5
quite likely,	4.6
not very likely,	5.3
or - not at all likely?	3.3
(Don't know)	0.5

32.a) ASK ALL EMPLOYEES

At your place of work are there unions, staff associations, or groups of unions recognised by the management for negotiating pay and conditions of employment?

	%
Yes	61.6
No	37.3
Don't know	0.9

IF YES

b) On the whole, do you think these unions or staff associations do their job well or not?

	%
Yes	37.3
No	22.3
Don't know	1.7

33.a) ASK ALL EMPLOYEES

In general how would you describe relations between management and other employees at your workplace ... READ OUT ...

	%
... very good,	33.5
quite good,	46.7
not very good,	13.9
or - not at all good?	4.9
Don't know	0.4

b) And in general, would you say your workplace was ... READ OUT ...

	%
... very well managed,	26.8
quite well managed,	51.5
or - not well managed?	20.4
Don't know	0.4

NOW GO TO SECTION 3 (p.18) - GREEN STRIPE

- 11 -

34.a) ALL SELF-EMPLOYED (CODE 2 AT Q.22): ASK Qs 34-38   N = 186

ROUND TO NEAREST HOUR   MEDIAN [5][0]

How many hours a week do you normally work in your (main) job?

(IF RESPONDENT CANNOT ANSWER, ASK ABOUT LAST WEEK)

	%	Skip to
	HOURS	
AND CODE: 10-15 hours a week	5.3	
16-23 hours a week	3.6	
24-29 hours a week	3.1	
30 or more hours a week	88.0	

b) During the last 5 years (that is since March 1981) have you been unemployed and seeking work for any period?

	%	Skip to
Yes	15.2	c)
No	34.5	Q.35

IF YES

c) For how many months in total during the last 5 years?

MONTHS [ ] OR YEARS [ ]

35. ALL SELF-EMPLOYED

If without having to work, you had what you would regard as a reasonable living income, do you think you would still prefer to do paid work, or wouldn't you bother?

	%	Skip to
still prefer paid work	75.2	
Wouldn't bother	22.6	
Don't know	0.6	
Other answer (SPECIFY)	1.1	

36.a) Have you, for any period in the last five years, worked as an employee as your main job rather than as self-employed?

	%	Skip to
Yes	31.9	b)
No	68.1	c)

IF YES, ASK b). IF NO, ASK c)

b) In total for how many months during the last five years have you been an employee?

MEDIAN [2][4] MONTHS OR YEARS [ ]

NOW SKIP TO Q.37   Q.37

IF NO AT a)

c) How seriously in the last five years have you considered getting a job as an employee ... READ OUT ...

	%	Skip to
... very seriously,	3.9	
quite seriously,	7.2	
not very seriously,	5.8	
or - not at all seriously?	51.3	

- 12 -

37.a) ASK ALL SELF-EMPLOYED   N = 186

Compared with a year ago, would you say your business is doing ... READ OUT ...

	%	Skip to
... very well,	11.1	
quite well,	27.3	
about the same,	41.8	
not very well,	9.6	
or - not at all well?	3.8	
(Business not in existence then)	6.4	

b) And over the coming year, do you think your business will do ... READ OUT ...

	%	Skip to
... better,	36.1	
about the same,	49.8	
or - worse than this year?	5.4	
(Don't know)	2.0	
Other (SPECIFY)	5.9	

38.a) Comparing yourself with people with the same level of education and training, would you say that your pay is ... READ OUT ...

	%	Skip to
... very high,	4.1	
a little high,	18.6	
about average,	49.2	
a little low,	19.7	
or - very low?	5.3	
(Don't know)	3.0	

b) And still comparing yourself with people with the same level of education and training, what would you say about the level of your job, that is, how quickly do you think you've got ahead ... READ OUT ...

	%	Skip to
... very quickly,	12.0	
quite quickly,	27.8	
about average,	44.6	
not very quickly,	7.3	
or - not at all quickly?	1.8	
(Don't know)	6.5	

c) And now thinking of people in similarly demanding jobs to yours, would you say that your pay is ... READ OUT ...

	%	Skip to
... very high,	1.1	
a little high,	4.1	
about average,	69.9	Q.53
a little low,	16.2	
or - very low?	6.0	
(Don't know)	2.7	

NOW GO TO SECTION 3 (p.18) - GREEN STRIPE

- 13 -

ALL ON GOVERNMENT SCHEMES OR WAITING TO TAKE UP PAID WORK (CODES 02 OR 04 AT Q.21): ASK Qs 39-40

N = 27

		%	Skip to
39.a)	During the last five years (that is since March 1981) have you been unemployed and seeking work for any period?		
	Yes		b)
	No		Q.40
	IF YES ASK b)		
	b) For how many months in total during the last five years?		
	MONTHS [ ] OR YEARS [ ]		

40. ASK ALL ON GOVERNMENT SCHEMES OR WAITING TO TAKE UP PAID WORK

If without having to work, you had what you would regard as a reasonable living income, do you think you would still prefer to have a paid job or wouldn't you bother?

	%	Skip to
Still prefer paid job		
Wouldn't bother		
Other answer (SPECIFY)		Q.53
Don't know		

NOW GO TO SECTION 3 (p.18) - GREEN STRIPE

ALL IN FULL-TIME EDUCATION (CODE 01 AT Q.21): ASK Qs 41-42

N = 58

		%	Skip to
41.a)	When you leave full-time education, do you think you will start looking for a job, will you wait several months or longer before you start looking, or will you decide not to look for a job?		
	Start looking	68.2	b)
	Wait several months or longer	6.6	
	Decide not to look	18.6	Q.42
	Don't know	4.3	
	Other answer (SPECIFY)		

IF START LOOKING ASK b). OTHERS GO TO Q.42.

	%	Skip to
b) How long do you think it will take you to find an acceptable job?		
MONTHS [ ] OR YEARS [ ]		
Never		
Don't know	10.2	

IF 3 MONTHS OR MORE, NEVER OR D.K. ASK c). OTHERS GO Q.42.

	%
c) How willing do you think you would be in these circumstances to take what you now consider to be an unacceptable job? ... READ OUT ...	
... very willing,	
quite willing,	19.6
or - not very willing?	22.4
(Don't know)	
Other answer (SPECIFY)	

42. ASK ALL IN FULL-TIME EDUCATION

If without having to work, you had what you would regard as a reasonable living income, do you think you would prefer to have a paid job, or wouldn't you bother?

	%	Skip to
Prefer paid job	84.3	
Wouldn't bother	15.7	
Other answer (SPECIFY)	-	Q.53
Don't know	-	

NOW GO TO SECTION 3 (p.18) - GREEN STRIPE

- 14 -

N = 195

ALL UNEMPLOYED AND LOOKING FOR JOB - (CODES 05 AND 06 AT Q.21): ASK Qs 43-44

		%	Skip to
43.a)	In total how many months in the last five years (that is, since March 1981) have you been unemployed and seeking work?		
	MEDIAN [2][4] MONTHS OR YEARS [ ]		
b)	How long has this present period of unemployment and seeking work lasted so far?		
	MEDIAN [1][2] MONTHS OR YEARS [ ]		
c)	How confident are you that you will find a job to match your qualifications ... READ OUT ...		
	... very confident,	3.9	
	quite confident,	29.3	
	not very confident,	26.8	
	or - not at all confident?	38.6	
d)	Although it may be difficult to judge, how long from now do you think it will be before you find an acceptable job?		
	MEDIAN [2][4] MONTHS OR YEARS [ ]		
	Never	20.0	
	Don't know	24.7	

IF 3 MONTHS OR MORE, NEVER, OR D.K. (ASK e)- g). OTHERS GO TO Q.44

	%
e) How willing do you think you would be in these circumstances to retrain for a different job ... READ OUT ...	
... very willing,	32.8
quite willing,	26.8
or - not very willing?	19.1
(Don't know)	-
f) How willing would you be to move to a different area to find an acceptable job ... READ OUT ...	
... very willing,	13.6
quite willing,	14.2
or - not very willing?	51.0
(Don't know)	-
g) And how willing do you think you would be in these circumstances to take what you now consider to be an unacceptable job ... READ OUT ...	
... very willing,	9.2
quite willing,	23.5
or - not very willing?	43.1
(Don't know)	2.9

ASK ALL UNEMPLOYED AND LOOKING FOR JOB

		%	Skip to
44.	If without having to work, you had what you would regard as a reasonable living income, do you think you would still prefer to have a paid job or wouldn't you bother?		
	still prefer paid job	77.5	
	Wouldn't bother	19.7	Q.53
	Don't know	0.9	
		0.5	
	Other answer (SPECIFY)		

NOW GO TO SECTION 3 (p.18) - GREEN STRIPE

* Filter condition changed from previous year.

- 15 -

N = 30

ALL WHO ARE UNEMPLOYED BUT NOT ACTIVELY LOOKING FOR A JOB (CODE 07 AT Q.21): ASK Qs 45-47

		Skip to
45.a)	In total how many months in the last five years (that is, since March 1981) have you been unemployed and seeking work? WRITE IN MONTHS [ ] OR YEARS [ ]	
b)	How long has this present period of unemployment lasted so far? WRITE IN MONTHS [ ] OR YEARS [ ]	
c)	You said you were unemployed but not actively looking for a job. Could you say why not? PROBE FULLY FOR MAIN REASON. RECORD VERBATIM	
46.a)	Although it may be difficult to judge, how long from now do you think it will be before you find an acceptable job? WRITE IN MONTHS [ ] OR YEARS [ ] — Never — Don't know	

IF 3 MONTHS OR MORE, NEVER, OR D.K. ASK b)-d). OTHERS GO TO Q.47

b)	How willing do you think you would be in these circumstances to retrain for a different job ... READ OUT ...	... very willing, quite willing, or - not very willing? (Don't know)
c)	How willing would you be to move to a different area to find an acceptable job ... READ OUT ...	... very willing, quite willing, or - not very willing? (Don't know)
d)	And how willing do you think you would be in these circumstances to take what you now consider to be an unacceptable job ... READ OUT ...	... very willing, quite willing, or - not very willing? (Don't know)

ASK ALL UNEMPLOYED BUT NOT ACTIVELY LOOKING FOR A JOB

		Skip to
47.	If without having to work, you had what you would regard as a reasonable living income, do you think you would still prefer to have a paid job or wouldn't you bother?	still prefer paid job — Wouldn't bother } Q.53 — Other answer (SPECIFY) _____ — Don't know

NOW GO TO SECTION 3 (p.18) - GREEN STRIPE

- 16 -

N = 462

ALL WHOLLY RETIRED FROM WORK (CODE 09 AT Q.21): ASK Q.48

			%	Skip to
48.a)	Do you (or does your husband/wife) receive a pension from any past employer?	Yes	58.3	
		No	41.4	c)
b)	(Can I just check) are you over 65 (men)/60 (women)?	Yes	90.7	
		No	9.1	e)
	IF YES ASK c) AND d). IF NO GO TO e)			
c)	On the whole would you say the present state pension is on the low side, reasonable, or on the high side? IF 'On the low side': Very low or a bit low?	Very low	35.6	
		A bit low	31.0	
		Reasonable	22.9	
		On the high side	-	
d)	Do you expect your state pension in a year's time to purchase more than it does now, less, or about the same?	More	3.5	
		Less	52.6	Q.53
		About the same	31.4	
		Don't know	2.7	
	IF NO AT b)			
e)	At what age did you retire from work?	MEDIAN 5 8 YEARS		
		Never worked	-	

NOW GO TO SECTION 3 (p.18) - GREEN STRIPE

ALL LOOKING AFTER HOME (CODE 10 AT Q.21): ASK Qs 49-52

N = 534

			%	Skip to
49.a)	Do you currently have a paid job of less than 10 hours a week? INCLUDE THOSE TEMPORARILY AWAY FROM A PAID JOB OF LESS THAN 10 HOURS A WEEK	Yes	11.3	Q.50
		No	87.7	b)
	IF NO AT a)			
b)	What are the main reasons you do not have a paid job outside the home? PROBE FULLY FOR MAIN REASONS AND RECORD VERBATIM			
	Raising children		31.5	
	Retired/too old		21.0	
	Prefer looking after home/family		17.6	
	No jobs available		3.4	
	Unsuited for jobs		1.7	
	Wives shouldn't work		2.9	
	Husband agin working		1.4	
	Voluntary worker		2.7	
	Pregnant/ill health		2.8	
	Dependent relative		5.7	
	Poverty trap		4.6	
	Unpaid work/family business		1.9	
	Childcare costs		0.1	
	Other		4.3	

- 17 -

50.a) ASK ALL LOOKING AFTER THE HOME | N = 534 |

Have you, during the last five years, ever had a full or part-time job of 10 hours per week or more?

	%	Skip to
Yes	26.0	b)
No	73.2	Q.51

IF YES

b) How long ago was it that you left that job?

NO. OF MONTHS AGO   OR   NO. OF YEARS AGO

MEDIAN | 2 | 4 |

NOW GO TO Q.52   Q.52

51.a) IF NO AT Q.50a)

How seriously in the past five years have you considered getting a full-time job?

... READ OUT ...

PROMPT, IF NECESSARY: FULL TIME IS 30 HRS + PER WEEK

	%	Skip to
... very seriously,	2.8	Q.52
quite seriously,	1.3	Q.52
not very seriously,	4.9	b)
or - not at all seriously?	63.4	b)

IF NOT VERY OR NOT AT ALL SERIOUSLY ASK b)

b) How seriously, in the past five years, have you considered getting a part-time job?
... READ OUT ...

	%
... very seriously,	1.9
quite seriously,	3.7
not very seriously,	7.3
or - not at all seriously?	54.9

52. ASK ALL LOOKING AFTER THE HOME

Do you think you are likely to look for a paid job in the next 5 years?

IF YES: Full-time or part-time?

	%
Yes - full-time	7.2
Yes - part-time	26.5
No	60.7
Other (SPECIFY) _____	0.7
Don't know	3.6

| NOW GO TO SECTION 3 (p.18) - GREEN STRIPE |

- 18 -

SECTION THREE

| N = 3100 |

ASK ALL

CARD H

53. Here are some items of government spending. Which of them, if any, would be your highest priority for extra spending? And which next? Please read through the whole list before deciding.

ONE CODE ONLY IN EACH COL.

	1st Priority %	2nd Priority %
Education	27.0	29.9
Defence	1.1	2.6
Health	47.2	27.5
Housing	7.0	13.8
Public transport	0.4	1.7
Roads	1.2	2.1
Police and prisons	2.6	5.0
Social security benefits	4.5	6.9
Help for industry	8.0	8.4
Overseas aid	0.5	0.9
(NONE OF THESE)	0.2	0.8
(Don't know)	0.3	0.1

CARD I

54. Thinking now only of the government's spending on social benefits like those on the card. Which, if any, of these would be your highest priority for extra spending? And which next?

ONE CODE ONLY IN EACH COL.

	1st Priority %	2nd Priority %
Retirement pensions	40.4	24.2
Child benefits	10.5	12.5
Benefits for the unemployed	16.0	16.8
Benefits for disabled people	25.0	33.0
Benefits for single parents	6.8	11.1
(NONE OF THESE)	0.4	0.7
(Don't know)	0.9	1.6

55. I will read two statements. For each one please say whether you agree or disagree? strongly or slightly?

ONE CODE ONLY IN EACH COL.

a) Large numbers of people these days falsely claim benefits.

b) Large numbers of people who are eligible for benefits these days fail to claim them.

	(a) Falsely claim %	(b) Fail to claim %
Agree strongly	44.8	48.7
Agree slightly	25.4	33.6
Disagree slightly	11.0	8.0
Disagree strongly	10.1	3.2
(Don't know)	8.6	6.5

- 19 -

N = 3100

56. Opinions differ about the level of benefits for the unemployed. Which of these two statements comes closest to your own ... READ OUT ...

	%	Skip to
OR ... benefits for the unemployed are too low and cause hardship,	44.2	
OR - benefits for the unemployed are too high and discourage people from finding jobs?	33.4	
(Neither)	6.1	
Both, because wages are low	1.1	
Both, it varies	7.5	
About right	1.6	
Don't know	4.8	

CARD J

57. Suppose the government had to choose between the three options on this card. Which do you think it should choose?

Reduce taxes and spend less on health, education and social benefits	4.8	
Keep taxes and spending on these services at the same level as now	43.6	
Increase taxes and spend more on health, education and social benefits	46.0	
(None)	3.4	
(Don't know)	2.1	

CARD K

58. All in all, how satisfied or dissatisfied would you say you are with the way in which the National Health Service runs nowadays? Choose a phrase from this card.

Very satisfied	6.4	
Quite satisfied	34.0	
Neither satisfied nor dissatisfied	19.3	
Quite dissatisfied	23.3	
Very dissatisfied	16.5	

- 20 -

N = 3100

CARD K AGAIN

59. From your own experience, or from what you have heard, please say how satisfied or dissatisfied you are with the way in which each of these parts of the National Health Service runs nowadays?
READ OUT i-vi BELOW AND RING ONE CODE FOR EACH

	Very satisfied	Quite satisfied	Neither satisfied nor dis-satisfied	Quite dis-satisfied	Very dis-satisfied	Col./Code Don't know	Skip to
i) First, local doctors/GPs?	% 26.7	50.7	8.3	9.6	4.4	0.3	
ii) National Health Service dentists?	% 19.1	54.9	13.7	6.5	3.0	2.7	
iii) Health visitors?	% 12.3	36.9	28.8	6.3	2.2	13.5	
iv) District nurses?	% 18.6	40.5	25.3	2.5	0.6	12.3	
v) Being in hospital as an inpatient?	% 24.9	42.3	15.2	10.1	3.2	4.3	
vi) Attending hospital as an outpatient?	% 13.9	40.8	14.0	18.7	10.0	2.6	

60.a) Are you covered by a private health insurance scheme, that is an insurance scheme that allows you to get private medical treatment?

Yes	13.9	b)
No	86.0	Q-61
Don't know	0.1	

IF YES

b) Does your employer (or your husband's/wife's employer) pay the majority of the cost of membership of this scheme?

Yes	7.2	
No	6.0	
Don't know	0.3	

ASK ALL

61.a) Do you think that the existence of private medical treatment in National Health Service hospitals is a good or bad thing for the National Health Service, or doesn't it make any difference to the NHS?

Good thing	26.7	
Bad thing	39.8	
No difference	28.2	
Don't know	5.1	

b) And do you think the existence of private medical treatment in private hospitals is a good thing or bad thing for the National Health Service, or doesn't it make any difference to the NHS?

Good thing	37.1	
Bad thing	18.5	
No difference	40.0	
Don't know	4.3	

- 21 -

CARD L [N = 3100]

62. Which of the views on this card comes closest to your own views about private medical treatment in hospitals?

	%	Skip to
Private medical treatment in all hospitals should be abolished	10.9	
Private medical treatment should be allowed in private hospitals, but not in National Health Service hospitals	46.3	
Private medical treatment should be allowed in both private and National Health Service hospitals	40.8	
(Don't know)	1.8	

Now thinking of GPs and dentists.

	Should	Should not	Don't know
63.a) Do you think that National Health Service GPs should or should not be free to take on private patients?	57.3	38.3	4.0
b) And do you think that National Health Service dentists should or should not be free to give private treatment?	62.0	33.1	4.6

64. It has been suggested that the National Health Service should be available only to those with lower incomes. This would mean that contributions and taxes could be lower and most people would then take out medical insurance or pay for health care. Do you support or oppose this idea?

	%
Support	26.9
Oppose	67.3
(Don't know)	5.8

65.a) And, generally speaking, what is your opinion about private schools in Britain? Should there be ... READ OUT ...

	%
... more private schools,	13.4
about the same number as now,	63.8
fewer private schools,	9.1
or - no private schools at all?	10.3
Other answer (SPECIFY)	1.1
Don't know	2.3

b) If there were fewer private schools in Britain today do you think, on the whole, that state schools would ... READ OUT ...

	%
... benefit,	19.2
suffer,	15.7
or - would it make no difference?	60.2
(Don't know)	4.7

- 22 -

SECTION FOUR

[N = 3100]

Now moving on to the subject of social class in Britain.

66.a) To what extent do you think a person's social class affects his or her opportunities in Britain today ... READ OUT ...

	%	Skip to
... a great deal,	24.0	
quite a lot,	39.5	
not very much,	28.3	
or - not at all?	5.5	
Don't know	0.4	
Other answer (SPECIFY)	2.3	

b) Do you think social class is more or less important now in affecting a person's opportunities than it was 10 years ago, or has there been no real change?

	%
More important now	24.2
Less important now	29.5
No change	43.7
Don't know	2.5

c) Do you think that in 10 years time social class will be more or less important than it is now in affecting a person's opportunities, or will there be no real change?

	%
More important in 10 years time	20.7
Less important in 10 years time	26.4
No change	48.4
Don't know	4.3

CARD M

67.a) Most people see themselves as belonging to a particular social class. Please look at this card and tell me which social class you would say you belong to? RECORD ANSWER IN COL (a)

b) And which social class would you say your parents belonged to when you started at primary school? RECORD ANSWER IN COL (b)

	(a) Self %	(b) Parents %
Upper middle	1.2	1.8
Middle	24.4	16.6
Upper working	20.8	12.2
Working	47.8	58.9
Poor	3.2	8.2
(Don't know)	2.0	1.9

– 24 –

Skip to

ASK ALL   N = 3100

Now I would like to ask you some questions about racial prejudice in Britain.

70.a) First, thinking of Asians - that is, people whose families were originally from India and Pakistan - who now live in Britain. Do you think there is a lot of prejudice against them in Britain nowadays, a little or hardly any?   RECORD IN COL (a)

b) And black people - that is people whose families were originally from the West Indies or Africa - who now live in Britain. Do you think there is a lot of prejudice against them in Britain nowadays, a little, or hardly any?   RECORD IN COL (b)

	(a) Asians %	(b) Blacks %
A lot	61.3	55.4
A little	30.2	34.7
Hardly any	5.6	6.6
Don't know	2.7	3.0

c) Do you think there is generally more racial prejudice in Britain now than there was 5 years ago, less, or about the same amount?

	%
More now	48.6
Less now	12.4
About the same	35.9
Don't know	0.5
Other answer (SPECIFY)	2.2

d) Do you think there will be more, less or about the same amount of racial prejudice in Britain in 5 years time compared with now?

	%
More in 5 years	46.3
Less	13.1
About the same	35.6
Don't know	1.2
Other answer (SPECIFY)	3.7

e) How would you describe yourself:
... READ OUT ...

	%	Skip to
... as very prejudiced against people of other races,	3.7	} f)
a little prejudiced,	31.9	}
or - not prejudiced at all?	63.4	} Q.71
Don't know	0.6	
Other answer (SPECIFY)	0.1	

IF 'VERY' OR ' A LITTLE' PREJUDICED

f) Against any race in particular?   PROBE FOR RACES AND RECORD.
IF 'BLACK' OR 'COLOURED' MENTIONED, PROBE FOR WHETHER WEST INDIAN, ASIAN, GENERAL, ETC.   RECORD VERBATIM EVERYTHING MENTIONED

– 23 –

N = 3100

68.a) Do you regard yourself as belonging to any particular religion?
IF YES: Which?   IF 'Christian' PROBE FOR DENOMINATION

ONE CODE ONLY

	%	Skip to
No religion	33.9	Q.69
Christian - no denomination	2.8	
Roman Catholic	10.2	
Church of England/Anglican	37.1	
CHRISTIAN DENOMINATIONS: United Reform Church (URC)/Congregational	1.4	
Baptist	1.7	
Methodist	3.3	
Presbyterian/Church of Scotland	4.4	
Other Christian (SPECIFY)	2.2	b)
OTHER RELIGIONS: Hindu	0.8	
Jew	0.4	
Islam/Muslim	1.0	
Sikh	0.2	
Buddhist	0.2	
Other non-Christian (SPECIFY)	0.2	
Don't know	*	

IF RELIGION ENTERED AT a) ASK b).   OTHERS SKIP TO Q.69

b) Apart from such special occasions as weddings, funerals and baptisms, how often nowadays do you attend services or meetings connected with your religion?

PROBE AS NECESSARY

	%
Once a week or more	12.5
Less often but at least once in two weeks	2.5
Less often but at least once a month	5.4
Less often but at least twice a year	10.2
Less often but at least once a year	5.2
Less often	4.5
Never or practically never	24.8
Varies	0.5

69. INTERVIEWER: CODE FROM OBSERVATION FOR ALL RESPONDENTS

	%
White/European	95.6
Indian/East African Asian/Pakistani/Bangladeshi/Sri Lankan	2.1
Black/African/West Indian	1.6
Other (inc. Chinese)	0.5

- 25A -

SECTION FIVE

ASK ALL N = 1552

Now I'd like to ask you a few questions about families and children.

71.a) What would you say is the ideal number of children for a couple to have these days?

MEDIAN [U][2]

DO NOT PROMPT OR CODE:

	%	Skip to
There is no ideal/depends on couple	8.5	
(Don't know)	1.6	

b) Who do you think should decide how many children to have? Should it be ... READ OUT ...

	%	
... the father,	0.7	
the mother,	4.4	
a joint decision,	89.7	
or - left to nature?	4.1	
(Don't know)	0.6	

CARD N

72. Which of the statements on this card best describes your views?

	%	
Parents' duty is to do their best for their children, even at the expense of their own well-being	83.8	
Parents have a life of their own and should not be asked to sacrifice their own well-being for the sake of their children	10.8	
(Neither)	4.4	
Other answer (SPECIFY)	0.8	
Don't know	0.2	

73.a) Have you had, or do you have, any responsibility for bringing up a child?

PROBE FOR CORRECT PRECODE

	%	Skip to
Yes, used to	36.6	c)
Yes, now	38.6	b)
No	24.8	Q.75

IF 'YES, NOW' (CODE 2 AT a)

b) Are any of these children over 10 years old, and now living as part of your household?

	%	Skip to
Yes	23.9	} c)
No	14.4	}
Don't know	–	

INTERVIEWER: CHANGE WORDING OF (BRACKETED) PHRASE IN c) AS APPROPRIATE, USING PHRASE IN ITALICS IF CHILDREN OVER 1O IN HOUSEHOLD NOW

CARD O

c) Suppose there is/(was) a big decision being made, say, over going on holiday, or having someone come to live in your household for a while.

Please look at this card and tell me what you think (should happen)/(used to happen)/(usually happens) in your household?

	%	
The parent(s) decide and tell the child(ren) afterwards	19.1	
The parent(s) decide after discussing it with the child(ren)	20.8	
Everyone discusses it and the family decides together	33.0	
The children have the final say	0.5	
Depends on age of children	0.7	
(Don't know)	0.2	
Other answer (SPECIFY)	0.4	

- 26A -

N = 1552

IF EVER RESPONSIBLE FOR BRINGING UP A CHILD (CODE 1 OR 2 AT Q.73a)

CARD P

74. Compare the way you (brought)/(bring) up your own children with the way your parents brought you up. Who would be more likely to ... READ OUT ...

	I WITH MY CHILDREN	MY PARENTS WITH ME	NO DIFFER-ENCE	(DON'T KNOW)
... allow the child privacy, or is there no difference?	% 32.8	1.9	38.9	1.1
... let the child have a say in decisions?	% 49.9	1.1	22.7	0.9
... show affection towards the child?	% 29.5	1.2	43.4	0.6
... take a strong line on behaviour?	% 18.0	23.3	32.7	0.4
... show interest in the child's activities?	% 41.3	1.4	31.6	0.3
... allow the child to express him- or herself freely?	% 48.7	0.7	24.9	0.3
... treat the child as a friend?	% 41.8	1.4	30.6	6.7

ASK ALL

CARD Q

75.a) Thinking back to how you were brought up, do you remember how hard your parents tried to get you to share their own ... READ OUT ...

	VERY HARD	QUITE HARD	NOT VERY HARD	NOT AT ALL	(NEVER TALKED ABOUT)	(DON'T REMEM-BER)
... religious beliefs?	% 11.8	15.7	34.1	36.2	1.0	0.8
... views about sexual behaviour?	% 6.9	10.3	16.9	29.8	34.5	0.9
... attitudes towards right and wrong?	% 47.7	39.3	8.1	2.7	0.8	1.0
... political point of view?	% 3.3	7.1	25.6	52.4	9.6	1.4

IF EVER RESPONSIBLE FOR BRINGING UP A CHILD (CODE 1 OR 2 AT Q.73a). OTHERS GO TO Q.76
(CHANGE TENSES AS APPROPRIATE).

CARD Q AGAIN

b) And how hard (did)/(do)/(will) you try to get your children to share your own ... READ OUT ...

	VERY HARD	QUITE HARD	NOT VERY HARD	NOT AT ALL	(NEVER TALKED ABOUT)	(DON'T REMEM-BER)
... religious beliefs?	% 3.6	10.8	28.6	31.1	0.6	0.1
... views about sexual behaviour?	% 9.0	26.1	19.8	12.5	7.0	0.3
... attitudes towards right and wrong?	% 38.6	30.2	4.1	1.4	0.3	0.1
... political point of view?	% 1.8	4.6	19.3	46.1	2.9	0.1

- 28A -

N = 1552

INTERVIEWER: CHECK MARITAL STATUS

	%	Skip to
78,a) Can I just check are you currently married or living as married?		
Yes	71.5	b)
No	28.5	Q.79

IF CURRENTLY MARRIED/LIVING AS MARRIED
CARD T

b) How do you and your partner organise the money that comes into your household? Please choose the phrase on this card that comes closest.

	%	Skip to
I manage all the money and give my partner his/her share	12.5	
My partner manages all the money and gives me my share	11.1	
We pool all the money and each take out what we need	36.3	
We pool some of the money and keep the rest separate	7.0	c)
We each keep our own money separate	3.8	
	0.4	
Other answer (SPECIFY)	0.1	Q.79

IF ANY METHOD NAMED AT b (CODES 01-97)

c) Do you remember how your parents organised the money that came into their household? Was it ... READ OUT ...

	%
... in the same way,	23.9
or - differently?	37.1
(Does not apply)	1.4
	0.1
Other answer (SPECIFY)	
(Don't remember)	8.4

ASK ALL

79. Please tell me which of these you think are sufficient reasons for divorce ... READ OUT ...

	YES	NO	DON'T KNOW
... when either partner is ill for a long time?	3.3	95.3	1.1
... when they are financially broke?	3.6	94.9	1.1
... when either partner consistently drinks too much?	59.2	35.9	4.5
... when either partner is violent?	92.4	5.7	1.4
... when either partner is consistently unfaithful?	93.7	4.8	1.1
... when the sexual relationship is not satisfactory?	27.5	64.9	6.9
... when either partner has ceased to love the other?	74.9	20.6	4.0
... when they can't get along with each other's relatives?	4.0	94.9	0.7
... when they can't have children?	7.0	88.8	3.8
... when their personalities don't match?	42.0	52.0	5.5

- 27A -

ASK ALL
N = 1552
CARD R

76,a) For a family with children under 5 years old, which one of the arrangements on this card do you think is best? RECORD ONE ONLY IN COL a) BELOW

b) And for a family with children in their early teens, which one of these arrangements is best? RECORD ONE ONLY UNDER b)

	(a) UNDER FIVE %	(b) EARLY TEENS %
Both parents working full-time	1.0	14.7
Father working full-time and mother at home	76.3	18.9
Mother working full-time and father at home	0.2	0.4
Both parents working part-time	2.3	2.8
Father working full-time and mother part-time	16.9	60.0
Mother working full-time and father part-time	0.1	0.3
	2.2	2.0
Other answer (SPECIFY a) b)		
(Don't know)	0.6	0.8

ASK ALL
CARD S

77. As I read from this list, please look at the card and tell me how important you think each one is to a successful marriage ... READ OUT ...

	VERY IMPORTANT	QUITE IMPORTANT	NOT VERY IMPORTANT	NOT AT ALL IMPORTANT	DON'T KNOW
... faithfulness?	86.3	12.4	0.9	0.1	0.1
... an adequate income?	34.0	57.0	8.3	0.4	0.1
... coming from the same social background?	11.4	36.7	42.9	7.7	1.0
... mutual respect and appreciation?	76.6	21.5	1.1	0.1	0.4
... shared religious beliefs?	9.2	26.9	42.9	19.6	1.1
... good housing?	33.1	57.6	8.4	0.4	0.2
... agreement on politics?	2.5	12.4	55.5	28.3	1.1
... understanding and tolerance?	68.8	26.9	1.5	-	0.5
... living apart from in-laws?	55.1	30.1	11.5	2.2	1.0
... a happy sexual relationship?	50.3	44.2	4.2	0.1	0.7
... sharing household chores?	25.3	51.7	19.2	2.9	0.8
... having children?	31.1	40.7	22.3	4.6	0.9
... tastes and interests in common?	20.7	58.6	18.5	1.8	0.2

- 29A -

SECTION SIX

N = 1552

Now I would like to ask some questions about the law.

HAND RESPONDENT 8 'CRIME' CARDS

On these cards are various things which are against the law. Please look at them all.

90.

a) Please tell me which one you think is the most serious, and pass me the card. CODE '1' BELOW IN APPROPRIATE BOX

b) And which one is the least serious? Please pass me the card. CODE '8' IN APPROPRIATE BOX BELOW

c) Now please look at the six cards left, and sort them into order, starting at the most serious and ending with the least serious. Then pass them back to me in that order. TAKE BACK CARDS, ONE BY ONE, CODING '2' – '7' IN APPROPRIATE BOXES BELOW. CHECK THAT CODES RUN FROM 1 TO 8

	% saying most serious	MEAN* SCORE
X = Driving after drinking too much	35	2.6
S = Driving through a red traffic light	1	5.8
N = Burgling from a house while the owners are away	18	3.2
K = Driving after disqualification by a Court	4	4.6
V = Vandalising a telephone box	1	5.7
J = Injuring a pedestrian while driving carelessly	39	2.3
H = Driving at 50 mph in a 30 mph limit	1	6.6
P = Shoplifting from a supermarket	*	5.8

81.

INTERVIEWER INSTRUCTION

REFER TO RESPONDENT SELECTION DIGIT.

IF ODD: ASK Q.82-84 AND RING CODE ⟶ 49.1   Q.82

IF EVEN OR O: ASK Q.85-87 AND RING CODE ⟶ 50.2   Q.85

* This score was computed by assigning the value '1' to the most serious offence through to '8' for the least serious offences for each respondent. Therefore it provides a measure of the distribution of responses.

The following two pages show only the punishment mentioned most frequently as "most suitable" for the offence, and where appropriate the levels of punishment mentioned. (See p.32 of the questionnaire for the showcards used.) Q.82-84 and Q.85-87 were each asked of a random sub-sample of the 1552 respondents to Version A. For further information, contact SCPR.

- 30A -

IF CODE 1 RINGED AT Q.81, ASK Q.82-84   N = 770

OTHERS GO TO Q.85

82.a) Now I would like you to think of someone driving at 50 mph, knowing that the speed limit on that road is 30 mph.

CARD U

Suppose there are no other cars or pedestrians around when the driver is caught for speeding, which one of these punishments would be the most suitable?

Formal warning by police   3   9%

IF PUNISHMENTS O1, O2, O3 OR O4 SHOW APPROPRIATE PENALTY LEVEL CARD W

b) At which of these three levels?   LEVEL

ASK ALL

CARD U AGAIN

c) And would you want any other punishments from the card along with the one you have already suggested? Any others? PROBE UNTIL 'No'. RECORD PUNISHMENT NO. OF ALL MENTIONED ('NONE' = 'OO' IN FIRST BOX)

ENTER PUNISHMENT NO(S)   [ ][ ][ ]   NA

83.a) Still thinking of someone driving at 50 mph, knowing that the speed limit on that road is 30 mph.

CARD U

Suppose now that the driver causes an accident in which another person is badly bruised. Which one of these punishments would be the most suitable?

Court order for compensation   3   6%

IF PUNISHMENTS O1, O2, O3 OR O4 SHOW APPROPRIATE PENALTY LEVEL CARD W

b) At which of these three levels?   LEVEL

ASK ALL

CARD U AGAIN

c) And would you want any other punishments from the card along with the one you have already suggested? Any others? PROBE UNTIL 'No'. AND RECORD PUNISHMENT NO. OF ALL MENTIONED ('NONE' = 'OO' IN FIRST BOX)

ENTER PUNISHMENT NO(S)   [ ][ ][ ]   NA

84.a) Still thinking of someone driving at 50 mph knowing that the speed limit on that road is 30 mph.

CARD U

Suppose finally that the driver causes an accident in which another person is killed, which one of these punishments would be the most suitable?

Disqualification   4   2%

IF PUNISHMENTS O1, O2, O3 OR O4 SHOW APPROPRIATE PENALTY LEVEL CARD W

b) At which of these three levels?   LEVEL: Up to 6 mths   1

    Between 6 months - 2 years   15

    Over 2 years   27

ASK ALL

CARD U AGAIN

c) And would you want any other punishments from the card along with the one you have already suggested? Any others? PROBE UNTIL 'No'. AND RECORD PUNISHMENT NO. OF ALL MENTIONED ('NONE' = 'OO' IN FIRST BOX)

ENTER PUNISHMENT NO(S)   [ ][ ][ ]   NOW GO TO Q.88

- 32A -

ASK ALL N = 1552

			Skip to
			%
88.a)	Have you yourself driven a car or van, within the past year?	Yes	60.7
		No	39.1
b)	Have you yourself ridden a motorcycle on the roads, within the past year?	Yes	5.9
		No	93.8
c)	Have you yourself ridden a pedal cycle on the roads, within the past year?	Yes	26.6
		No	73.1
d)	Have you yourself ever been stopped by the police, while driving a motor vehicle or riding a bike or cycle, because they said you had committed a traffic offence?	Yes	27.5
		No	72.2
e)	Have you, or has a relative or close friend of yours, been involved in a serious road accident within the past five years?	Yes	18.0
		No	81.8

(INTERVIEWER REFERENCE ONLY)

CARD U   Q.82-87

01 Prison
02 Fine
03 Disqualification from driving
04 Licence endorsed with penalty points (12 points in three years means disqualification)
05 Court order for driver to compensate the victim or his/her family
06 Court order for driver to do some work helpful to the community
07 Court order for driver to retake the driving test
08 No court action: just a formal warning by the police

PENALTY LEVEL CARDS

PRISON W/01	FINE W/02
1. ... UP TO TWO YEARS	1. ... UP TO £100
2. ... BETWEEN TWO AND FIVE YEARS	2. ... BETWEEN £100 AND £900
3. ... OVER FIVE YEARS	3. ... £1000 AND OVER

DISQUALIFICATION W/03	PENALTY POINTS (12 POINTS IN 3 YEARS MEANS DISQUALIFICATION) W/04
1. ... UP TO SIX MONTHS	1. ... UP TO THREE POINTS
2. ... BETWEEN SIX MONTHS AND TWO YEARS	2. ... BETWEEN FOUR AND EIGHT POINTS
3. ... OVER TWO YEARS	3. ... NINE POINTS OR OVER

- 31A -

IF CODE 2 RINGED AT Q.81,ASK Q.85-87 N = 772 OTHERS GO TO Q.88.

			Skip to
			%
85.a)	Now I would like you to think of someone driving at 50 mph, not realising that the speed limit on that road is 30 mph. CARD U Suppose there are no other cars or pedestrians around when the driver is caught for speeding, which one of these punishments would be the most suitable? Formal warning by police 54%		
	IF PUNISHMENTS 01, 02, 03 OR 04 SHOW APPROPRIATE PENALTY LEVEL CARD W		
b)	At which of these three levels? LEVEL ☐		NA
c)	ASK ALL CARD U AGAIN And would you want any other punishments from the card along with the one you have already suggested? Any others? PROBE UNTIL 'No' RECORD PUNISHMENT NO. OF ALL MENTIONED ('NONE' = '00' IN FIRST BOX) ☐☐ ☐☐ ☐☐ ENTER PUNISHMENT NO(S)		
86.a)	Still thinking of someone driving at 50 mph not realising that the speed limit on that road is 30 mph. CARD U Suppose now that the driver causes an accident in which another person is badly bruised. Which one of these punishments would be the most suitable? Court order for compensation 35%		
	IF PUNISHMENTS 01, 02, 03 OR 04 SHOW APPROPRIATE PENALTY LEVEL CARD W		
b)	At which of these three levels? LEVEL ☐		NA
c)	ASK ALL CARD U AGAIN And would you want any other punishments from the card along with the one you have already suggested? Any others? PROBE UNTIL 'No' AND RECORD PUNISHMENT NO. OF ALL MENTIONED ('NONE' = '00' IN FIRST BOX) ☐☐ ☐☐ ☐☐ ENTER PUNISHMENT NO(S)		
87.a)	Still thinking of someone driving at 50 mph not realising that the speed limit on that road is 30 mph. CARD U Suppose finally that the driver causes an accident in which another person is killed, which one of these punishments would be the most suitable? Disqualification 42%		
	IF PUNISHMENTS 01, 02, 03 OR 04 SHOW APPROPRIATE PENALTY LEVEL CARD W		
b)	At which of these three levels? LEVEL: Up to 6 months 1 Between 6 months - 2 years 15 Over 2 years 27		
c)	ASK ALL CARD U AGAIN And would you want any other punishments from the card along with the one you have already suggested? Any others? PROBE UNTIL 'No' AND RECORD PUNISHMENT NO. OF ALL MENTIONED ('NONE' = '00' IN FIRST BOX) ☐☐ ☐☐ ☐☐ ENTER PUNISHMENT NO(S)		

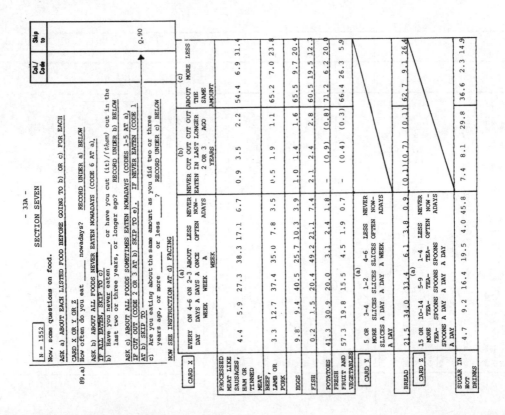

- 33A -

SECTION SEVEN

N = 1552

Now, some questions on food.

89.a) ASK a) ABOUT EACH LISTED FOOD BEFORE GOING TO b) OR c) FOR EACH

CARD X OR Y OR Z
How often do you eat _____ nowadays? RECORD UNDER a) BELOW

ASK b) ABOUT ALL FOODS NEVER EATEN NOWADAYS (CODE 6 AT a),
IF ALL EATEN, SKIP TO c)
b) Have you never eaten _____, or have you cut (it)/(them) out in the last two or three years, or longer ago? RECORD UNDER b) BELOW

ASK c) ABOUT ALL FOODS SOMETIMES EATEN NOWADAYS (CODES 1-5 AT a),
IF CUT OUT (CODE 2 OR 3 AT b) SKIP TO e). IF NEVER EATEN (CODE 1
AT b) SKIP TO _____
c) Are you eating about the same amount as you did two or three years ago, or more or less _____ ? RECORD UNDER c) BELOW

NOW SEE INSTRUCTION AT d) FACING

	(a)						(b)			(c)			Col./Code	Skip to
	EVERY DAY	ON 4-6 DAYS A WEEK	ON 2-3 DAYS A WEEK	ABOUT ONCE A WEEK	LESS OFTEN	NEVER NOW-ADAYS	NEVER EATEN	CUT OUT IN LAST 2 OR 3 YEARS	CUT OUT LONGER AGO	ABOUT THE SAME AMOUNT	MORE	LESS		
PROCESSED MEAT LIKE SAUSAGES, HAM OR TINNED MEAT	4.4	5.9	27.3	38.3	17.1	6.7	0.9	3.5	2.2	54.4	6.9	31.4		
BEEF, LAMB OR PORK	3.3	12.7	37.4	35.0	7.8	3.5	0.5	1.9	1.1	65.2	7.0	23.8		
EGGS	9.8	9.4	40.5	25.7	10.3	3.9	1.0	1.4	1.6	65.5	9.7	20.4		
FISH	0.2	1.5	20.4	49.2	21.1	7.4	2.1	2.4	2.8	60.5	19.5	12.3		
POTATOES	41.3	30.9	20.0	3.1	2.4	1.8	-	(0.9)	(0.8)	71.2	6.2	20.0		
FRESH FRUIT AND VEGETABLES	57.3	19.8	15.5	4.5	1.9	0.7	-	(0.4)	(0.3)	66.4	26.3	5.9		

CARD Y

	5 OR MORE SLICES A DAY	3-4 SLICES A DAY	1-2 SLICES A DAY	4-6 SLICES A WEEK	LESS OFTEN	NEVER NOW-ADAYS								
	(a)													
BREAD	21.5	34.0	33.4	6.1	3.8	0.9	(0.1)	(0.7)	(0.1)	62.7	9.1	26.4		

CARD Z

	15 OR MORE TEA-SPOONS A DAY	10-14 TEA-SPOONS A DAY	5-9 TEA-SPOONS A DAY	1-4 TEA-SPOONS A DAY	LESS OFTEN	NEVER NOW-ADAYS								
	(a)													
SUGAR IN HOT DRINKS	4.7	9.2	16.4	19.5	4.0	45.8	7.4	8.1	29.8	36.6	2.3	14.9		Q.90

- 34A -

N = 1552

ASK d) ABOUT ALL FOODS EATEN ABOUT THE SAME AMOUNT' (CODE 1 AT c)
IF EATEN 'MORE' OR 'LESS', SKIP TO e)
d) (is)/are _____ on the whole good for one, bad for one or neither? RECORD UNDER d) BELOW. NOW SKIP TO

ASK e) ABOUT ALL FOODS 'CUT OUT' (CODE 2 OR 3 AT b) OR
EATEN MORE OR LESS (CODE 2 OR 3 AT c)
CARD AA
e) You said that you had changed the amount of _____ you eat. Have you changed for any of these reasons? PROBE: Any other of these reasons? UNTIL 'No'. RECORD UNDER e) BELOW

IF REASON(S) CHOSEN FROM CARD, SKIP TO
IF NONE OF THESE REASONS (CODE 0 AT e), ASK f) OVERLEAF

	(d)			(e)							Col./Code	Skip to
	GOOD FOR ONE	BAD FOR ONE	NEITHER	TO HELP CONTROL MY WEIGHT	I WAS TOLD TO FOR MEDICAL REASONS	IT IS GOOD VALUE FOR MONEY	IT IS POOR VALUE FOR MONEY	I WANTED TO KEEP HEALTHY	I JUST DON'T LIKE IT	I JUST LIKE IT AS MUCH	NONE OF THESE REASONS		
PROCESSED MEAT	12.4	7.9	33.1	5.6	3.0	1.9	4.7	11.9	2.3	11.2	7.3		
BEEF, LAMB	42.8	2.0	19.8	1.8	2.0	1.5	9.6	7.3	2.7	4.9	5.7		
EGGS	47.7	2.4	15.0	1.7	2.6	3.1	0.1	7.3	3.3	8.9	6.4		
FISH	55.0	*	4.9	2.2	1.7	3.6	3.5	7.8	7.3	6.5	7.0		
POTATOES	45.6	3.8	21.1	10.1	1.3	1.7	0.1	4.5	2.2	3.4	6.1		
FRESH FRUIT	63.4	0.1	2.3	4.1	1.3	2.6	1.7	16.7	7.0	2.2	3.5		Q.90
BREAD	43.7	2.1	16.1	12.0	1.9	1.2	0.2	6.0	3.1	5.4	7.9		
SUGAR IN HOT DRINKS	9.4	16.5	10.2	16.2	4.3	0.1	0.3	13.8	1.0	11.9	4.8		Q.90

- 36A -

SECTION EIGHT

N = 1552

ASK ALL

Now a few questions on housing.

		%	Skip to
91.a)	How long have you lived in your present neighbourhood? ... READ OUT ...		
	... less than a year	4.6	Q.92
	or - one year or more?	95.3	b)
	Don't know	0.1	

IF ONE YEAR OR MORE (CODE 2 AT a)

b) How many years? PROBE FOR BEST ESTIMATE

MEDIAN [1][4] YEARS

ASK ALL
CARD BB

		%	
92.	In general how satisfied or dissatisfied are you with your own house/flat? Choose a phrase from the card.		
	Very satisfied	41.8	
	Quite satisfied	45.9	
	Neither satisfied nor dissatisfied	4.4	
	Quite dissatisfied	4.5	
	Very dissatisfied	3.3	

		%	Skip to
93.	Does your household own or rent this accommodation? PROBE AS NECESSARY TO CLASSIFY N = 3100		
	ONE CODE ONLY OWN: Own leasehold or freehold outright	28.6	Q.96
	Buying leasehold or freehold on mortgage	39.1	
	RENTED FROM: Local authority (Inc. GLC)	24.0	Q.94
	New Town Development Corporation	0.2	
	Housing Association	1.6	
	Property company	0.7	
	Employer	0.8	Q.95
	Other organisation	1.3	
	Relative	0.4	
	Other individual	3.0	
	Don't know	0.?	

		%	
94.	IF LOCAL AUTHORITY OR NEW TOWN DEVELOPMENT CORPORATION TENANT (CODES O3 OR O4 AT Q.93).		
	Is it likely or unlikely that you - or the person responsible for paying the rent - will buy this accommodation at some time in the future? IF LIKELY OR UNLIKELY: Very or quite?		
	Very likely	1.6	
	Quite likely	2.6	
	Quite unlikely	2.6	
	Very unlikely	16.1	
	Not allowed to buy	0.8	
	(Don't know)	0.5	

		%	Skip to
95.	ASK ALL RENTERS (CODES O3-1O AT Q.93) N = 1552		
	How would you describe the rent - not including rates - for this accommodation? Would you say it was ... READ OUT ...		
	... on the high side,	14.?	Q.97
	reasonable,	15.?	
	or - on the low side?	0.8	

-35A -

N = 1552

ASK f) ABOUT EACH FOOD CODED 0 -'NONE OF THESE REASONS'- AT e)

f) For what reason of your own did you change the amount of ____ you eat? PROBE FULLY. RECORD VERBATIM BELOW

	Col/Code	Skip to
PROCESSED MEAT LIKE SAUSAGES HAM OR TINNED MEAT		
BEEF, LAMB OR PORK		
EGGS		
FISH		
POTATOES		
FRESH FRUIT AND VEGETABLES		
BREAD		
SUGAR IN HOT DRINKS		

ASK ALL

90. Compared with two or three years ago, would you say you are now....
READ OUT EACH STATEMENT IN TURN

	YES	NO	DON'T KNOW
... using more low fat spreads or soft margarine instead of butter, or not?	%54.4	44.8	0.2
... eating more grilled food instead of fried food, or not?	%56.3	42.7	0.5
... eating more fish and poultry instead of red meat, or not?	%43.6	55.6	0.3
... drinking or using more semi-skimmed or skimmed milk instead of full cream milk, or not?	%32.5	66.9	0.1
... eating more wholemeal bread instead of white bread, or not?	%55.5	43.9	*

- 37A -

N = 3100

96.a IF CURRENTLY OWNS ACCOMMODATION (CODES 01 OR 02 AT Q.93)

Did you, or the person responsible for the mortgage, buy your present home from the local authority as a tenant?

	%	Skip to
Yes	6.9	c) &d)
No	60.5	b)

'LOCAL AUTHORITY' INCLUDES GLC AND NEW TOWN DEVELOPMENT CORPORATION

IF NO (CODE 2 AT a)

b) Have you ever lived in rented accommodation?

	%	Skip to
Yes	37.2	c) &d)
No	23.5	Q.97

IF YES, (CODE 1 AT a) OR b)

c) How long ago was it that you last lived in rented accommodation?
INCLUDES PRESENT HOUSE/FLAT

MEDIAN 1 4 YEARS

d) Were you renting then from a local authority or from someone else?
'LOCAL AUTHORITY' INCLUDES GLC AND NEW TOWN DEVELOPMENT CORPORATION

	%
Local authority	19.1
Private company	22.1
Someone else (SPECIFY)	2.7
(Don't know)	0.2

97.a ASK ALL

If you had a free choice, would you choose to stay in your present home, or would you choose to move out?

	%	Skip to
Would choose to stay	62.1	Q.98
Would choose to move out	35.8	b)
(Don't know)	1.6	Q.98

IF MOVE OUT (CODE 2 AT a)

b) How keen are you to move out? Are you ... READ OUT ...

	%
... very keen,	12.0
fairly keen,	13.8
or - not that keen?	9.7
(Don't know)	0.3

98.a ASK ALL

And apart from what you would like, where do you expect to be living in two years' time - do you expect to .. ... READ OUT ...

	%	Skip to
... stay in this house/flat,	76.4	Q.99
or - move elsewhere?	20.5	b)
(Don't know)	2.9	Q.99

IF ELSEWHERE (CODE 2 AT a)

b) Which do you think is most likely - that you will buy or rent your next home?

	%
Buy	14.1
Rent: from local authority/council	3.7
Rent from other landlord	1.8
(Don't know)	0.8

IF RENT: PROBE FOR COUNCIL/OTHER

99.a IF CURRENTLY RENTING FROM ANY LANDLORD (CODES 03-10 AT Q.93), ASK (Q.99-101), OTHERS GO TO Q.102

If you had a free choice would you choose to rent accommodation, or would you choose to buy?

	%
Would choose to rent	10.0
Would choose to buy	20.8
(Don't know)	0.5

b) And apart from what you would like, do you expect to buy a house or a flat in the next two years, or not?

	%
Yes - expect to buy	5.8
No - do not expect to buy	24.3
(Don't know)	1.0

INCLUDES BUYING PRESENT HOUSE/FLAT

- 38A -

N = 1552

10(.a ASK ALL RENTERS (CODES 03-10 AT Q.93)

Have you ever owned your own accommodation? That is, lived in a house or flat, which was in your sole or joint name?

	%	Skip to
Yes	4.2	b)
No	27.1	Q.101
Don't know	0.3	

IF YES (CODE 1 AT a)

b) How long ago was it that you last owned your own accommodation?
PROBE FOR BEST ESTIMATE

MEDIAN 1 4 YEARS

101. ASK ALL RENTERS (CODES 03-10 AT Q.93)

Here are some reasons people might give for not wanting to buy a home. As I read out each one, please tell me whether or not it applies to you, at present. ... READ OUT ...

	APPLIES %	DOES NOT APPLY %	(DON'T KNOW) %
... I could not afford the deposit	22.7	8.4	0.1
... I would not be able to get a mortgage	19.5	10.5	1.3
... It might be difficult to keep up the repayments	22.2	8.4	0.7
... I can't afford any of the properties I'd want to buy	22.0	8.7	0.5
... I do not have a secure enough job	18.2	12.8	0.2
... I would not want to be in debt	22.2	8.9	0.1
... It would cost too much to repair and maintain	19.8	10.8	0.6
... I might not be able to resell the property when I wanted to	12.2	17.8	1.2
... It is just too much of a responsibility	16.9	14.1	0.3
... At my age, I would not want to change	45.1	15.9	0.2

102. ASK ALL

When you were a child, did your parents own their home, rent it from a local authority, or rent it from someone else?

	%
Owned it	36.1
Rented from local authority	35.3
Rented from someone else	25.1
Other (SPECIFY)	2.6
Don't know	0.5

IF DIFFERENT TYPES OF TENURE, PROBE FOR ONE RESPONDENT LIVED IN LONGEST

103. CODE FROM OBSERVATION AND CHECK WITH RESPONDENT   N = 3100

Would I be right in describing this accommodation as a -

	%
Detached house or bungalow	21.5
Semi-detached house or bungalow	37.2
Terraced house	25.0
Self-contained, purpose-built flat/maisonette (inc. in tenement block)	12.0
Self-contained converted flat/maisonette	2.6
Room(s) - not self-contained	0.6
Other (SPECIFY)	0.8

- 39A -

104.a)

N = 1552

How long have you lived in your present home? ... READ OUT ...

	%	Skip to
... less than a year,	7.0	Q.105
or - one year or more?	92.8	b)
Don't know	0.1	

IF ONE YEAR OR MORE (CODE 2 AT a)

b) How many years?

PROBE FOR BEST ESTIMATE

MEDIAN [1][0] YEARS

NOW GO TO Q.105 (p.40A)

- 40A -

SECTION NINE

N = 3100

105a) Finally, a few questions about you and your household. Including yourself, how many people live here regularly as members of this household? INTERVIEWER: CHECK INTERVIEWER MANUAL FOR DEFINITION OF HOUSEHOLD IF NECESSARY.

MEDIAN [0][3]

	%	Skip to
	CARD 15	
	PEOPLE	

b) And can I just check your own marital status? At present are you ... READ OUT ...

	%
... married,	66.8
living as married,	2.8
separated or divorced,	4.8
widowed,	8.7
or - not married?	16.5

106. Now I'd like to ask for a few details about each person in your household. Starting with yourself, what was your age last birthday? WORK DOWN COLUMNS OF GRID FOR EACH HOUSEHOLD MEMBER.

	Respondent %
a) Sex: Male	46.9
Female	53.1
b) Age last birthday	
c) Relationship to respondent:	
Spouse/partner	
Son/daughter	
Parent/parent-in-law	
Other relative	
Not related	
d) HOUSEHOLD MEMBERS WITH LEGAL RESPONSIBILITY FOR ACCOMMODATION (INC. JOINT AND SHARED) SOLE	25.6
SHARED	51.5

CHECK THAT NUMBER OF PEOPLE IN GRID EQUALS NUMBER GIVEN AT Q.105a

ASK ALL

107a) Have you ever attended a private primary or secondary school in the United Kingdom? 'PRIVATE' INCLUDES PUBLIC AND DIRECT GRANT SCHOOLS, BUT EXCLUDES NURSERY SCHOOLS AND VOLUNTARY-AIDED SCHOOLS. CODE YES OR NO IN COL a) BELOW

IF MARRIED OR LIVING AS MARRIED ASK b). OTHERS GO TO c)

b) And has your (husband/wife/partner) ever attended a private primary or secondary school in the United Kingdom? CODE YES OR NO IN COL b) BELOW

IF SON OR DAUGHTER OVER 5 YRS IN HH, ASK c). OTHERS GO TO Q.108

c) And (have any of your children/has your child) ever attended a private primary or secondary school in the United Kingdom? CODE YES OR NO IN COL c)

	(a) Self %	(b) Partner %	(c) Children %
Yes	11.3	7.4	4.4
No	88.6	61.6	36.2
Don't know	0.1	0.4	0.9

-41A-

N = 3100

108 ASK ALL

How old were you when you completed your continuous full-time education?

	%	Skip to
15 or under	50.3	
16	24.6	
17	7.7	
18	6.1	
19 or over	9.3	
Still at school	0.2	
Still at college, polytechnic, or university	1.8	
Other answer (SPECIFY)	-	

109a) ASK ALL
CARD CC

Have you passed any exams or got any of the qualifications on this card?

	%	Skip to
Yes	55.0	b)
No, none	44.8	Q.110

IF YES (CODE 1 AT a)
b) Which ones? Any others?
CODE ALL THAT APPLY

	%
CSE Grades 2-5	12.1
CSE Grade 1 / GCE 'O' level / School certificate / Scottish (SCE) Ordinary	34.8
GCE 'A' level/'S' level / Higher certificate / Matriculation / Scottish (SCE) Higher	14.0
Overseas School Leaving Exam/Certificate	0.8
Recognised trade apprenticeship completed	6.3
RSA/other clerical, commercial qualification	8.1
City & Guilds Certificate - Craft/Intermediate/Ordinary/Part I	6.4
City & Guilds Certificate - Advanced/Final/Part II or Part III	3.2
City & Guilds Certificate - Full technological	1.6
BEC/TEC General/Ordinary National Certificate (ONC) or Diploma (OND)	2.5
BEC/TEC Higher/Higher National Certificate (HNC) or Diploma (HND)	2.4
Teachers training qualification	3.0
Nursing qualification	3.1
Other technical or business qualification/certificate	5.9
University or CNAA degree or diploma	6.7
Other (SPECIFY)	1.8

110a) IS THIS A SINGLE PERSON HOUSEHOLD?   Yes → SKIP TO Q.111
       No → ASK a)

Who is the person mainly responsible for general domestic duties in this household?

	%
Respondent mainly	37.5
Someone else mainly (SPECIFY RELATIONSHIP TO RESP.)	39.1
Duties shared equally (SPECIFY BY WHOM)	11.6

IS THERE A CHILD UNDER 16 IN THE HOUSEHOLD?   Yes → ASK b)
       No → SKIP TO Q.111

b) Who is the person mainly responsible for the general care of the child(ren) here?

	%
Respondent mainly	16.2
Someone else mainly (SPECIFY RELATIONSHIP TO RESP.)	12.6
Duties shared equally (SPECIFY BY WHOM)	5.9

-42A-

N = 3100

REFER TO ECONOMIC POSITION OF RESPONDENT (Q.21) PAGE 6.
IF:
- IN PAID WORK (CODE O3) ASK a) TO h) ABOUT PRESENT MAIN JOB
- WAITING TO TAKE UP JOB OFFERED (CODE O4) ASK a) TO h) ABOUT FUTURE JOB
- UNEMPLOYED (CODES O5, O6 OR O7) OR RETIRED (CODE O9) OR LOOKING AFTER HOME (CODE 10) ASK a) TO h) ABOUT LAST JOB
- NEVER HAD A JOB, WRITE IN AT a)
- OTHERS GO TO Q.112

Now I want to ask you about your (present/future/last) job.
CHANGE TENSES FOR (BRACKETED) WORDS AS APPROPRIATE

111 a) What (is) your job?   PROBE AS NECESSARY.
What (is) the name or title of the job?

b) What kind of work (do) you do most of the time? IF RELEVANT: What materials/machinery (do) you use?

c) What training or qualifications do you have that (are) needed for that job?

d) (Do) you supervise or (are) you responsible for the work of any other people?   IF YES: How many?
    Yes:
    No: RING: 0000

e) Can I just check: (are) you ... READ OUT ...

	%	Skip to
... an employee,	82.6	f)
or - self-employed?	8.4	g)

f) IF EMPLOYEE (CODE 1)
CARD DD
Which of the types of organisation on this card (do) you work for?

	%
Private firm or company	52.6
Nationalised industry/public corporation	7.0
Local Authority/Local Education Authority	11.2
Health Authority/hospital	4.9
Central Government/Civil Service	3.8
Charity or trust	0.9
Other (SPECIFY)	2.0

g) ASK ALL
What (does) your employer (IF SELF-EMPLOYED: you) make or do at the place where you usually (work)? IF FARM, GIVE NO. OF ACRES

h) Including yourself, how many people (are) employed at the place you usually (work) from? IF SELF-EMPLOYED: (Do) you have any employees? IF YES: How many?

	%
(No employees)	4.0
Under 10	19.2
10-24	13.5
25-99	18.2
100-499	14.1
500 or more	20.2
Don't know	0.8

N = 3100

ASK ALL

112 a) Are you _now_ a member of a trade union or staff association?

		Skip to
Yes: trade union	23.9	c)
Yes: staff association	2.9	
No	73.0	

IF NO AT a)

b) Have you ever been a member of a trade union or staff association?

Yes: trade union	27.3	c)
Yes: staff association	3.0	
No	42.6	

IF NOW OR EVER A MEMBER (CODES 1 OR 2 AT a OR b)

c) Have you ever ... READ OUT ... (RING ONE CODE FOR EACH)

	YES	NO
... attended a union or staff association meeting?	37.9	19.0
... voted in a union or staff association election or meeting?	35.0	21.9
... put forward a proposal or motion at a union or staff association meeting?	14.0	42.9
... gone on strike?	19.0	38.0
... stood in a picket line?	7.9	49.0
... served as a lay representative such as a shop steward or branch committee member?	8.8	48.0

IF RESPONDENT IS MARRIED OR LIVING AS MARRIED, ASK Q.113
ABOUT HUSBAND/WIFE/PARTNER. OTHERS GO TO Q.115

CARD EE

113 a) Which of these descriptions applied to what your (husband/wife/partner) was doing last week, that is the seven days ending last Sunday? PROBE: Any others? CODE ALL THAT APPLY IN COL. I

IF ONLY ONE CODE AT I, TRANSFER IT TO COL. II
IF MORE THAN ONE AT I, TRANSFER HIGHEST ON LIST TO II

	COL. I	COL.II ECONOMIC POSITION %	Skip to
In full-time education (not paid for by employer, including on vacation)		0.1	b)
On government training/employment scheme (e.g. Community Programme, Youth Training Scheme etc.)		0.1	
In paid work (or away temporarily) for at least 10 hours in the week		42.8	
Waiting to take up paid work already accepted		0.2	
Unemployed and registered at a benefit office		2.4	Q.414
Unemployed, not registered, but actively looking for a job		0.1	
Unemployed, wanting a job (of at least 10 hrs per week), but not actively looking for a job		0.4	
Permanently sick or disabled		1.8	
Wholly retired from work		7.6	
Looking after the home		14.0	b)
Doing something else (SPECIFY)		0.1	

IF CODES 01-02, OR 08-11 AT a)

b) How long ago did your (husband/wife/partner) last have a paid job (other than the government scheme you mentioned) of at least 10 hours a week?

Within past 12 months	2.4	
Over 1-5 years ago	6.4	
Over 5-10 years ago	5.1	
Over 10-20 years ago	4.3	Q.114
Over 20 years ago	3.8	
Never had a paid job of 10+ hours a week	1.3	Q.115
Don't know	0.1	

N = 3100

- 44A -

(REFER TO ECONOMIC POSITION OF RESPONDENT'S SPOUSE/PARTNER (Q.113)

IF:

- SPOUSE IS IN PAID WORK (CODE 03) - ASK a) TO i) ABOUT PRESENT MAIN JOB
- SPOUSE IS WAITING TO TAKE UP JOB OFFERED (CODE 04) - ASK a) TO i) ABOUT FUTURE JOB
- SPOUSE IS UNEMPLOYED (CODES 05, 06 OR 07), OR RETIRED (CODE 09) OR LOOKING AFTER HOME (CODE 10), OR DOING SOMETHING ELSE (CODES 01-02, 08, 11), ASK a) TO i) ABOUT LAST JOB

Now I want to ask you about your (husband's/wife's/partner's) job.

114a) What (is) the name or title of that job?

		Skip to

b) What kind of work (does) he/she do most of the time? IF RELEVANT:
What materials/machinery (does) he/she use?

c) What training or qualifications does he/she have that (are) needed for that job?

d) (Does) he/she supervise or (is) he/she responsible for the work of any other people?

Yes:	
No: (RING) :	
IF YES: How many?	☐☐☐☐

e) (Is) he/she ... READ OUT ...

... an employee,		56.6	f)
or - self-employed?		7.3	g)

IF EMPLOYEE (CODE 1)
CARD FF

f) Which of the types of organisation on this card (does) he/she work for?

Private firm or company	35.2
Nationalised industry/public corporation	6.0
Local Authority/Local Education Authority	8.2
Health Authority/hospital	3.0
Central Government/Civil Service	2.7
Charity or trust	0.6
Other (SPECIFY)	0.8
Don't know	0.1

ASK ALL

g) What (does) the employer (IF SELF-EMPLOYED: he/she) make or do at the place where he/she usually (works)? IF FARM GIVE NO. OF ACRES

h) Including him/herself, roughly how many people (are) employed at the place where he/she usually (works) (from)? IF SELF-EMPLOYED: Do you have any employees? IF YES: How many?

(No employees)	3.9
Under 10	11.5
10-24	8.7
25-99	11.9
100-499	14.5
500 or more	10.6
Don't know	2.4

i) (Is) the job ... READ OUT ...

... full-time (30 hours+)	49.3	
or - part-time (10-29 hours)?	13.3	

- 45A -

N = 3100

ASK ALL

115 a) Do you remember which political party your father usually voted for when you were growing up?
ONE CODE IN COL a)

b) And your mother? ONE CODE IN COL b)

	(a) Father %	(b) Mother %	Skip to
Conservative	23.1	23.8	
Labour	45.1	41.3	
Liberal	5.1	6.2	
Scottish Nationalist	0.2	0.2	
Plaid Cymru	*	0.1	
Other (SPECIFY) a) b)	0.2	0.1	
Varied	0.6	0.7	
Not applicable/Not brought up in Britain	3.5	3.2	
Refused to disclose	0.3	0.3	
Did not vote	1.9	3.8	
Can't remember/Don't know	19.6	19.8	

116 Do you, or does anyone else in your household, own or have the regular use of a car or a van?

	%	
Yes	68.3	
No	30.5	

ASK ALL
CARD GG

117 Have you or anyone in this household been in receipt of any of the benefits on this card during the last five years?
IF YES: Which ones? Any others?
CODE ALL THAT APPLY

	%
Child benefit (family allowance)	46.8
Maternity benefit or allowance	10.6
One parent benefit	2.9
Family Income Supplement	2.2
State retirement or widow's pension	23.1
Supplementary pension	3.2
Invalidity or disabled pension or benefit	6.2
Attendance/Invalid care/Mobility allowance	3.0
Sickness or injury benefit	13.5
Unemployment benefit	20.6
Supplementary benefit	14.7
Rate or rent rebate or allowance	18.9
Other benefit(s) volunteered (SPECIFY)	0.4
NO, NONE	15.1

- 46A -

N = 3100

ASK ALL
CARD HH

118 a) Which of the letters on this card represents the total income from all sources of your household? ONE CODE IN COLUMN a)
IF IN PAID WORK (ECONOMIC POSITION CODE 03 AT Q.21) ASK b). OTHERS GO TO Q.119

b) Which of the letters on this card represents your own gross or total earnings, before deduction of income tax and national insurance? ONE CODE IN COLUMN b)

	a) Household Income	b) Own Earnings
Less than £2,000	2.3	4.3
£2,000-£2,999	6.8	4.9
£3,000-£3,999	6.9	3.7
£4,000-£4,999	6.7	4.6
£5,000-£5,999	5.6	5.5
£6,000-£6,999	5.3	4.3
£7,000-£7,999	5.4	4.1
£8,999-£9,999	9.7	6.5
£10,000-£11,999	9.1	5.5
£12,000-£14,999	9.6	4.1
£15,000-£17,999	6.9	1.7
£18,000-£19,999	4.2	0.7
£20,000+	9.1	2.2
Don't know	8.3	0.3

ASK ALL

119 Do you (or your husband/wife/partner) own any shares quoted on the Stock Exchange, including unit trusts?

	%	Skip to
Yes	16.5	
No	82.7	

ASK ALL

120 a) Is there a telephone in (your part of) this accommodation?

	%	Skip to
Yes	86.6	c)
No	13.3	b)

IF NO ASK b)

b) Do you have easy access to a 'phone where you can receive incoming calls? IF YES, ASK: Is this a home or a work number? IF BOTH, CODE HOME ONLY

	%	Skip to
Yes - home ONLY	1.0	c)
Yes - work	0.6	c)
No	11.1	Q.121

IF YES AT a) OR b)

c) A few interviews on any survey are checked by a supervisor to make sure that people are satisfied with the way the interview was carried out. In case my supervisor needs to contact you, it would be helpful if we could have your telephone number. Number given 81.4
RECORD HOME OR WORK NUMBER ON ADDRESS SLIP ONLY - NOT HERE
Number refused 4.9

ASK ALL

121 In a year's time we may be doing a similar interview and we may wish to include you again. Would this be all right?

	%
Yes	90.1
No	8.9

	Code	to

INTERVIEWER TO CODE:

SELF-COMPLETION QUESTIONNAIRE

122 a) Was it ...   ... filled in immediately after interview
      in interviewer's presence, — 10.7

ONE CODE ONLY   or <u>left behind</u> to be filled in after interview? — 82.5

No S/C — 4.3

Other (SPECIFY) _____ — 0.3

b) Was it ...   ... (to be) collected by interviewer, — 60.1

or to be posted back? — 25.5

No S/C — 11.2

Time interview completed — 24 hour clock [ ][ ] [ ][ ]

MEDIAN DURATION OF INTERVIEW — Minutes | 0 | 6 | 5 | [ ][ ][ ]

Name of interviewer _____   No: [ ]

DATE OF INTERVIEW: DAY [ ]   MONTH [0]   YEAR [8][6]

PLEASE REMEMBER TO WRITE THE NAME OF THE
RESPONDENT ON THE BACK OF THE ARF SLIP!

B

SCPR

SOCIAL AND   COMMUNITY PLANNING RESEARCH

Head Office 35 Northampton Square London EC1V 0AX. Tel: 01-250 1866
Northern Field Office Charaxel House Gainford Darlington Co. Durham DL2 3EG. Tel: 0325 730 888

P.860

April 1986

BRITISH SOCIAL ATTITUDES:

1986 SURVEY

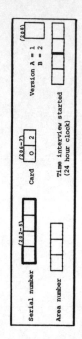

Serial number   (202-5)

Area number

Card (206-7) | 0 | 2 |

Version A = 1
        B = 2   (208)

Time interview started
(24 hour clock)

Col./Code	Skip to

- 25B -

71.a) ASK ALL   N = 1548

On the whole, do you think people of Asian origin in Britain are not given jobs these days because of their race ... READ OUT ...

... a lot,	23.6
a little,	38.2
or - hardly at all?	28.1
(Don't know)	9.4

b) And on the whole, do you think people of West Indian origin in Britain are not given jobs these days because of their race ... READ OUT ...

... a lot,	28.7
a little,	37.7
or - hardly at all?	23.4
(Don't know)	9.4

72.a) There is a law in Britain against racial discrimination, that is against giving unfair preference to a particular race in housing, jobs and so on. Do you generally support or oppose the idea of a law for this purpose?

Support	64.6
Oppose	31.8
Don't know	3.1

b) Do you think, on the whole, that Britain gives too little or too much help to Asians and West Indians who have settled in this country, or are present arrangements about right?

Too little	10.2
Present arrangements right	50.2
Too much	32.6
Other answer (SPECIFY) ____	0.5
Don't know ____	0.3

73.a) INTERVIEWER: CHECK CODE AT Q.69.

		Skip to
RESPONDENT IS WHITE/EUROPEAN (CODE 1 AT Q.69)	94.8	b)
OTHER (CODES 2-4 AT Q.69)	5.2	Q.75

IF RESPONDENT IS WHITE/EUROPEAN
INTERVIEWER:
b) REFER TO RESPONDENT SELECTION DIGIT.

IF ODD: ASK VERSION A OF Q.74 AND RING CODE: A → 43.5

IF EVEN OR O: ASK VERSION B OF Q.74 AND RING CODE: B → 45.4

- 26B -

IF SERIAL NUMBER IS ODD, ASK VERSION A

VERSION A   N = 744

74.a) Do you think most white people in Britain would mind or not mind if a suitably qualified person of Asian origin were appointed as their boss? IF 'WOULD MIND': A lot or a little? RECORD IN COL. (a)

b) And you personally? Would you mind or not mind?
IF 'WOULD MIND': A lot or a little? RECORD IN COL. (b)

c) Do you think that most white people in Britain would mind or not mind if one of their close relatives were to marry a person of Asian origin? IF 'WOULD MIND': A lot or a little? RECORD IN COL. (c)

d) And you personally? Would you mind or not mind?
IF 'WOULD MIND': A lot or a little? RECORD IN COL. (d) THEN GO TO Q.75

IF SERIAL NUMBER IS EVEN, ASK VERSION B

VERSION B   N = 719

74.a) Do you think most white people in Britain would mind or not mind if a suitably qualified person of black or West Indian origin were appointed as their boss? IF 'WOULD MIND': A lot or a little? RECORD IN COL. (a)

b) And you personally? Would you mind or not mind?
IF 'WOULD MIND': A lot or a little? RECORD IN COL. (b)

c) Do you think that most white people in Britain would mind or not mind if one of their close relatives were to marry a person of black or West Indian origin? IF 'WOULD MIND': A lot or a little? RECORD IN COL. (c)

d) And you personally? Would you mind or not mind?
IF 'WOULD MIND': A lot or a little? RECORD IN COL. (d)

	BOSS		MARRIAGE	
	(a) Most people	(b) Self	(c) Most people	(d) Self
	Asian Black	Asian Black	Asian Black	Asian Black
Mind a lot	23.0 27.6	8.9 7.0	44.8 45.5	26.3 27.0
Mind a little	31.1 28.7	9.0 9.7	31.4 33.6	19.8 23.1
Not mind	42.1 38.7	80.8 82.0	18.6 15.6	51.4 46.6
Other answer	1.6 1.6	0.5 0.4	1.0 1.4	1.8 2.0
Don't know	2.0 3.4	0.5 0.6	4.2 3.9	0.6 1.1

- 27B -

ASK ALL [N = 1548]

75.a) Some people say there is very little real poverty in Britain today. Others say there is quite a lot. Which comes closest to your view ... READ OUT ...

	%	Skip to
... that there is very little real poverty in Britain,	41.0	
or - that there is quite a lot?	55.4	
(Don't know)	3.5	

b) Over the last ten years, do you think that poverty in Britain has been increasing, decreasing or staying at about the same level?

	%	
Increasing	51.1	
Decreasing	15.2	
Staying at same level	29.9	
(Don't know)	3.8	

c) And over the next ten years, do you think that poverty in Britain will ... READ OUT ...

	%	
... increase,	44.5	
decrease,	12.5	
or - stay at about the same level?	35.8	
(Don't know)	7.2	

76. Would you say someone in Britain was or was not in poverty if ... ... READ OUT EACH STATEMENT BELOW AND CODE FOR EACH ...

	Yes	No	(Don't know)
... they had enough to buy the things they really needed, but not enough to buy the things most people take for granted?	%24.6	71.6	3.6
... they had enough to eat and live, but not enough to buy other things they needed?	%54.6	42.6	2.6
... they had not got enough to eat and live without getting into debt?	%95.1	3.1	1.6

77. CARD N

Why do you think there are people who live in need? Of the four views on this card, which one comes closest to your own? CODE ONE ONLY

	%	
Because they have been unlucky	11.1	
Because of laziness or lack of willpower	18.8	
Because of injustice in our society	25.0	
It's an inevitable part of modern life	36.8	
(None of these)	4.3	
(Don't know)	1.1	
OTHER ANSWER (SPECIFY) _____	2.8	

- 28B -

[N = 1548]

78.a) How often do you and your household feel poor nowadays ... READ OUT ...

	%	Skip to
... never,	40.1	
every now and then,	42.1	
often,	9.4	
or - almost all the time?	7.7	
(Don't know)	0.6	

b) What would you say is the minimum income - after tax - that households like yours would need just to make ends meet? PROBE FOR BEST ESTIMATE OF MINIMUM HOUSEHOLD INCOME NEEDED

£ [ ][ ][ ] per week

£ [ ][ ][ ] per month

MEDIAN £ [6][2][4][0] per year

OR RING CODE: Don't know/Can't say

79.a) Think of a married couple without children living only on unemployment benefit. Would you say that they are ... READ OUT ...

	%	
... really poor,	12.3	
hard up,	46.9	
have enough to live on,	28.3	
or - have more than enough?	0.7	
(Don't know)	11.6	

b) Now thinking of a married couple living only on the state pension. Would you say they are ... READ OUT ...

	%	
... really poor,	19.3	
hard up,	50.9	
have enough to live on,	23.1	
or - have more than enough?	0.4	
(Don't know)	6.2	

- 29B-

N = 1548

		%	Skip to
80.a)	Now thinking of a married couple without children living on £50 per week. Would you say they are ... READ OUT ...		
	... really poor,	38.5	
	hard up,	50.5	
	have enough to live on,	7.7	
	or - have more than enough?	0.5	
	(Don't know)	2.5	
b)	And what about a pensioner couple living on £62 per week. Would you say they are ... READ OUT ...		
	... really poor,	23.1	
	hard up,	48.7	
	have enough to live on,	24.5	
	or - have more than enough?	0.5	
	(Don't know)	2.5	
81.a)	Do you think that health care should be the same for everyone, or should people who can afford it be able to pay for better health care?		
	Same for everyone	45.6	
	Able to pay for better health	53.1	
	(Don't know)	1.2	
b)	Should the quality of education be the same for all children, or should parents who can afford it be able to pay for better education?		
	Same for everyone	46.6	
	Able to pay for better	51.9	
	(Don't know)	1.3	
c)	And do you think that pensions should be the same for everyone, or should people who can afford it be able to pay for better pensions?		
	Same for everyone	36.2	
	Able to pay for better	60.6	
	(Don't know)	3.1	

- 30B-

SECTION FIVE

N = 1548

Now I'd like to ask some questions about politics.

ASK ALL

		%	Skip to
82.	How much interest do you generally have in what is going on in politics ... READ OUT ...		
	... a great deal,	7.2	
	quite a lot,	21.8	
	some,	31.1	
	not very much,	26.7	
	or - not at all?	12.8	
	(Don't know)	0.3	
83.	CARD O. Which of the four statements on this card comes closest to the way you vote in a general election?		
	ONE CODE ONLY		
	I vote for a Party, regardless of the candidate	53.6	
	I vote for a Party, only if I approve of the candidate	23.1	
	I vote for a candidate, regardless of his or her Party	4.4	
	I do not generally vote at all	17.0	
	Not yet voted	0.9	
	Don't know	0.4	
	Other answer (SPECIFY) _____	0.3	
84.a)	Which do you think is generally better for Britain ... READ OUT ...		
	... to have a government formed by one political party	52.4	Q.85
	or - for two or more parties to get together to form a government?	43.0	b)
	Don't know	3.9	
	IF TWO OR MORE PARTIES (CODE 2 AT a)		
b)	Which of these party groupings do you think would provide the best government for Britain ... READ OUT ...		
	... Conservative and Alliance,	13.3	
	Labour and Alliance,	13.0	
	Conservative and Labour,	7.6	
	or - some other grouping?	6.1	
	(Don't know)	2.9	
85.	ASK ALL. Some people say that we should change the voting system to allow smaller political parties to get a fairer share of MPs. Others say that we should keep the voting system as it is, to produce more effective government. Which view comes closest to your own ... READ OUT ... IF ASKED, REFERS TO 'PROPORTIONAL REPRESENTATION'		
	... that we should change the voting system,	32.3	
	or - keep it as it is?	59.7	
	(Don't know)	7.7	

- 31B -

CARD P | N = 1548

86.a) Suppose a law was being considered by Parliament which you thought was really unjust and harmful. Which, if any, of the things on this card do you think you would do? Any others? RECORD IN COL a) BELOW, THEN ASK b). MORE THAN ONE CODE MAY BE RINGED

b) And have you ever done any of the things on this card about a government action which you thought was unjust or harmful? Which ones? Any others? RECORD IN COL b) BELOW. MORE THAN ONE CODE MAY BE RINGED

	(a) Would do %	(b) Ever done %
Contact my MP	51.7	10.9
Speak to influential person	14.5	3.2
Contact a government department	11.5	2.7
Contact radio, TV or newspaper	15.0	2.8
Sign a petition	64.6	34.3
Raise the issue in an organisation I already belong to	10.1	4.8
Go on a protest or demonstration	10.5	5.7
Form a group of like-minded people	8.2	1.5
(NO - NONE OF THESE)	10.0	55.5

87. CARD Q

Please use a phrase from this card to say how effective you think each of the following would be in influencing a government to change its mind? How effective would it be to ...
READ OUT ITEMS a)-h) BELOW AND CODE FOR EACH

	Very effective	Quite effective	Not very effective	Not at all effective	(Don't know)
a) ... Contact your MP? %	6.9	43.0	38.0	6.7	4.6
b) ... Speak to an influential person? %	4.5	33.4	44.8	10.6	6.0
c) ... Contact a government department? %	3.3	23.0	48.2	18.9	5.9
d) ... Contact radio, TV or newspaper? %	10.2	48.2	27.2	9.3	4.3
e) ... Sign a petition? %	4.3	40.7	40.0	11.2	3.1
f) Raise the issue in an organisation you already belong to? %	2.5	29.8	41.4	13.1	12.3
g) ... Go on a protest or demonstration? %	2.2	18.4	45.5	28.6	4.6
h) ... Form a group of like-minded people? %	1.7	24.4	44.2	21.3	7.6

- 32B -

N = 1548

88.a) In general would you say that people should obey the law without exception, or are there exceptional occasions on which people should follow their consciences even if it means breaking the law?

	%
Obey law without exception	54.9
Follow conscience on occasions	43.0
(Don't know)	1.5

b) Are there any circumstances in which you might break a law to which you were very strongly opposed?

	%
Yes	31.0
No	60.7
Don't know	7.1

89. CARD R

Please choose a phrase from this card to say how you feel about ... READ OUT ...

	Very strongly in favour	Strongly in favour	In favour	Neither in favour nor against	Against	Strongly against	Very strongly against	(DK/Can't say)
a) .. the Conservative Party? %	3.6	6.3	22.1	20.2	17.0	10.5	16.6	3.1
b) .. the Labour Party? %	5.6	7.7	23.8	23.4	22.0	7.6	6.3	2.9
c) .. The Social Democrat Party? %	1.2	2.5	20.0	43.6	18.5	4.5	2.9	6.2
d) .. the Liberal Party? %	1.6	3.8	22.7	46.0	14.4	3.6	2.4	4.9
SCOTLAND e) .. the Scottish Nationalist Party? %	0.4	0.5	2.5	3.4	2.5	0.4	0.4	0.4
WALES f) .. Plaid Cymru? %	0.1	0.1	1.3	1.6	0.9	0.2	0.9	0.2

90.a) ASK ALL

On the whole, would you describe the Conservative Party nowadays as extreme or moderate? Is it extreme or moderate?

b) And the Labour Party nowadays, is it extreme or moderate?

c) And the SDP/Liberal Alliance nowadays, is it extreme or moderate?

RECORD IN APPROPRIATE COL.

	(a) Conservative	(b) Labour	(c) Alliance
Extreme	56.1	39.5	5.1
Moderate	35.1	46.0	72.0
(Neither or both)	2.8	5.1	4.8
(Don't know)	7.2	8.5	17.0

d) On the whole, would you describe the Conservative Party as good for one class, or good for all classes?

e) And the Labour Party, is it good for one class or good for all classes?

f) And the Alliance, is it good for one class or good for all classes?

	(d) Conservative	(e) Labour	(f) Alliance
Good for one class	64.4	48.8	9.9
Good for all classes	28.4	39.4	60.1
(Neither or both)	2.6	6.1	8.8
(Don't know)	3.8	4.9	20.4

- 33B -

91.a) Are you generally in favour of
... READ OUT ...

N = 1548

	%	Skip to
... more **nationalisation** of companies by government,	13.6	b)
... more **privatisation** of companies by government,	28.4	
or - should things be left as they are now?	50.9	Q.92
(Don't know)	0.7	
Other (SPECIFY)	5.4	

IF MORE NATIONALISATION OR PRIVATISATION (CODES 1 OR 2 AT a)

	%	
b) A lot more (nationalisation)/(privatisation) A lot more	19.2	
or a little more? A little more	22.7	
Don't know	0.5	

92. ASK ALL
CARD S
Please choose a phrase from this card to say how much you agree or disagree with the following statements ... READ OUT a)-d)
BELOW AND CODE FOR EACH

	Agree strongly	Agree	Neither agree nor dis-agree	Dis-agree	Disagree strongly	(Don't know)
	%					
a) ... People like me have no say in what the government does.	22.7	48.4	8.6	17.4	1.3	0.9
b) ... Sometimes politics and government seem so complicated that a person like me cannot really understand what is going on.	17.2	51.5	7.1	20.1	2.6	0.8
c) ... Generally speaking, those we elect as MPs lose touch with people pretty quickly.	16.4	53.4	10.7	15.4	0.4	3.0
d) ... Parties are only interested in people's votes, not in their opinions.	18.6	47.5	12.4	17.4	1.2	2.0

93. CARD T
How much do you trust a British government of any party to place the needs of this country above the interests of their own political party? Please choose a phrase from this card.

	%
Just about always	4.5
Most of the time	33.5
Only some of the time	45.7
Almost never	11.2
(Don't know/Can't say)	4.2

- 34B -

SECTION SIX

N = 1548
ASK ALL

94. Now I'd like to ask a few questions about industry and jobs.
Suppose you were advising a young person who was looking for his or her first job.

CARD U
Which one of these would you say is the most important, and which **next**?

ONE CODE ONLY IN EACH COLUMN

	MOST IMPOR-TANT	NEXT MOST IMPOR-TANT
	%	%
Good starting pay	3.1	8.9
A secure job for the future	56.5	17.8
Opportunities for promotion	9.3	29.1
Interesting work	26.4	28.0
Good working conditions	3.9	15.1
(Don't know)	0.5	0.7

95. CARD V
Suppose this young person could choose between different kinds of jobs anywhere in Britain.
From what you know or have heard, which **one** of these kind of jobs is most likely to offer him or her ...
READ OUT AND RECORD UNDER a)-e) BELOW

a) ... good starting pay?
b) ... a secure job for the future? You may choose the same one again or a different one.
c) ... opportunities for promotion?
d) ... interesting work?
e) ... good working conditions?

ONE CODE ONLY IN EACH COLUMN

	(a) Good starting pay	(b) Secure job	(c) Promotion	(d) Inter-esting work	(e) Good working conditions
	%	%	%	%	%
A building society	9.2	13.4	8.5	6.2	24.0
A large firm of accountants	12.9	13.4	16.6	9.9	11.9
A large engineering factory	13.4	4.7	8.9	16.3	3.6
A department store	1.8	1.3	5.3	8.7	6.2
The Civil Service	24.2	49.2	34.2	15.8	31.6
A large firm making computers	29.9	14.1	17.9	30.1	13.5
(None of these)	0.5	0.7	0.3	0.3	0.3
(Don't know)	7.7	2.8	7.9	9.8	8.3

- 35B -

N = 1548

CARD V AGAIN

96.a) Now taking everything together, which job would you be most likely to advise this young person to choose? RECORD UNDER a) BELOW

b) And which next? RECORD UNDER b) BELOW

c) And which would you be least likely to advise him or her to choose? RECORD UNDER c) BELOW

ONE CODE ONLY IN EACH COLUMN

	(a) Most likely	(b) Next	(c) Least likely
	%	%	%
A building society	11.0	19.5	4.7
A large firm of accountants	17.9	20.6	3.3
A large engineering factory	7.0	10.5	20.1
A department store	1.4	4.0	50.2
The Civil Service	31.5	19.8	5.6
A large firm making computers	24.1	15.8	7.2
(None of these)	1.2	1.6	0.8
(Don't know)	4.8	6.8	7.0

CARD W

97.a) How good do you think Britain is at selling its goods abroad, compared with other countries that compete with us? Please choose a phrase from this card. RECORD IN GRID BELOW

b) And in inventing new products? RECORD IN GRID BELOW

REPEAT FOR EACH STATEMENT a)-i)

Britain is ...	better than most	worse than most	about the same	(Don't know/ varies)
a) .. in selling its goods abroad? %	9.5	46.0	38.1	5.5
b) .. in inventing new products? %	52.4	14.0	27.4	5.3
c) .. in making well-designed products? %	46.9	10.1	36.1	5.8
d) .. in investing in new machinery and technology? %	11.6	48.7	30.7	7.9
e) .. in attracting the best people to manage its industries? %	12.0	38.5	39.0	9.7
f) .. in attracting the best people to work in manufacturing industries? %	10.5	33.0	45.2	10.1
g) .. in making goods that people really want to buy? %	22.8	22.9	47.6	5.6
h) .. in keeping good relations between management and other employees? %	11.0	42.5	39.2	6.4
i) .. in training employees in new skills? %	17.0	34.8	38.9	8.3

- 36B -

N = 1548

CARD X

Suppose a big British firm made a large profit in a particular year.

98.a) Which one of these things do you think it would be most likely to do? RECORD IN COL a) BELOW

b) And which one would it be next most likely to do? RECORD IN COL b) BELOW

c) Now which one do you think should be its first priority? RECORD IN COL c) BELOW

d) And which should be its next priority? RECORD IN COL d) BELOW

CODE ONE ONLY IN EACH COLUMN

	Likely to do		Should be	
	(a) Most	(b) Next	(c) First priority	(d) Next priority
	%	%	%	%
Increase dividends to the shareholders	36.1	17.5	4.1	2.1
Give the employees a pay rise	3.4	5.2	20.7	12.1
Cut the prices of its products	2.1	3.8	12.6	11.8
Invest in new machinery or new technology	19.5	20.3	30.9	16.7
Improve the employees' working conditions	1.7	3.0	6.8	14.7
Research into new products	10.2	19.9	10.3	18.6
Invest in training for the employees	2.4	4.0	11.5	19.4
Give a bonus to top management	18.9	18.8	0.3	0.9
(None of these)	0.1	0.1	-	-
(Don't know)	4.9	6.1	2.1	2.6

99.a) Do you think that British industry is more efficient than it was five years ago, less efficient, or about the same? CODE UNDER a) BELOW

b) And do you think that, in five years' time, British industry will be more efficient or less efficient compared with now, or about the same? CODE UNDER b)

	(a) 5 years ago	(b) 5 years time
	%	%
More	31.7	35.7
Less	24.3	13.4
About the same	36.8	41.6
(Don't know)	6.3	8.3

- 37B -

SECTION SEVEN

N = 1548

Now I'd like to ask you a few questions about the countryside.

CARD Y

100a) On this card are some activities people do in their leisure time. Have you taken part in any of these leisure activities in the last four weeks?

	%	Skip to
Yes	63.9	b) Q.-101
No	35.7	

IF NO AT a)
CARD Y AGAIN

b) Can you remember when you last did any of these activities in the countryside? IF YES: How long ago was that?

PROBE FOR CORRECT CODE

	%
Within past month	0.8
1-3 months ago	5.7
4-6 months ago	5.0
7-12 months ago	11.7
More than one year ago	8.7
No, can't remember	3.7

ASK ALL

101.a Do you think the countryside generally is much the same as it was twenty years ago, or do you think it has changed? IF CHANGED: has it changed a bit or a lot?

	%	Skip to
Much the same	21.8	Q.-02
Changed a bit	24.8	b)
Changed a lot	47.9	
(Don't know)	5.1	Q.-02

IF CHANGED A BIT OR A LOT (CODES 2 OR 3 AT a)

b) Do you think the countryside generally has changed for the better or worse?

	%
Better	13.1
Worse	50.9
(Better in some ways/worse in others)	7.9
Don't know	0.3

ASK ALL

102. Are you personally concerned about things that may happen to the countryside, or does it not concern you particularly? IF CONCERNED: Are you very concerned, or just a bit concerned?

	%
Very concerned	39.9
A bit concerned	34.5
Does not concern me particularly	25.2

- 38B -

N = 1548

ASK ALL

103a) Suppose you heard that a housing development was being planned in a part of the countryside you knew and liked. Would you be concerned by this, or not?

	%	Skip to
Yes, concerned	71.4	b)
No	22.1	Q.-104
(Don't know/Depends)	6.2	

IF CONCERNED AT a)
CARD Z

b) Would you personally be likely to do any of these things about it? Any others?

CODE ALL THAT APPLY

	%
Would take no action	14.3
Contact MP or councillor	23.2
Contact a government or planning department	10.8
Contact radio, TV or a newspaper	6.9
Sign a petition	44.6
Join a conservation group	8.1
Give money to a campaign	10.3
Volunteer to work for a campaign	7.5
Go on a protest march or demonstration	5.7

ASK ALL

104a) Now suppose you heard that a protected site where wildflowers grew was going to be ploughed for farmland. Would you be concerned by this, or not?

	%	Skip to
Yes, concerned	54.7	b)
No	39.6	Q.-105
(Don't know/Depends)	5.3	

IF CONCERNED AT a)
CARD Z AGAIN

b) Would you personally be likely to do any of these things about it? Any others?

CODE ALL THAT APPLY

	%
Would take no action	12.0
Contact MP or councillor	15.5
Contact a government or planning department	6.7
Contact radio, TV or a newspaper	4.8
Sign a petition	33.1
Join a conservation group	7.9
Give money to a campaign	7.5
Volunteer to work for a campaign	4.7
Go on a protest march or demonstration	3.4

- 39B -

N = 1548

ASK ALL

105a) And suppose you read a report that forests in Britain were in danger of being damaged by acid rain. Would you be concerned by this, or not?

	%	Skip to
Yes, concerned	83.5	
No	12.3	b)
(Don't know/depends)	3.9	Q.106

IF CONCERNED AT a)
CARD Z AGAIN

b) Would you personally be likely to do any of the things on this card about it? Any others?

CODE ALL THAT APPLY

	%
Would take no action	18.1
Contact MP or councillor	21.5
Contact a government or planning department	9.3
Contact radio, TV or a newspaper	7.5
Sign a petition	50.6
Join a conservation group	9.5
Give money to a campaign	13.2
Volunteer to work for a campaign	7.7
Go on a protest march or demonstration	4.8

ASK ALL
CARD AA

106a) Have you ever done any of the things on the card about a countryside issue?

	%	Skip to
Yes	24.7	b)
No	74.9	Q.107

IF YES AT a)

b) Which ones have you ever done about a countryside issue? Any others?

CODE ALL THAT APPLY

	%
Contacted MP or councillor	4.2
Contacted a government or planning department	3.8
Contacted radio, TV or a newspaper	0.9
Signed a petition	18.1
Joined a conservation group	3.5
Given money to a campaign	7.2
Volunteered to work for a campaign	2.3
Gone on a protest march or demonstration	1.0

- 40B -

N = 1548

ASK ALL

107a) Which political party's views on the environment would you say come closest to your own views?

DO NOT PROMPT
ONE CODE ONLY

	%	Skip to
Conservative	12.8	
Labour	13.6	
Liberal	3.6	
SDP/Social Democrat	3.2	
(Alliance)	2.0	
Green Party/Ecology Party	4.3	
Other (SPECIFY)	0.9	
Don't know	54.2	
None	4.8	

CARD BB

b) Are you, or anyone in your household, a member of any of the groups, clubs or organisations listed on this card?

IF YES: Which ones?   YES - MEMBER OF:

	%
National Trust	7.8
Royal Society for the Protection of Birds	5.4
Other wildlife or countryside protection group	4.5
Countryside sports/leisure organisation	6.6
NO - NONE OF THESE	80.3

(INTERVIEWER REFERENCE ONLY)

CARD Y   Q.100

In the last four weeks have you ...

... been for a drive, outing or picnic in the countryside

... been for a long walk, ramble or hike (of more than 2 miles) in the countryside

... visited any historic or stately homes, gardens, zoos or wildlife parks in the countryside

... gone fishing, horse riding, shooting or hunting in the countryside

... visited seacoast or cliffs

- 41B -

SECTION EIGHT

N = 1548

	%	Skip to

108a) INTERVIEWER: CODE FROM OBSERVATION AND CHECK WITH RESPONDENT

Can I just check, would you describe the place where you live as being ... READ OUT ...

	%	Skip to
... in a big city,	10.5	
in the suburbs or outskirts of a city,	33.6	b) & c)
in a small city or town,	33.4	
in a country village or town,	18.9	c)
or - in the countryside?	3.6	Q.109

IF RESPONDENT LIVES IN CITY, SUBURBS, OR SMALL CITY/TOWN (CODES 1-3 AT a)

b) Have you ever lived in the countryside, or in a country village or town - for instance, when you were a child or at some time before now?

	%
Yes	31.7
No	45.3

IF RESPONDENT LIVES IN CITY, SUBURBS, OR ANY CITY/VILLAGE/TOWN (CODES 1-4 AT a).

c) About how far do you live from the nearest open countryside that you can visit or walk in? Please do not include city parks.

IF NOT SURE, PROBE FOR ESTIMATE

	%
Less than ½ mile (15 mins. walk)	29.7
½, up to 1 mile (15-30 mins. walk)	12.8
Over 1 mile, up to 3 miles	22.7
Over 3 miles, up to 10 miles	22.3
Over 10 miles	5.9
Don't know	1.9

A

SCPR

SOCIAL AND COMMUNITY PLANNING RESEARCH

Head Office 35 Northampton Square London EC1V 0AX Tel: 01-250 1866
Northern Field Office Charazel House Ganford Darlington Co Durham DL2 3EG Tel: 0325 730 888

Interviewer to enter:

Area No. ☐ ☐

Serial No. ☐ ☐ ☐

BRITISH SOCIAL ATTITUDES: 1986

SELF-COMPLETION QUESTIONNAIRE

April 1986   P.860A

To the selected respondent

We hope very much that you will agree to participate in this important study - the fourth in an annual series of surveys to be published each summer. The study consists of this self-completion questionnaire and an interview. Some of the questions are also being asked in America, West Germany, Austria and Australia, as part of an international survey of social attitudes.

Completing the questionnaire

The questions inside cover a wide range of subjects, but each one can be answered simply by placing a tick (✓) in one or more of the boxes provided. No special knowledge is required: we are confident that everyone will be able to offer an opinion on all questions. And we want _all_ people to take part, not just those with strong views or particular viewpoints. The questionnaire should not take very long to complete, and we hope you will find it interesting and enjoyable. It should be completed by the person selected by the interviewer at your address. Your participation will be treated as confidential and anonymous.

Returning the questionnaire

Your interviewer will arrange with you the most convenient way of returning the questionnaire. If the interviewer has arranged to call back for it, please complete it and keep it safely until then. If not, please complete it and post it back in the stamped, addressed envelope _as soon as you possibly can._

Thank you for your help.

Social and Community Planning Research is an independent social research institute registered as a charitable trust. Its projects are funded by government departments, local authorities, universities and foundations to provide information on social issues in Britain. SCPR interviewers carry out around 50,000 interviews per year. This study has been funded mainly by the Monument Trust, a Sainsbury foundation and the Nuffield Foundation, with contributions also from government departments, universities and industry. Please contact us if you require further information.

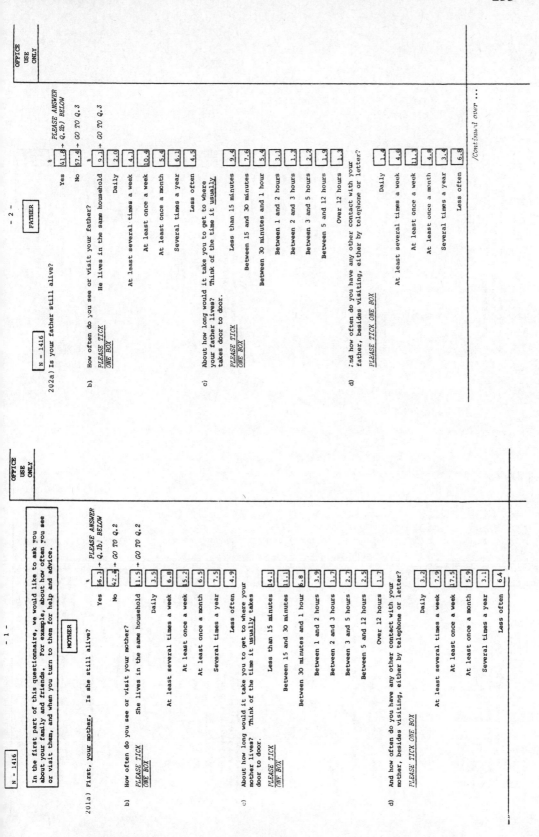

OFFICE USE ONLY

- 1 -

N = 1416

In the first part of this questionnaire, we would like to ask you about your family and friends. For example, about how often you see or visit them, and when you turn to them for help and advice.

MOTHER

201a) First, __your mother__, Is she still alive?

Yes [56.3] → *PLEASE ANSWER Q.1b) BELOW*
No [42.6] → *GO TO Q.2*

b) How often do you see or visit your mother?

She lives in the same household [11.5] → *GO TO Q.2*
Daily [3.5]
At least several times a week [6.8]
At least once a week [5.2]
At least once a month [6.5]
Several times a year [7.5]
Less often [4.9]

PLEASE TICK ONE BOX

c) About how long would it take you to get to where your mother lives? Think of the time it usually takes door to door.

PLEASE TICK ONE BOX
Less than 15 minutes [14.1]
Between 15 and 30 minutes [11.1]
Between 30 minutes and 1 hour [6.8]
Between 1 and 2 hours [3.9]
Between 2 and 3 hours [1.7]
Between 3 and 5 hours [2.7]
Between 5 and 12 hours [2.5]
Over 12 hours [1.7]

d) And how often do you have any other contact with your mother, besides visiting, either by telephone or letter?

PLEASE TICK ONE BOX
Daily [3.2]
At least several times a week [7.9]
At least once a week [17.5]
At least once a month [5.9]
Several times a year [3.1]
Less often [6.4]

OFFICE USE ONLY

- 2 -

FATHER

N = 1416

202a) Is your father still alive?

Yes [41.8] → *PLEASE ANSWER Q.2b) BELOW*
No [57.4] → *GO TO Q.3*

b) How often do you see or visit your father?

He lives in the same household [9.1] → *GO TO Q.3*
Daily [2.0]
At least several times a week [4.1]
At least once a week [10.4]
At least once a month [5.4]
Several times a year [6.1]
Less often [4.5]

PLEASE TICK ONE BOX

c) About how long would it take you to get to where your father lives? Think of the time it usually takes door to door.

PLEASE TICK ONE BOX
Less than 15 minutes [9.4]
Between 15 and 30 minutes [7.6]
Between 30 minutes and 1 hour [5.4]
Between 1 and 2 hours [3.1]
Between 2 and 3 hours [1.3]
Between 3 and 5 hours [2.2]
Between 5 and 12 hours [1.9]
Over 12 hours [1.3]

d) And how often do you have any other contact with your father, besides visiting, either by telephone or letter?

PLEASE TICK ONE BOX
Daily [1.4]
At least several times a week [4.6]
At least once a week [11.3]
At least once a month [4.8]
Several times a year [3.4]
Less often [6.8]

/Continued over .../

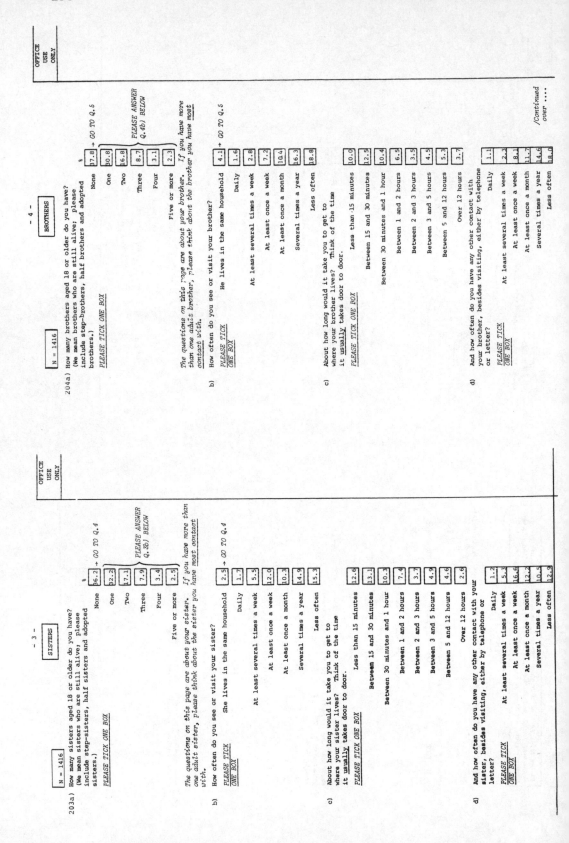

- 3 -

SISTERS

N = 1416

203a) How many sisters aged 18 or older do you have? (We mean sisters who are still alive; please include step-sisters, half sisters and adopted sisters.)
PLEASE TICK ONE BOX

	%
None	36.2 → GO TO Q.4
One	32.2
Two	17.1
Three	7.9 } PLEASE ANSWER Q.3b) BELOW
Four	3.4
Five or more	2.5

The questions on this page are about your sister. If you have more than one adult sister, please think about the sister you have most contact with.

b) How often do you see or visit your sister?
PLEASE TICK ONE BOX

	%
She lives in the same household	2.5 → GO TO Q.4
Daily	1.7
At least several times a week	5.5
At least once a week	12.0
At least once a month	10.3
Several times a year	14.9
Less often	15.3

c) About how long would it take you to get to where your sister lives? Think of the time it usually takes door to door.
PLEASE TICK ONE BOX

	%
Less than 15 minutes	12.6
Between 15 and 30 minutes	13.1
Between 30 minutes and 1 hour	10.3
Between 1 and 2 hours	7.4
Between 2 and 3 hours	3.7
Between 3 and 5 hours	4.9
Between 5 and 12 hours	4.6
Over 12 hours	2.6

d) And how often do you have any other contact with your sister, besides visiting, either by telephone or letter?
PLEASE TICK ONE BOX

	%
Daily	1.2
At least several times a week	5.3
At least once a week	16.6
At least once a month	12.2
Several times a year	10.5
Less often	12.9

- 4 -

BROTHERS

N = 1416

204a) How many brothers aged 18 or older do you have? (We mean brothers who are still alive; please include step-brothers, half brothers and adopted brothers.)
PLEASE TICK ONE BOX

	%
None	37.8 → GO TO Q.5
One	30.8
Two	16.8
Three	8.7 } PLEASE ANSWER Q.4b) BELOW
Four	3.1
Five or more	2.3

The questions on this page are about your brother. If you have more than one adult brother, please think about the brother you have most contact with.

b) How often do you see or visit your brother?
PLEASE TICK ONE BOX

	%
He lives in the same household	4.1 → GO TO Q.5
Daily	1.6
At least several times a week	2.8
At least once a week	7.2
At least once a month	10.4
Several times a year	16.3
Less often	18.8

c) About how long would it take you to get to where your brother lives? Think of the time it usually takes door to door.
PLEASE TICK ONE BOX

	%
Less than 15 minutes	10.0
Between 15 and 30 minutes	12.5
Between 30 minutes and 1 hour	10.4
Between 1 and 2 hours	6.5
Between 2 and 3 hours	3.5
Between 3 and 5 hours	4.5
Between 5 and 12 hours	5.3
Over 12 hours	3.7

d) And how often do you have any other contact with your brother, besides visiting, either by telephone or letter?
PLEASE TICK ONE BOX

	%
Daily	1.1
At least several times a week	2.3
At least once a week	8.1
At least once a month	11.7
Several times a year	14.6
Less often	18.0

/Continued over ....

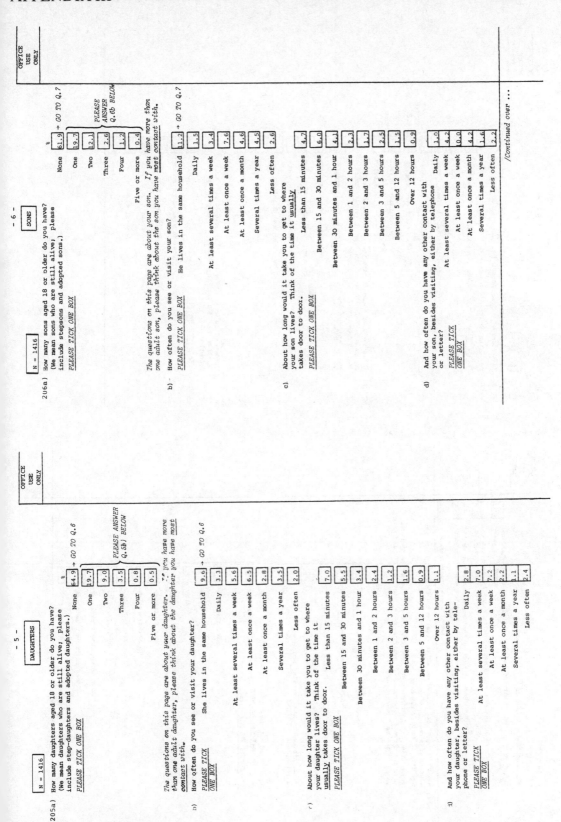

- 5 -

DAUGHTERS

N = 1416

205a) How many daughters aged 18 or older do you have? (We mean daughters who are still alive; please include step-daughters and adopted daughters.)
PLEASE TICK ONE BOX

None	64.9	→ GO TO Q.6
One	19.7	
Two	9.0	
Three	3.5	*PLEASE ANSWER Q.5b) BELOW*
Four	0.8	
Five or more	0.5	

The questions on this page are about your daughter. If you have more than one adult daughter, please think about the daughter you have most contact with.

b) How often do you see or visit your daughter? She lives in the same household
PLEASE TICK ONE BOX

She lives in the same household	9.6 → GO TO Q.6
Daily	3.3
At least several times a week	5.6
At least once a week	6.5
At least once a month	2.8
Several times a year	3.5
Less often	2.0

c) About how long would it take you to get to where your daughter lives? Think of the time it usually takes door to door.
PLEASE TICK ONE BOX

Less than 15 minutes	7.0
Between 15 and 30 minutes	5.5
Between 30 minutes and 1 hour	3.4
Between 1 and 2 hours	2.4
Between 2 and 3 hours	1.2
Between 3 and 5 hours	1.6
Between 5 and 12 hours	0.9
Over 12 hours	1.1

f) And how often do you have any other contact with your daughter, besides visiting, either by telephone or letter?
PLEASE TICK ONE BOX

Daily	2.8
At least several times a week	7.0
At least once a week	7.2
At least once a month	2.2
Several times a year	1.1
Less often	2.4

- 6 -

SONS

N = 1416

206a) How many sons aged 18 or older do you have? (We mean sons who are still alive; please include stepsons and adopted sons.)
PLEASE TICK ONE BOX

None	61.9	→ GO TO Q.7
One	19.7	
Two	12.1	
Three	2.6	*PLEASE ANSWER Q.6b BELOW*
Four	1.2	
Five or more	0.4	

The questions on this page are about your son. If you have more than one adult son, please think about the son you have most contact with.

b) How often do you see or visit your son? He lives in the same household
PLEASE TICK ONE BOX

He lives in the same household	11.2 → GO TO Q.7
Daily	1.5
At least several times a week	3.4
At least once a week	7.6
At least once a month	4.6
Several times a year	4.5
Less often	2.6

c) About how long would it take you to get to where your son lives? Think of the time it usually takes door to door.
PLEASE TICK ONE BOX

Less than 15 minutes	4.7
Between 15 and 30 minutes	6.0
Between 30 minutes and 1 hour	4.1
Between 1 and 2 hours	2.3
Between 2 and 3 hours	1.7
Between 3 and 5 hours	2.5
Between 5 and 12 hours	1.5
Over 12 hours	0.9

d) And how often do you have any other contact with your son, besides visiting, either by telephone or letter?
PLEASE TICK ONE BOX

Daily	1.0
At least several times a week	4.2
At least once a week	10.0
At least once a month	4.2
Several times a year	1.6
Less often	2.2

OFFICE USE ONLY

/Continued over ...

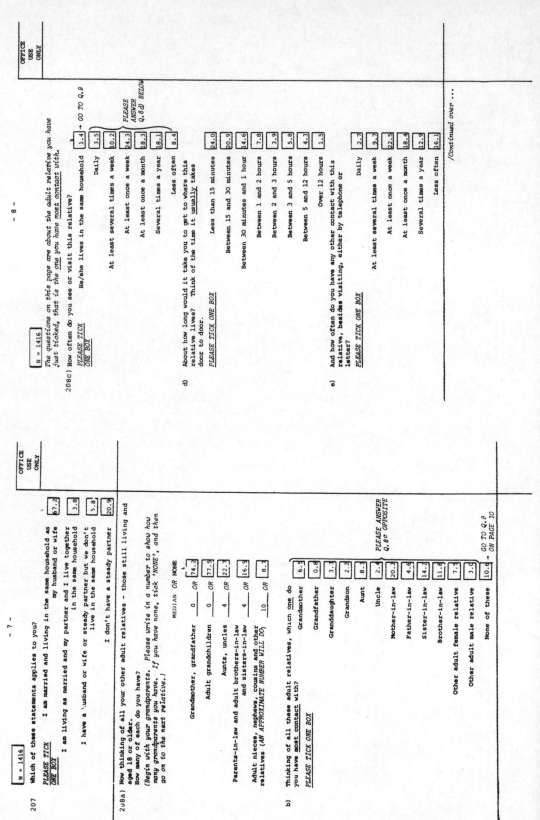

- 7 -

OFFICE USE ONLY

N = 1416

207 Which of these statements applies to you?

PLEASE TICK ONE BOX

I am married and living in the same household as my husband or wife	67.2
I am living as married and my partner and I live together in the same household	3.8
I have a 'usband or wife or steady partner but we don't live in the same household	5.8
I don't have a steady partner	20.9

208a) Now thinking of all your other adult relatives – those still living and aged 18 or older.
How many of each do you have?
(Begin with your grandparents. Please write in a number to show how many grandparents you have. If you have none, tick 'NONE', and then go on to the next relative.)

	MEDIAN	OR	NONE
Grandmother, grandfather	0	OR	74.2
Adult grandchildren	0	OR	77.5
Aunts, uncles	4	OR	22.7
Parents-in-law and adult brothers-in-law and sisters-in-law	4	OR	16.5
Adult nieces, nephews, cousins and other relatives *(AN APPROXIMATE NUMBER WILL DO)*	10	OR	8.1

b) Thinking of all these adult relatives, which **one** do you have **most** contact with?

PLEASE TICK ONE BOX

Grandmother	6.5
Grandfather	0.8
Granddaughter	3.3
Grandson	2.2
Aunt	8.3
Uncle	2.4
Mother-in-law	20.2
Father-in-law	4.6
Sister-in-law	14.2
Brother-in-law	11.8
Other adult female relative	7.5
Other adult male relative	3.4
None of these	10.6 → GO TO Q.9 ON PAGE 10

PLEASE ANSWER Q.8c OPPOSITE

- 8 -

OFFICE USE ONLY

N = 1416

The questions on this page are about the adult relative you have just ticked, that is the one you have most contact with.

208c) How often do you see or visit this relative?

PLEASE TICK ONE BOX

He/she lives in the same household	1.4 → GO TO Q.9
Daily	3.5
At least several times a week	10.2
At least once a week	24.3 } *PLEASE ANSWER Q.8d) BELOW*
At least once a month	18.3
Several times a year	18.1
Less often	8.4

d) About how long would it take you to get to where this relative lives? Think of the time it usually takes door to door.

PLEASE TICK ONE BOX

Less than 15 minutes	24.0
Between 15 and 30 minutes	20.9
Between 30 minutes and 1 hour	14.6
Between 1 and 2 hours	7.8
Between 2 and 3 hours	3.9
Between 3 and 5 hours	5.8
Between 5 and 12 hours	4.3
Over 12 hours	1.5

e) And how often do you have any other contact with this relative, besides visiting, either by telephone or letter?

PLEASE TICK ONE BOX

Daily	2.7
At least several times a week	9.7
At least once a week	22.5
At least once a month	18.4
Several times a year	12.9
Less often	16.1

/Continued over ...

- 9 -

N = 1416

209 Thinking now of close friends - not your husband, or wife, or partner, or family members - but people you feel fairly close to.

a) How many close friends would you say you have?

MEDIAN 4

PLEASE WRITE IN NUMBER ___   OR   NONE % 13.6

b) How many of these friends are people you work with now?

PLEASE WRITE IN NUMBER 0   OR   NONE 53.4

c) How many of these friends are your close neighbours?

PLEASE WRITE IN NUMBER 1   OR   NONE 42.1

d) Now thinking of your best friend, or the friend you feel closest to. Is this friend a man or a woman?

PLEASE TICK ONE BOX

Man	34.1
Woman	46.4

e) How often do you see or visit this friend?

PLEASE TICK ONE BOX

He/she lives in the same household	0.4 → GO TO Q.10
Daily	10.6
At least several times a week	19.8
At least once a week	22.8
At least once a month	14.4
Several times a year	9.8
Less often	4.1

f) About how long would it take you to get to where this friend lives? Think of the time it usually takes door to door.

PLEASE TICK ONE BOX

Less than 15 minutes	39.7
Between 15 and 30 minutes	20.0
Between 30 minutes and 1 hour	11.1
Between 1 and 2 hours	3.3
Between 2 and 3 hours	2.0
Between 3 and 5 hours	2.0
Between 5 and 12 hours	1.9
Over 12 hours	1.1

g) And how often do you have any other contact with this friend, besides visiting, either by telephone or letter?

PLEASE TICK ONE BOX

Daily	5.9
At least several times a week	12.3
At least once a week	25.4
At least once a month	14.5
Several times a year	9.2
Less often	13.1

OFFICE USE ONLY

- 10 -

N = 1416

210 Now we'd like to ask you about some problems that can happen to anyone.

First, there are some household and garden jobs you really can't do alone - for example, you may need someone to hold a ladder, or to help you move furniture.

a) Who would you turn to first for help?

b) And who would you turn to second?

PLEASE TICK ONLY ONE AS YOUR FIRST CHOICE AND ONE AS YOUR SECOND CHOICE

	a) FIRST %	b) SECOND %
Husband/wife/partner	52.0	3.3
Mother	2.7	5.4
Father	6.0	6.9
Daughter	3.9	8.3
Son	10.0	18.8
Sister	0.7	3.1
Brother	3.1	5.1
Other relative, including in-laws	2.3	8.7
Closest friend	2.6	11.1
Other friend	0.9	5.5
Neighbour	2.9	15.8
Someone you work with	0.4	0.8
Social services, or home help	0.3	0.6
Someone you pay to help	0.8	1.7
Other (PLEASE WRITE IN) FIRST	0.1	
Other (PLEASE WRITE IN) SECOND		0.1
No-one	0.5	1.6

BEFORE GOING ON TO THE NEXT QUESTION, PLEASE CHECK TO SEE THAT YOU HAVE ONLY ONE FIRST CHOICE AND ONE SECOND CHOICE

/Continued over ...

OFFICE USE ONLY

- 11 -

N = 1416

211 Suppose you had the 'flu and you had to stay in bed for a few days, and needed help around the home, with shopping and so on.

a) Who would you turn to first for help?

b) And who would you turn to second?

PLEASE TICK ONLY ONE AS YOUR FIRST CHOICE AND ONE AS YOUR SECOND CHOICE

	a) FIRST %	b) SECOND %
Husband/wife/partner	64.1	3.7
Mother	12.2	10.6
Father	0.8	4.6
Daughter	8.0	19.2
Son	3.1	9.7
Sister	1.9	6.8
Brother	0.6	2.2
Other relative, including in-laws	0.9	8.8
Closest friend	2.7	10.5
Other friend	0.5	4.0
Neighbour	2.5	11.7
Someone you work with	0.1	0.5
Health visitor	0.1	0.1
Church, clergy or priest	-	0.1
Someone you pay to help	-	0.8
Other (PLEASE WRITE IN) FIRST	0.6	
Other (PLEASE WRITE IN) SECOND		0.4
No one	0.8	3.4

BEFORE GOING ON TO THE NEXT QUESTION, PLEASE CHECK TO SEE THAT YOU HAVE ONLY ONE FIRST CHOICE AND ONE SECOND CHOICE

- 12 -

N = 1416

212 Suppose you needed to borrow a large sum of money.

a) Who would you turn to first for help?

b) And who would you turn to second?

PLEASE TICK ONLY ONE AS YOUR FIRST CHOICE AND ONE AS YOUR SECOND CHOICE

	a) FIRST %	b) SECOND %
Husband/wife/partner	21.8	3.0
Mother	8.8	8.4
Father	8.0	8.7
Daughter	2.3	3.8
Son	3.6	4.4
Sister	1.9	3.0
Brother	2.0	5.3
Other relative, including in-laws	2.2	10.3
Closest friend	1.4	4.8
Other friend	0.1	0.8
Neighbour	0.1	-
Someone you work with	0.1	0.2
Bank, building society or other financial institution	37.6	18.3
Employer	0.6	4.4
Government or social services	1.6	3.0
Other (PLEASE WRITE IN) FIRST	0.1	
Other (PLEASE WRITE IN) SECOND		0.1
No-one	6.3	16.1

BEFORE GOING ON TO THE NEXT QUESTION, PLEASE CHECK TO SEE THAT YOU HAVE ONLY ONE FIRST CHOICE AND ONE SECOND CHOICE

/Continued over ...

OFFICE USE ONLY

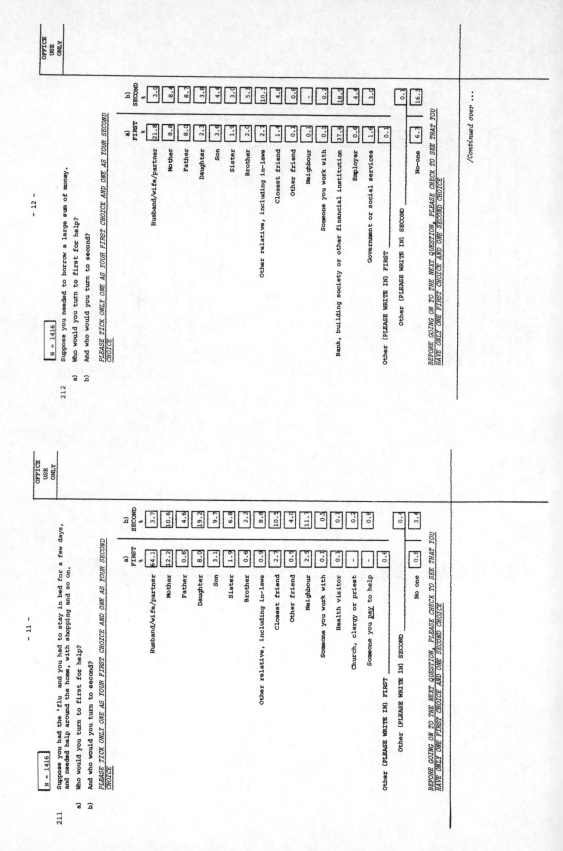

- 13 -

N = 1416

213 Suppose you were very upset about a problem with your husband, wife or partner, and haven't been able to sort it out with them.

Even if you are not married or have no partner, what would you do if you were?

a) Who would you turn to first for help?

b) And who would you turn to second?

PLEASE TICK ONLY ONE AS YOUR FIRST CHOICE AND ONE AS YOUR SECOND CHOICE

	a) FIRST %	b) SECOND %
Husband/wife/partner	12.7	0.7
Mother	15.1	7.4
Father	2.9	4.0
Daughter	10.1	6.3
Son	7.2	7.3
Sister	9.1	6.4
Brother	2.1	5.2
Other relative, including in-laws	4.0	8.5
Closest friend	18.5	14.8
Other friend	1.2	6.3
Neighbour	0.5	1.0
Someone you work with	0.6	1.8
Church, clergy or priest	1.9	2.7
Family doctor (GP)	2.7	5.7
Psychologist, psychiatrist, marriage guidance or other professional counsellor	1.7	4.4
Other (PLEASE WRITE IN) FIRST ————	0.1	0.1
Other (PLEASE WRITE IN) SECOND ————		
No-one	7.5	13.2

BEFORE GOING ON TO THE NEXT QUESTION, PLEASE CHECK TO SEE THAT YOU HAVE ONLY ONE FIRST CHOICE AND ONE SECOND CHOICE

- 14 -

N = 1416

214 Now suppose you felt just a bit down or depressed, and you wanted to talk about it.

a) Who would you turn to first for help?

b) And who would you turn to second?

PLEASE TICK ONLY ONE AS YOUR FIRST CHOICE AND ONE AS YOUR SECOND CHOICE

	a) FIRST %	b) SECOND %
Husband/wife/partner	52.6	3.8
Mother	6.8	10.1
Father	0.6	2.9
Daughter	6.5	9.8
Son	2.5	6.9
Sister	5.3	7.2
Brother	1.0	3.2
Other relative, including in-laws	0.9	4.9
Closest friend	14.1	21.0
Other friend	1.2	5.9
Neighbour	0.5	1.6
Someone you work with	0.4	3.2
Church, clergy or priest	0.6	1.0
Family doctor (GP)	3.1	6.2
Psychologist, psychiatrist, or other professional counsellor	0.4	1.1
Other (PLEASE WRITE IN) FIRST ————	0.1	0.2
Other (PLEASE WRITE IN) SECOND ————		
No-one	2.6	8.5

BEFORE GOING ON TO THE NEXT QUESTION, PLEASE CHECK TO SEE THAT YOU HAVE ONLY ONE FIRST CHOICE AND ONE SECOND CHOICE

/Continued over ...

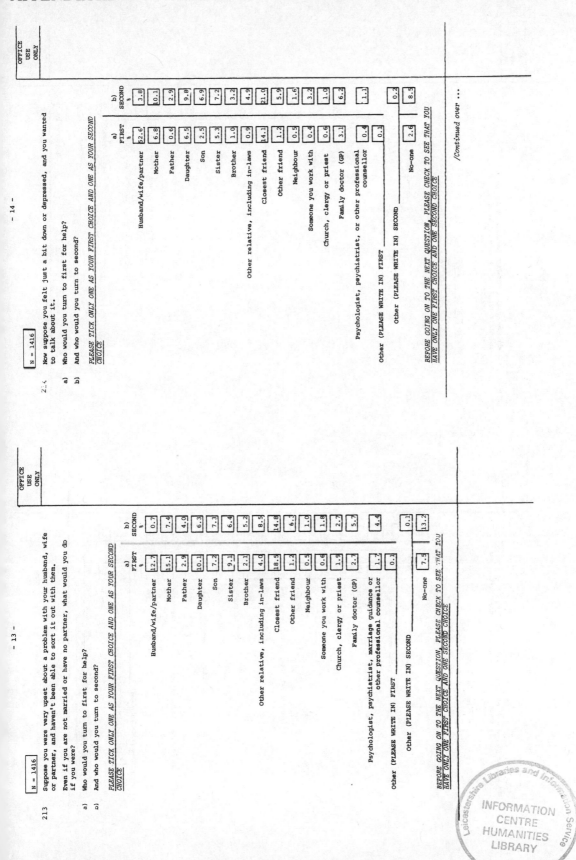

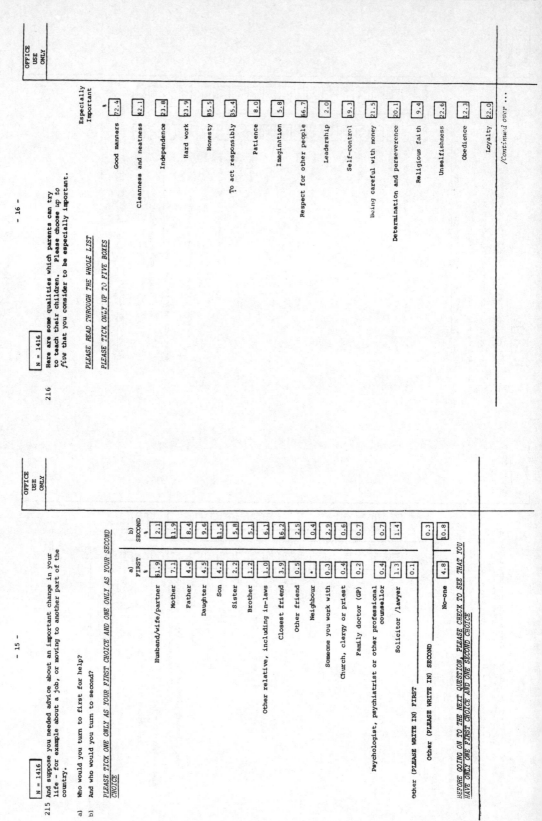

OFFICE USE ONLY

- 15 -

N = 1416

215 And suppose you needed advice about an important change in your life - for example about a job, or moving to another part of the country.

a) Who would you turn to first for help?

b) And who would you turn to second?

PLEASE TICK ONE ONLY AS YOUR FIRST CHOICE AND ONE ONLY AS YOUR SECOND CHOICE

	a) FIRST %	b) SECOND %
Husband/wife/partner	51.9	2.1
Mother	7.1	11.9
Father	4.6	8.4
Daughter	4.5	9.6
Son	4.2	11.5
Sister	2.2	5.8
Brother	1.2	5.1
Other relative, including in-laws	1.0	6.1
Closest friend	3.9	16.2
Other friend	0.5	2.5
Neighbour	*	0.4
Someone you work with	0.3	2.9
Church, clergy or priest	0.4	0.6
Family doctor (GP)	0.2	0.7
Psychologist, psychiatrist or other professional counsellor	0.4	0.7
Solicitor/lawyer	1.3	1.4
Other (PLEASE WRITE IN) FIRST	0.1	0.3
Other (PLEASE WRITE IN) SECOND		
No-one	4.8	10.8

BEFORE GOING ON TO THE NEXT QUESTION, PLEASE CHECK TO SEE THAT YOU HAVE ONLY ONE FIRST CHOICE AND ONE SECOND CHOICE

- 16 -

N = 1416

216 Here are some qualities which parents can try to teach their children. Please choose up to five that you consider to be especially important.

PLEASE READ THROUGH THE WHOLE LIST

PLEASE TICK ONLY UP TO FIVE BOXES

Quality	Especially Important %
Good manners	72.4
Cleanness and neatness	42.1
Independence	23.8
Hard work	23.9
Honesty	85.5
To act responsibly	35.4
Patience	8.0
Imagination	5.8
Respect for other people	56.7
Leadership	2.0
Self-control	19.3
Being careful with money	21.5
Determination and perseverance	20.1
Religious faith	9.4
Unselfishness	22.6
Obedience	12.3
Loyalty	22.0

/Continued over....

- 17 -

N = 1416

217 Please tick one box for each statement to show how much you agree or disagree with it.

PLEASE TICK ONE BOX ON EACH LINE

	AGREE STRONGLY	JUST AGREE	NEITHER AGREE NOR DISAGREE	JUST DISAGREE	DISAGREE STRONGLY	DON'T KNOW (OFFICE USE ONLY)
Divorce in Britain should be made more difficult to obtain than it is now	16.7	22.4	33.0	16.2	10.8	0.4
Most young couples start their married life well prepared for its ups and downs	6.1	23.4	27.1	36.3	6.2	0.2
As a society, we ought to do more to safeguard the institution of marriage	36.9	34.2	21.4	5.0	1.3	0.3
To grow up happily, children need a home with both their own father and mother	51.3	27.1	8.6	8.2	4.1	0.1
Most people nowadays take marriage too lightly	37.7	36.6	15.4	7.6	1.7	*

218a) Central government provides financial support to housing in two main ways.
First, by means of allowances to low income tenants.
Second, by means of tax relief to people with mortgages.

On the whole, which of these three types of family would you say benefits *most* from central government support for housing?

PLEASE TICK ONE BOX

	%
Families with high incomes	33.1
Families with middle incomes	22.0
Families with low incomes	40.3
Don't know	1.8

b) Which of these three views comes closest to your own on the sale of council houses and flats to tenants?

PLEASE TICK ONE BOX

	%
Council tenants *should not* be allowed to buy their houses or flats	7.9
Council tenants *should* allowed to buy but *only* in areas with no housing shortage	27.6
Council tenants *should generally* be allowed to buy their houses or flats	62.9
Don't know	0.5

- 18 -

N = 1416

219 Which of the following statements do you think are generally true and which false?

PLEASE TICK ONE BOX ON EACH LINE

	True	False	Don't know (OFFICE USE ONLY)
Council tenants pay low rents	25.6	54.5	1.8
Councils give a poor standard of repairs and maintenance	65.5	27.8	1.6
Council estates are generally pleasant places to live	37.3	54.7	1.5

22a) Suppose a newly-married young couple, both with steady jobs, asked your advice about whether to buy or rent a home. If they had the choice, what would you advise them to do?

PLEASE TICK ONE BOX

	%
To buy a home as soon as possible	74.3
To wait a bit, then try to buy a home	19.7
Not to plan to buy a home at all	0.9
Can't choose	4.2

b) Still thinking of what you might say to this young couple, please tick one box for *each* statement below to show how much you agree or disagree with it.

PLEASE TICK ONE BOX ON EACH LINE

	AGREE STRONGLY	JUST AGREE	NEITHER AGREE NOR DIS-AGREE	JUST DIS-AGREE	DISAGREE STRONGLY	DON'T KNOW
Owning your home can be a risky investment	5.4	19.6	15.6	23.5	33.5	0.2
Over time, buying a home works out less expensive than paying rent	44.1	38.6	8.3	4.9	2.0	0.2
Owning your home makes it easier to move when you want to	27.4	36.2	18.9	11.8	3.6	0.2
Owning a home ties up money you may need urgently for other things	7.3	27.4	22.5	26.4	13.6	0.2
Owning a home gives you the freedom to do what you want to it	40.1	42.1	8.4	5.9	1.4	0.1
Owning a home is a big financial burden to repair and maintain	15.7	34.0	22.1	20.7	5.3	0.3
Your own home will be something to leave your family	39.2	41.1	12.4	2.7	2.1	0.1
Owning a home is just too much of a responsibility	4.2	7.8	15.6	34.3	35.9	0.1
Owning a home is too much of a risk for couples without secure jobs	24.2	35.2	14.1	19.0	5.1	0.2
Couples who buy their own homes would be wise to wait before starting a family	23.1	36.0	22.8	11.6	4.4	0.1

/Continued over ...

- 19 -

221   N = 1416

Please tick one box for each statement below, to show how much you agree or disagree with it.

PLEASE TICK ONE BOX ON EACH LINE

	AGREE STRONGLY	JUST AGREE	NEITHER AGREE NOR DISAGREE	JUST DISAGREE	DISAGREE STRONGLY	DON'T KNOW
The courts are too hard on people who break traffic laws %	6.5	17.5	28.5	28.2	17.4	
Most traffic offences occur because of lack of concentration, rather than drivers deliberately breaking the law %	20.5	49.5	13.3	11.7	3.7	0.5
Drivers should be prosecuted even for minor traffic offences %	5.4	17.9	19.1	35.8	20.4	0.3
The roads would be safer if speed limits were lower %	15.3	18.0	16.7	33.6	14.9	0.4
Police spend too much time and energy enforcing traffic laws %	17.3	25.9	25.0	22.1	8.1	0.5
Road traffic laws are too complicated for the average driver to understand %	7.4	17.5	20.3	36.5	16.7	0.5
The roads would be safer if drivers kept to the speed limit %	38.4	40.6	11.8	7.0	1.0	0.3
Parking regulations should be more strictly enforced %	18.6	29.0	26.6	16.5	7.7	0.3

- 20 -

222   N = 1416

Please tick one box for each statement, to show how much you agree or disagree with it.

PLEASE TICK ONE BOX ON EACH LINE

	AGREE STRONGLY	JUST AGREE	NEITHER AGREE NOR DISAGREE	JUST DISAGREE	DISAGREE STRONGLY	DON'T KNOW
Food that is good for you generally tastes nicer than other food %	8.1	19.0	34.3	27.9	9.4	0.1
Food that is good for you is usually more expensive %	7.9	30.8	16.2	25.6	8.4	0.1
Food that is good for you in supermarkets %	3.9	15.5	25.2	37.8	16.1	0.1
It is easy to find food that is good for you generally takes too long to prepare %	15.9	48.5	15.1	15.9	3.1	0.2
Many people would eat healthier food if the rest of their families would let them %	10.5	31.9	31.9	17.7	6.0	0.4
As long as you take enough exercise you can eat whatever foods you want %	9.9	20.9	16.7	33.8	17.1	0.2
If heart disease is in your family, there is little you can do to reduce your chances of getting it %	4.1	11.0	12.7	38.6	31.6	0.4
The experts contradict each other over what makes a healthy diet %	30.4	42.1	14.9	7.8	3.3	0.2
People worry too much about their weight %	16.3	43.7	16.2	17.9	4.2	0.1
Good health is just a matter of good luck %	4.3	12.4	13.0	36.4	32.1	0.1
A proper meal should include meat and vegetables %	30.5	31.2	14.7	16.5	5.8	0.1

223   Here are a number of circumstances in which a woman might consider an abortion. Please say whether or not you think the law should allow an abortion in each case.

PLEASE TICK ONE BOX ON EACH LINE

	Should abortion be allowed by law?		
	Yes	No	DON'T KNOW
The woman decides on her own she does not wish to have the child %	46.1	53.2	0.6
The couple agree they do not wish to have the child %	56.1	40.0	0.7
The woman is not married and does not wish to marry the man %	50.9	45.2	0.7
The couple cannot afford any more children %	50.6	45.2	0.9
There is a strong chance of a defect in the baby %	85.4	11.5	0.8
The woman's health is seriously endangered by the pregnancy %	92.3	4.9	0.9
The woman became pregnant as a result of rape %	90.6	6.5	1.0

OFFICE USE ONLY

/Continued over ...

- 21 -

N = 1416

224 To help us plan better in future, please tell us about
how long it took you to complete this questionnaire?

PLEASE TICK ONE BOX

		%
Less than 15 minutes		12.9
Between 15 and 20 minutes		31.5
Between 20 and 30 minutes		31.2
Between 30 and 45 minutes		15.4
Between 45 and 60 minutes		5.2
Over one hour		2.9

THANK YOU VERY MUCH FOR YOUR HELP

Please keep the completed questionnaire for the interviewer
if he or she has arranged to call for it. Otherwise,
please post it as soon as possible in the stamped, addressed
envelope provided.

OFFICE
USE
ONLY

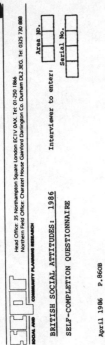

B

Head Office: 35 Northampton Square London EC1V 0AX. Tel: 01-250 1866
Northern Field Office: Charzel House Gainford Darlington Co. Durham DL2 3EG. Tel: 0325 730 868

Interviewer to enter:

Area No.

Serial No.

BRITISH SOCIAL ATTITUDES: 1986

SELF-COMPLETION QUESTIONNAIRE

April 1986   P.860B

To the selected respondent

We hope very much that you will agree to participate in this important study -
the fourth in an annual series of surveys to be published each summer. The
study consists of this self-completion questionnaire and an interview.

Completing the questionnaire

The questions inside cover a wide range of subjects, but each one can be
answered simply by placing a tick (✓) or a number in one or more of the boxes
provided. No special knowledge is required: we are confident that everyone
will be able to offer an opinion on all questions. And we want *all* people
to take part, not just those with strong views or particular viewpoints. The
questionnaire should not take very long to complete, and we hope you will find
it interesting and enjoyable. It should be completed by the person selected
by the interviewer at your address. Your participation will be treated as
confidential and anonymous.

Returning the questionnaire

Your interviewer will arrange with you the most convenient way of returning
the questionnaire. If the interviewer has arranged to call back for it, please
complete it and keep it safely until then. If not, please complete it and
post it back in the stamped, addressed envelope as soon as you possibly can.

Thank you for your help.

*Social and Community Planning Research is an independent social research
institute registered as a charitable trust. Its projects are funded by
government departments, local authorities, universities and foundations to
provide information on social issues in Britain. SCPR interviewers carry
out around 50,000 interviews per year. This study has been funded mainly
by the Monument Trust, a Sainsbury foundation, with contributions also from
government departments, universities and industry. Please contact us if
you require further information.*

OFFICE USE ONLY

- 1 -

201 N = 1321

Please tick one box on each line to show how important or unimportant each of these has been as a cause of Britain's economic difficulties.

PLEASE TICK ONE BOX ON EACH LINE

	Very important	Quite important	Not very important	Not at all important	Don't know
A. People are not working hard enough	33.2	45.6	14.4	4.9	0.1
B. Employers are not investing enough	47.7	42.6	6.6	1.3	0.2
C. There has been a decline in world trade	43.5	41.4	10.7	2.3	0.2
D. Wages are too high	13.1	40.4	31.6	12.2	0.2
E. Energy costs are too high for the industry	39.9	43.7	12.4	1.2	0.2
F. Government spending has been too high	29.6	34.8	23.5	8.7	0.2
G. British industry is badly managed	47.5	41.0	7.8	1.2	0.4
H. British workers are reluctant to accept new ways of working	38.6	41.9	14.2	3.0	0.3
I. The government has not done enough to create jobs	58.7	27.6	8.9	2.4	0.1
J. The best school and college leavers don't seek jobs in manufacturing industry	35.2	37.2	19.8	5.5	0.3

202 There are many ways people or organisations can protest against a government action they strongly oppose. Please show which you think should be allowed and which should not be allowed by ticking a box on each line.

PLEASE TICK ONE BOX ON EACH LINE

Should it be allowed?

	Definitely	Probably	Probably not	Definitely not	Can't choose
A. Organising public meetings to protest against the government	54.8	28.0	6.4	5.6	4.3
B. Publishing pamphlets to protest against the government	42.7	35.5	9.9	7.1	3.3
C. Organising protest marches and demonstrations	30.2	27.4	17.9	20.7	2.7
D. Occupying a government office and stopping work there for several days	3.7	6.4	24.6	61.4	2.9
E. Seriously damaging government buildings	1.4	0.7	3.8	91.3	1.8
F. Organising a nationwide strike of all workers against the government	12.5	15.2	14.3	53.5	3.8

Please continue ...

- 2 -

203 N = 1321

All systems of justice make mistakes, but which do you think is worse?

PLEASE TICK ONE BOX

to convict an innocent person? 57.8

OR

to let a guilty person go free? 26.0

Can't choose 15.9

204 Some people think those with high incomes should pay a larger proportion (percentage) of their earnings in taxes than those who earn low incomes. Other people think that those with high incomes and those with low incomes should pay the same proportion (percentage) of their earnings in taxes.

Do you think those with high incomes should ...

PLEASE TICK ONE BOX

... pay a much larger proportion, 21.1

pay a larger proportion, 55.5

pay the same proportion as those who earn low incomes, 18.7

pay a smaller proportion, 0.6

or - pay a much smaller proportion? 0.4

Can't choose 2.6

205 What is your opinion of the following statement: It is the responsibility of the government to reduce the differences in income between people with high incomes and those with low incomes.

PLEASE TICK ONE BOX

Agree strongly 24.3

Agree 34.8

Neither agree nor disagree 19.6

Disagree 16.9

Disagree strongly 4.1

- 3 -

N = 1321

206 Please show whether you agree or disagree with each of the following statements.

PLEASE TICK ONE BOX ON EACH LINE

	Agree strongly	Agree	Neither agree nor disagree	Disagree	Disagree strongly	Don't know
A. A person whose parents are rich has a better chance of earning a lot of money than a person whose parents are poor	29.7	39.6	12.1	15.1	2.3	0.1
B. A person whose father is a professional person has a better chance of earning a lot of money than a person whose parents are poor	23.6	43.0	14.0	16.4	1.9	0.1
C. In Britain what you achieve in life depends largely on your family background	13.9	35.3	19.4	26.3	4.0	0.2

207 Do you consider the amount of income tax that your household has to pay is ...

PLEASE TICK ONE BOX

	%
... much too high,	20.3
too high,	14.1
about right,	23.7
too low,	0.4
or - much too low?	-
Can't choose	2.0
Does not apply	12.4

208 Do you consider the amount of tax that business and industry have to pay is too high or too low?

PLEASE TICK ONE BOX

	%
Much too high	10.0
Too high	37.6
About right	28.9
Too low	5.3
Much too low	0.6
Can't choose	17.2

/Please continue ...

- 4 -

N = 1321

209 Do you think that trade unions in this country have too much power or too little power?

PLEASE TICK ONE BOX

	%
Far too much power	18.6
Too much power	34.6
About the right amount of power	30.0
Too little power	9.3
Far too little power	1.8
Can't choose	5.5

210 How about business and industry? Do they have too much power or too little power?

PLEASE TICK ONE BOX

	%
Far too much power	4.8
Too much power	22.3
About the right amount of power	45.5
Too little power	14.6
Far too little power	0.7
Can't choose	11.6

211 And what about the government, does it have too much power or too little power?

PLEASE TICK ONE BOX

	%
Far too much power	19.1
Too much power	31.0
About the right amount of power	40.6
Too little power	4.3
Far too little power	0.3
Can't choose	4.5

- 5 -

212. **What do you think the government's role in each of these industries and services should be?**

N = 1321

PLEASE TICK ONE BOX ON EACH LINE

| | The government should | | | |
	Own it	Control prices and profits but not own it	Neither own it nor control its prices and profits	Can't choose
A. Electricity	% 27.7	41.6	24.2	4.9
B. Local public transport	% 20.3	34.5	38.3	5.4
C. Gas	% 28.1	40.2	25.0	4.6
D. Banking and insurance	% 6.3	31.8	50.4	9.9
E. The car industry	% 7.7	27.3	54.9	8.2
F. The telephone system	% 27.2	38.2	33.0	5.3

213. **Do you think big businesses or small businesses are generally better at each of these things, or is there no difference?**

PLEASE TICK ONE BOX ON EACH LINE

	Big businesses are better	Small businesses are better	There is no difference	Don't know
Inventing new products	% 42.1	26.4	28.8	0.6
Making well-designed products	% 26.0	39.2	31.9	0.5
Investing in new machinery and technology	% 47.4	7.7	42.7	0.5
Attracting the best people to work in them	% 68.9	7.5	20.8	0.6
Making goods that people really want to buy	% 19.3	40.8	37.4	0.6
Keeping good relations between management and other employees	% 5.3	57.3	35.2	0.5
Training employees in new skills	% 49.2	26.2	22.4	0.6
Paying their employees a fair wage	% 36.9	36.6	24.5	0.6
Charging fair prices for their products	% 21.7	39.3	36.7	0.5
Caring about their customers	% 4.6	71.3	22.2	0.5

OFFICE USE ONLY

Please continue ...

- 6 -

214. **Who do you think benefits most from the profits made by British firms?**

N = 1321

PLEASE TICK ONE BOX

	%
Mainly their owners or shareholders	71.4
Mainly their directors and managers	19.8
Mainly their employees	2.3
The public generally	4.6
Don't know	0.3

215. **Please tick one box for *each* statement to show how much you agree or disagree with it.**

N = 1321

PLEASE TICK ONE BOX ON EACH LINE

	Agree Strongly	Agree	Neither agree nor disagree	Disagree	Disagree strongly	Don't know
Consumers are given too little protection by the law	% 17.2	41.7	23.9	15.5	1.0	0.2
Too much of industry's profits go abroad	% 16.0	37.2	33.3	10.9	0.8	0.4
We would all be better off if British firms made bigger profits	% 10.1	36.5	22.7	18.3	11.5	0.1
Britain's economy can prosper without manufacturing industry	% 1.7	5.3	11.5	52.3	27.5	0.3
British firms make too much profit	% 4.7	13.6	32.5	39.9	7.9	0.2
Britain's schools fail to teach the kind of skills that British industry needs	% 25.6	46.5	15.1	10.0	1.8	0.1
Employees who have shares in their companies tend to work harder	% 23.7	51.8	14.2	8.4	0.9	0.2
The less profitable British industry is, the less money there is for governments to spend on things like education and health	% 16.8	47.9	19.2	13.5	1.4	0.2
British people should try to buy British goods even when they have to pay a bit more for them	% 20.6	38.4	17.3	19.2	3.3	0.1

OFFICE USE ONLY

- 7 -

216 N = 1321

Please tick one box on each line to show your views on government help for industry. Remember that if you say 'definitely' or 'probably', it might require an increase in income tax to pay for it.

Do you think the government should ...

PLEASE TICK ONE BOX ON EACH LINE

	Definitely	Probably	Probably not	Definitely not	Don't know
... help industry pay for research into new products?	22.8	38.1	28.5	8.0	0.4
... help pay for new factories in areas of high unemployment?	42.6	41.1	10.8	3.6	0.3
... help industry pay for the cost of replacing out-dated machinery and equipment?	18.5	35.8	32.1	11.7	0.3
... help industry pay the wages of people working in declining industries?	11.3	26.8	40.3	19.0	0.3
... give people grants to start their own businesses?	37.4	46.9	10.8	2.8	0.3
... give firms more help in selling goods abroad?	38.1	36.6	18.5	5.1	0.3
... help industry pay for training employees in new skills?	36.2	42.8	16.2	3.1	0.3

217 Listed below are some of Britain's institutions. From what you know or have heard about each one, can you say whether, on the whole, you think it is well run or not well run?

PLEASE TICK ONE BOX ON EACH LINE

	Well run	Not well run	Don't know
The National Health Service	36.3	52.5	0.1
The press	48.0	48.9	1.0
Local government	34.5	63.0	0.6
The civil service	47.2	50.0	0.6
Manufacturing industry	41.1	54.8	1.0
Nationalised industries	30.6	66.0	0.9
Banks	91.8	6.5	0.6
The trade unions	27.3	69.8	0.8
The BBC	69.7	28.4	0.4
Independent TV and radio	83.6	14.4	0.3
The police	73.6	24.9	

Please continue ...

- 8 -

218 N = 1321

How serious an effect on our environment do you think each of these things has?

PLEASE TICK ONE BOX ON EACH LINE

	Very serious	Quite serious	Not very serious	Not at all serious	Don't know
Noise from aircraft	9.2	33.1	46.4	9.8	0.2
Lead from petrol	42.2	42.5	12.8	1.1	0.2
Industrial waste in the rivers and sea	65.4	28.5	4.4	0.5	0.1
Waste from nuclear electricity stations	72.3	18.0	6.8	1.5	0.2
Industrial fumes in the air	45.8	43.1	8.6	1.0	0.1
Noise and dirt from traffic	24.6	48.5	23.6	2.1	0.1
Acid rain	53.6	32.6	10.3	2.0	0.3

219a) Which one of these three possible solutions to Britain's electricity needs would you favour most?

PLEASE TICK ONE BOX

	%
We should make do with the power stations we have already	34.1
We should build more coal-fuelled power stations	52.2
We should build more nuclear power stations	10.7
Don't know	0.6

b) As far as nuclear power stations are concerned, which of these statements comes closest to your own feelings?

PLEASE TICK ONE BOX

	%
They create very serious risks for the future	48.5
They create quite serious risks for the future	29.3
They create only slight risks for the future	16.6
They create hardly any risks for the future	3.8
Don't know	0.4

220 Which one of these two statements comes closest to your own views?

PLEASE TICK ONE BOX

	%
Industry should be prevented from causing damage to the countryside, even if this sometimes leads to higher prices	82.3
OR	
Industry should keep prices down, even if this sometimes causes damage to the countryside	16.3
Don't know	0.3

- 9 -

221 N = 1321

Here are some statements about the countryside. Please tick one box for each to show whether you agree or disagree with it.
PLEASE TICK ONE BOX ON EACH LINE

	Agree strongly	Agree	Dis-agree	Disagree strongly	Don't know
A. Modern methods of farming have caused damage to the countryside %	18.5	44.6	33.3	1.6	0.3
B. If farmers have to choose between producing more food and looking after the countryside, they should produce more food %	7.9	36.9	47.6	5.3	0.2
C. All things considered, farmers do a good job in looking after the countryside %	11.8	66.5	17.7	1.7	0.3
D. Government should withhold some subsidies from farmers and use them to protect the countryside, even if this leads to higher prices %	8.7	40.5	44.1	4.0	0.3

222

Which of these two statements comes closest to your own views?
PLEASE TICK ONE BOX ON EACH LINE

Looking after the countryside is too important to be left to farmers - government authorities should have more control over what's done and built on farms % — 33.6

OR

Farmers know how important it is to look after the countryside - there are enough controls and farmers should be left to decide what's done on farms — 47.0

Can't choose — 18.2

223

Please tick one box on each line to show how you feel about ...
PLEASE TICK ONE BOX ON EACH LINE

	It should be stopped altogether	It should be dis-couraged	Don't mind one way or the other	It should be encour-aged	Don't know
... Increasing the amount of countryside being farmed	7.7	44.8	34.9	10.3	0.3
... Building new housing in country areas	13.9	50.2	22.3	11.8	0.2
... Putting the needs of farmers before protection of wildlife	15.3	53.8	19.9	9.4	0.2
... Providing more roads in country areas	9.8	40.3	28.5	19.7	0.2
... Increasing the number of picnic areas and camping sites in the countryside	2.8	13.8	28.4	53.8	0.1

Please continue ...

- 10 -

224 N = 1321

Which of these three statements comes <u>closest</u> to your own views?
PLEASE TICK ONE BOX

I care about what happens to the countryside, and I get a lot of personal enjoyment from it — 72.1

I care about what happens to the countryside, but I don't get a lot of personal enjoyment from it — 23.7

I don't care much what happens to the countryside - I'm just not that bothered — 3.0

225

Here is a list of predictions. For each one, please say how likely or unlikely you think it is to come true *within the next ten years*?
PLEASE TICK ONE BOX FOR EACH PREDICTION

	Very likely	Quite likely	Not very likely	Not at all likely	Don't know
Acts of political terrorism in Britain will be common events %	25.1	48.6	23.9	1.5	0.2
Riots and civil disturbance in our cities will be common events %	19.8	44.4	31.8	2.5	0.3
There will be a world war involving Britain and Europe %	5.1	17.6	51.7	23.8	0.6
There will be a serious accident at a British nuclear power station %	16.5	42.0	34.4	5.8	0.3
The police in our cities will find it impossible to protect our personal safety on the streets %	19.3	39.3	34.8	5.6	0.2
The government in Britain will be overthrown by revolution %	2.0	7.5	40.7	48.7	0.3
A nuclear bomb will be dropped somewhere in the world %	7.9	26.8	38.8	25.1	0.3

- 11 -

226 On the whole, do you think it should or should not be the government's responsibility to ...

N = 1321

PLEASE TICK ONE BOX ON EACH LINE

	Definitely should be	Probably should be	Probably should not be	Definitely should not be	Can't choose	Don't know
A. ... provide a job for everyone who wants one? %	29.7	32.5	16.5	13.4	6.4	0.1
B. ... keep prices under control? %	52.1	37.3	5.8	2.6	1.2	0.4
C. ... provide health care for the sick? %	84.1	13.8	0.7	0.3	0.3	0.3
D. ... provide a decent standard of living for the old? %	80.0	17.9	0.9	0.4	0.2	
E. ... provide industry with the help it needs to grow? %	39.5	47.9	7.2	1.6	2.4	
F. ... provide a decent standard of living for the unemployed? %	38.8	44.3	10.2	3.1	2.6	
G. ... reduce income differences between the rich and poor? %	45.6	26.7	14.6	8.2	1.9	

227 Please say for each item whether you think its level is too high, too low or about right.

PLEASE TICK ONE BOX ON EACH LINE

	Too high	Too low	About right	Don't know
State pensions %	0.5	77.7	21.1	0.1
Unemployment benefit %	10.0	48.7	39.4	0.4
Child benefit %	3.5	38.8	46.3	0.3

228 Some people say that British governments nowadays - of whichever party - can actually do very little to change things. Others say they can do quite a bit. Please say whether you think that British governments nowadays can do very little or quite a bit ...

PLEASE TICK ONE BOX ON EACH LINE

	Very little	Quite a bit	Don't know
to keep prices down? %	29.1	70.0	0.1
to reduce unemployment? %	40.2	58.9	0.1
to improve the general standard of living? %	30.1	68.9	0.1
to improve the health and social services? %	15.4	83.8	0.1
to reduce poverty? %	26.9	72.0	0.1

[Please continue ...

- 12 -

229 Britain controls the numbers of people from abroad that are allowed to settle in this country. Please say, for each of the groups below, whether you think Britain should allow more settlement, less settlement, or about the same amount as now.

N = 1321

PLEASE TICK ONE BOX ON EACH LINE

	More Settlement	Less Settlement	About the same as now	Don't know
Australians and New Zealanders %	8.6	33.9	55.8	0.1
Indians and Pakistanis %	2.0	57.6	29.1	0.1
People from common market countries %	5.7	45.8	47.0	0.1
West Indians %	2.2	54.3	32.0	0.1

b) Now thinking about the families (husbands, wives, children, parents) of people who have *already* settled in Britain, would you say in general that Britain should ...

PLEASE TICK ONE BOX

	%
... be stricter in controlling the settlement of close relatives	58.1
or - less strict in controlling the settlement of close relatives	9.8
or - keep the controls about the same as now	30.5
Don't know	0.1

230 Please say whether you agree or disagree with each of these statements about industry today.

PLEASE TICK ONE BOX ON EACH LINE

	Agree strongly	Agree	Neither agree nor disagree	Disagree	Disagree strongly	Don't know
A. Industry should share more of its profits with its employees %	25.3	54.8	5.0	3.3	0.3	0.2
B. Full cooperation in firms is impossible because workers and management are really on opposite sides %	13.9	43.0	18.7	21.0	2.2	0.1
C. Managers generally know what's best for a firm and employees ought to go along with it %	5.0	27.1	24.1	36.5	6.3	0.1
D. Management will always try to get the better of employees if it gets the chance %	12.9	38.7	19.8	24.1	3.2	0.1
E. Employees need strong trade unions to protect their interests %	13.9	30.4	25.4	23.5	5.7	0.2

- 13 -

N = 1321

231 Please tick one box for each statement to show how much you agree or disagree with it.
PLEASE TICK ONE BOX ON EACH LINE

	Agree strongly	Agree	Neither agree nor disagree	Disagree	Disagree strongly	Don't know
When someone is unemployed it's usually his or her own fault	0.8	6.2	20.2	49.9	21.9	0.2
The government should spend more money to create jobs	28.1	51.3	11.4	6.8	1.3	0.1
Private enterprise is the best way to solve Britain's economic problems	10.7	33.8	35.3	15.0	3.5	0.2
There is one law for the rich and one for the poor	24.3	35.1	17.2	18.2	4.1	0.1
Big business benefits owners at the expense of workers	14.8	39.1	25.6	17.2	1.8	0.2
Ordinary working people do not get their fair share of the nation's wealth	20.2	45.3	19.1	13.3	1.2	0.2
Too many people these days like to rely on government handouts	16.0	40.7	16.5	19.8	5.6	0.2
More socialist planning is the best way to solve Britain's economic problems	6.9	18.5	36.2	28.3	7.9	0.6
Government should redistribute income from the better-off to those who are less well off	11.2	32.1	25.4	24.7	5.1	0.3
The police should be given more power	14.2	28.1	21.6	27.9	7.0	0.2
Britain should bring back the death penalty	38.2	28.0	10.5	10.2	11.8	0.4

Please continue ...

- 14 -

N = 1321

232 Please tick one box for each statement to show how much you agree or disagree with it.
PLEASE TICK ONE BOX ON EACH LINE

	Agree strongly	Agree	Neither agree nor disagree	Disagree	Disagree strongly	Don't know
Young people today don't have enough respect for traditional British values	24.5	41.5	20.3	11.4	1.7	0.1
Government should be allowed to tap telephone conversations of people who are politically active	4.5	20.3	17.9	36.5	19.8	0.1
For some crimes, the death penalty is the most appropriate sentence	41.0	33.0	6.4	9.5	9.3	0.2
Schools should teach children to obey authority	31.7	50.9	9.5	5.9	1.1	0.2
The law should always be obeyed, even if a particular law is wrong	12.4	32.8	22.2	27.3	4.2	0.2
The welfare state makes people nowadays less willing to look after themselves	11.6	38.1	19.6	24.7	5.1	0.2
People receiving social security are made to feel like second class citizens	14.4	38.3	21.8	21.8	2.9	0.6
The welfare state makes for a more caring society	6.4	36.5	29.9	22.9	3.0	0.3
Censorship of films and magazines is necessary to uphold moral standards	23.6	42.2	15.2	13.8	4.0	0.2
People who break the law should be given stiffer sentences	31.3	41.0	19.9	5.9	0.9	0.2
The government should be allowed to ban organisations which don't believe in democracy	14.0	24.7	29.4	25.1	5.5	0.4

- 15 -

N = 1321

233 Finally please tick one box for each statement below to show whether or not you think the government should ...

PLEASE TICK ONE BOX ON EACH LINE

The government	Definitely should	Probably should	Probably should not	Definitely should not	Don't know
... spend less on defence?	28.0	33.6	23.6	13.2	0.3
... get rid of private education in Britain?	10.1	17.0	39.7	31.7	0.2
... spend more money to get rid of poverty?	47.3	39.7	9.1	2.4	0.1
... encourage the growth of private medicine?	11.0	35.1	35.2	16.8	0.4
... introduce stricter laws to regulate the activities of trade unions?	18.7	36.0	30.0	14.0	0.3
... give workers more say in running the places where they work?	28.4	51.9	15.7	2.7	0.2

234 To help us plan better in future, please tell us about how long it took you to complete this questionnaire?

PLEASE TICK ONE BOX

	%
Less than 15 minutes	5.9
Between 15 and 20 minutes	22.5
Between 20 and 30 minutes	32.1
Between 30 and 45 minutes	9.6
Between 45 and 60 minutes	6.4
Over one hour	0.1

THANK YOU VERY MUCH FOR YOUR HELP

PLEASE KEEP THE COMPLETED QUESTIONNAIRE FOR THE INTER-VIEWER IF HE OR SHE HAS ARRANGED TO CALL FOR IT. OTHERWISE, PLEASE POST IT AS SOON AS POSSIBLE IN THE STAMPED, ADDRESSED ENVELOPE PROVIDED.

OFFICE USE ONLY

Subject index